Practical Deep Reinforcement Learning with Python

Concise Implementation of Algorithms, Simplified Maths, and Effective Use of TensorFlow and PyTorch

Ivan Gridin

www.bpbonline.com

Group Product Manager: Marianne Conor

Publishing Product Manager: Eva Brawn

Senior Editor: Connell

Content Development Editor: Melissa Monroe

Technical Editor: Anne Stokes

Copy Editor: Joe Austin

Language Support Editor: Justin Baldwin

Project Coordinator: Tyler Horan

Proofreader: Khloe Styles

Indexer: V. Krishnamurthy

Production Designer: Malcolm D'Souza

Marketing Coordinator: Kristen Kramer

First published: August 2022

Published by BPB Online
WeWork, 119 Marylebone Road
London NW1 5PU

UK | UAE | INDIA | SINGAPORE

ISBN 978-93-55512-055

www.bpbonline.com

Dedicated to

*My mom **Elena Gridina**
for her patience teaching me to play chess*

About the Author

Ivan Gridin is a researcher, author, developer, and artificial intelligence expert who has worked on distributive high-load systems and implemented different machine learning approaches in practice. One of the primary areas of his research is the design and development of predictive time series models. Ivan has fundamental math skills in random process theory, time series analysis, machine learning, reinforcement learning, neural architecture search, and optimization. He has published books on genetic algorithms and time series forecasting. He is a loving husband and father and collector of old math books.

You can learn more about him on LinkedIn.

(**https://www.linkedin.com/in/survex/**)

About the Reviewer

Satyajeet Dhawale is a professional Data Scientist having strong experience in machine learning, deep learning, computer vision, and inferential and descriptive statistical analysis. He has worked on many projects that involve complex machine learning and deep learning algorithms and used a variety of data sets from different domains. In his career, he has successfully delivered many machine learning and deep learning solutions for complex data problems.

You can find more professional details about Satyajeet on LinkedIn.

(**https://www.linkedin.com/in/satyajeet-dhawale/**)

Acknowledgement

There are a few people I want to thank for the idea and the motivation for writing this book. I thank my adorable wife Tamara; her patience and beauty inspired me every day. I thank my elder daughter Ksenia; her courage and determination motivated me in exhaustion moments. And my little daughter Elena for waking me up earlier – you're my energizer!

Thanks to my friends, who helped me in all my efforts. I want especially to thank Pavel Rogov for his valuable help when I started to make the first steps in programming. To Petr Rostov for his help in learning programming and mathematics. To Qamar Saitovski for his valuable English speech lessons. To Anatoliy Yalovik for his assistance in difficult life situations. Warm hug to Daria Kutsar. To my good old friend Julia Vaisman for helping me to relocate to another place. This book would be impossible without all of them.

My gratitude also goes to the book reviewer Satyajeet Dhawale. His participation and helpful advice have made this book much better.

Special thanks to BPB Publications for their support, advice, and assistance in creating and publishing this book.

Preface

Reinforcement learning is one of the most dynamic research areas in machine learning. It studies how an agent can adapt and learn perfect behavior in an unknown and constantly changing environment. Many scientists consider that reinforcement learning will take us closer to reaching artificial intelligence. In the past few years, reinforcement learning has evolved rapidly and has been used in complex applications ranging from stock trading to self-driving cars. The main reason for this growth is the involvement of deep reinforcement learning, which is a combination of deep learning and reinforcement learning.

Despite its popularity, reinforcement learning can seem like a rather complex area to study for a novice data scientist. Usually, many sources are overloaded with complicated mathematical concepts, proofs, and formulas. This book provides a practical introduction to reinforcement learning. Of course, the book contains math, but it doesn't try to overwhelm the reader, who is new to the topic. Each chapter is dedicated to a specific project, which is solved using a particular approach. So the book brings an exciting journey from the origins of reinforcement learning to the most advanced deep reinforcement learning methods using PyTorch and TensorFlow.

This book is divided into 2 parts. The first part introduces **classical reinforcement learning**. It covers the basics of reinforcement learning, explaining famous techniques like Q-learning, the Monte-Carlo method, and Thompson Sampling. The second part is dedicated to an advanced approach called **deep reinforcement learning**. It demonstrates how new achievements in neural networks and deep learning can help solve common real-life problems using Deep Q-Network, Double Deep Q-Network, Policy Gradient, and Actor-Critic methods.

Chapter 1 makes a short introduction to reinforcement learning. We will study the basics of reinforcement learning. Also, we will examine how reinforcement learning differs from other machine learning approaches. And finally, it shows some examples of reinforcement learning problems and their importance.

Chapter 2 will cover the basics of Markov reward process theory which makes the basis of whole reinforcement learning. We will study Markov reward processes using the example of the monopoly board game.

Chapter 3 introduces the Gym framework. Gym framework is a Python library that models an environment for reinforcement learning problems. Gym unifies the process of testing solutions to reinforcement learning problems and provides a lot of very fascinating environments that would be very useful for a beginner data scientist.

Chapter 4 will focus on the Multi-armed bandit problem. Despite the simplicity of the formulation and solution, this problem has great practical value. In this chapter, we will study two policies for solving the multi-armed bandit problem: epsilon greedy policy and Thompson sampling policy. The concepts covered in this chapter influence many aspects of reinforcement learning.

Chapter 5 illustrates the principles of the Monte Carlo method applied to blackjack. In this chapter, we will try to develop an optimal strategy for playing blackjack and then challenge the dealer. You will be introduced to the significant concept of the Q(s, a) action-value function, which is one of the cornerstones of reinforcement learning.

Chapter 6 introduces Q-learning and explains how this method can be used to find the shortest route to escape a maze. Q-learning is a very efficient reinforcement learning method, and the maze problem illustrates this method well.

Chapter 7 covers a handy discretization technique, which helps to adapt the environment with continuous state spaces to the classic reinforcement learning methods. This chapter provides a bridge from classical reinforcement learning to deep reinforcement learning.

Chapter 8 introduces the basic deep learning techniques with TensorFlow and PyTorch. It explains how to design and apply a neural network. And as the final step, we will demonstrate how to create a neural network for a handwritten digits recognition problem.

Chapter 9 shows one of the most popular deep reinforcement learning algorithms called Deep Q-Network or DQN. Many advanced deep reinforcement learning algorithms are based on DQN. DQN is the starting point where reinforcement learning and deep learning meet each other. This approach significantly expands the scope of reinforcement learning problems that can be practically solved.

Chapter 10 introduces the Double Deep Q-Network approach. We will apply this approach to train an agent playing video games!

Chapter 11 covers the Policy Gradient method. This approach allows us to solve the problems in which the Q-learning method is not good enough. We will study the pros and cons of this technique and apply it to the classical CartPole problem.

Chapter 12 tells us about the Actor-Critic method. The Actor-Critic approach combines the best of the policy gradient method and the Q-learning technique and is one of the most significant accomplishments of reinforcement learning. We will apply the Actor-Critic model to a real-life stock trading problem.

Chapter 13 finishes the book by making a global overview of reinforcement learning theory. In this chapter, we will see various directions a reader can follow after completing this book.

Code Bundle and Coloured Images

Please follow the link to download the
Code Bundle and the *Coloured Images* of the book:

https://rebrand.ly/fykbuvz

The code bundle for the book is also hosted on GitHub at **https://github.com/ bpbpublications/Practical-Deep-Reinforcement-Learning-with-Python**. In case there's an update to the code, it will be updated on the existing GitHub repository.

We have code bundles from our rich catalogue of books and videos available at **https://github.com/bpbpublications**. Check them out!

Errata

We take immense pride in our work at BPB Publications and follow best practices to ensure the accuracy of our content to provide with an indulging reading experience to our subscribers. Our readers are our mirrors, and we use their inputs to reflect and improve upon human errors, if any, that may have occurred during the publishing processes involved. To let us maintain the quality and help us reach out to any readers who might be having difficulties due to any unforeseen errors, please write to us at :

errata@bpbonline.com

Your support, suggestions and feedbacks are highly appreciated by the BPB Publications' Family.

Piracy

If you come across any illegal copies of our works in any form on the internet, we would be grateful if you would provide us with the location address or website name. Please contact us at **business@bpbonline.com** with a link to the material.

If you are interested in becoming an author

If there is a topic that you have expertise in, and you are interested in either writing or contributing to a book, please visit **www.bpbonline.com**. We have worked with thousands of developers and tech professionals, just like you, to help them share their insights with the global tech community. You can make a general application, apply for a specific hot topic that we are recruiting an author for, or submit your own idea.

Reviews

Please leave a review. Once you have read and used this book, why not leave a review on the site that you purchased it from? Potential readers can then see and use your unbiased opinion to make purchase decisions. We at BPB can understand what you think about our products, and our authors can see your feedback on their book. Thank you!

For more information about BPB, please visit **www.bpbonline.com**.

Table of Contents

Part - I

The first part of the book will be devoted to classical reinforcement learning methods. This part will consider the theoretical foundations of reinforcement learning problems and the primary techniques for solving them. One of the main concepts of the book's first part is the Q-Learning method. The Q-Learning method described in *Chapter 6: Escaping Maze With Q-Learning*, is the cornerstone for most reinforcement learning solutions. The book's first part can be considered as an introduction to reinforcement learning.

CHAPTER 1
Introducing Reinforcement Learning

Reinforcement learning (**RL**) is one of the most active research areas in machine learning. Many researchers think that RL will take us closer to reaching artificial general intelligence. In the past few years, RL has evolved rapidly and has been used in complex applications ranging from stock trading to self-driving cars. The main reason for this growth is the involvement of deep reinforcement learning, which is a combination of deep learning and reinforcement learning. Reinforcement learning is one of the most promising areas of machine learning that we will study in this book.

Structure

In this chapter, we will discuss the following topics:

- What is reinforcement learning?
- Reinforcement learning mechanism
- Reinforcement learning vs. supervised learning
- Applications of reinforcement learning

Objectives

After completing this chapter, you will have a basic understanding of reinforcement learning and its key definitions. You will also have learned how reinforcement learning works and how it differs from other machine learning approaches.

What is reinforcement learning?

Reinforcement learning is defined as a machine learning technique concerned with how agents should take actions in a surrounding environment depending on their current state. RL is a part of machine learning that helps an agent maximize the cumulative reward collected after making some sequence of actions. In RL, agents act in a known or unknown environment to constantly adapt and learn based on collected experience. The feedback of an environment might be positive, also known as rewards, or negative, also called **punishments**. At this point of time, all the above definitions may seem too abstract and unclear, but we will elaborate on them in this chapter.

The following figure represents the key concept of RL:

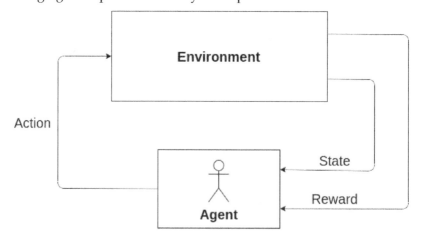

Figure 1.1: Reinforcement learning

Here, the agent is in some initial state in some environment. Then, the agent decides to take some action. The environment reacts to the agent's action, returns the agent some reward for his action, and transfers him to another state.

Most used reinforcement learning keywords are as follows:

- **Agent** is a decision-maker who defines what action to take.

  Examples: Self-driving car, chess player, stock trading robot

- **Action** is a concrete act in a surrounding environment that is taken by the agent.

  Examples: Turn car left, move chess pawn one cell forward, sell all assets

- **Environment** is a problem context that the agent cooperates with.

  Examples: Car track, chess board, stock market

- **State** is a position of the agent in the environment.

  Examples: Car coordinates on the track and its speed, arrangement of pieces on the chessboard, price of assets

- **Reward** is a numerical value returned by an environment as the reaction to the agent's action.

  Example: To reach a goal on the car without any accidents, to win chess play, to earn more money

RL is learning what to do or how to map situations to actions to maximize a reward. The agent doesn't know which actions to take but must learn which actions produce the most reward by trying them. Usually, actions may affect the immediate reward and the next situation and all subsequent rewards. It means that the agent should not think about the immediate reward only but about the reward in the long-term sense.

Reinforcement learning mechanics

In our life, we usually try to maximize our rewards. And it does not mean that we are always thinking about money or materialistic things. To give an example, when we read a new book to learn new skills, we understand that it is better to read a book carefully, without hurrying. Our way to read a book is a strategy, and the skills we gain are our reward. When we are negotiating with other people, we are trying to be polite, and the feedback we get is our reward.

The purpose of the reward is to tell our agent how well it has behaved. The main goal of RL is to find such strategy that maximizes the reward after some number of actions. Let's see some simple examples that help you illustrate the reinforcement learning mechanism.

Consider the following scientifically factual scenario. A robot has arrived on our planet. This robot is very good at designing posters but does not know how to negotiate with people. His target is *to get a job and make a lot of money in 5 years*. Good plan, why not? Every day, the robot makes a particular decision about how it will act today. At the end of the day, he checks his bank account and summarizes his state in the company.

Let's consider the first scenario. The robot decides to steal a computer from the office and sell it on the first working day. And it may seem that this is a pretty good decision because it will help the robot increase its balance significantly. But of course, we understand that the decision like this can be made only once, and the profits of our robot will stop there.

The following figure illustrates the first scenario:

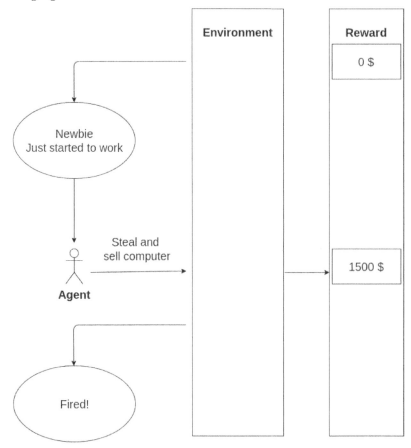

Figure 1.2: First strategy

Now, let's consider the second scenario. Every day the robot works hard and learns new things. In this case, his strategy is long-term. It may be inferior to other strategies in the short term, but it will be significantly more profitable in the long term.

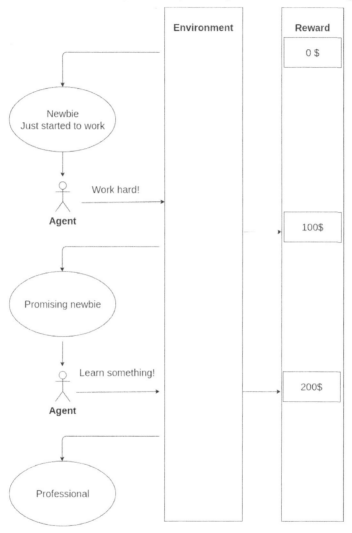

Figure 1.3: Second strategy

Of course, in real life, everything is much more complicated. But this example illustrates the principle when it is necessary to think several steps ahead. A solution that has a quick effect can be fatal in the long run. Reinforcement learning aims to find long-term strategies that maximize the agent's reward.

Here are some essential characteristics of reinforcement learning:

- There is no supervisor. Agent only receives a reward signal
- Sequential decision making
- Agent's actions determine the subsequent data it receives

The term reinforcement comes from the fact that a reward received by an agent should reinforce its behavior in a positive or negative direction. A local reward indicates the success of the agent's recent action and not overall successes achieved by the agent so far. Of course, getting a large reward for some action doesn't mean that you won't face dramatic consequences later due to your previous decisions. Remember our example with a robot that decides to rob a computer - it could look like a brilliant idea until you think about the next day.

The problem can be considered as RL problem if we can define the following:

- **Agent**: Define the subject, which takes some actions.
- **Environment**: Define the system that receives an agent's actions.
- **Set of states**: Define the set of states that an agent can receive. This set can be infinite.
- **Set of actions**: Define the set of actions an agent can take. This set can be infinite.
- **Reward**: Define what the agent's primary goal is and how it can be achieved with some reward system.

If all the above definitions can be obtained, you obviously deal with the reinforcement learning problem.

Reinforcement learning vs. supervised learning

When we have an intuitive understanding of reinforcement learning, we can examine how it differs from traditional supervised learning. A good rule of thumb is to treat reinforcement learning as a dynamic model and supervised learning as a static model. Let's elaborate on this.

We can use supervised learning as a statistical model that can extract some correlations and patterns from which they make predictions without being explicitly programmed. Generally speaking, supervised learning makes only one action. It takes input and returns the output. Its primary goal is to provide you with an automatically built function **F** that maps some input **X** into some output **Y**:

Figure 1.4: *Supervised learning*

While reinforcement learning builds an agent that makes a sequence of actions interacting with an environment, this agent cooperates with an environment and produces the sequence of actions:

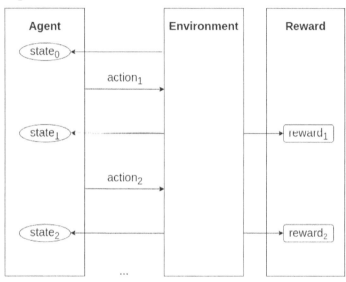

Figure 1.5: *Reinforcement learning*

Let's summarize all distinctions between reinforcement learning and supervised learning in the following table:

	Reinforcement learning	**Supervised learning**
Decision	RL takes decisions sequentially	SL makes only one decision applying function F to input X.
Input data	Environment provides input data.	Inputs are examples or sample data.
Action dependency	A decision is dependent on the previous ones.	A decision is independent of previous ones.
Example	Chess game	Object recognition

Table 1.1: *Reinforcement learning vs. supervised learning*

It is important to understand the difference between reinforcement learning and supervised learning. This knowledge will help you in the correct use of each of these methods.

Examples of reinforcement learning

In this section, we will see some popular examples of RL problems. In all these problems, we have the following: agent, environment, set of states, set of actions, and the reward.

Stock trading

This type of activity assumes making a profit by buying and selling shares of different companies. All traders tend to buy stocks of a company when they are cheap and sell when they are high:

Problem	Maximize profits by trading stocks on the stock market
Agent	Trader
Environment	Stock market
Action	Buy or sell stock
State	Actual stock price and quote history
Reward	An amount of profit is a reward for a trader buying and selling stocks

Table 1.2: Stock trading as RL problem

Chess

Chess is one of the oldest games. This game has many different styles and approaches. However, chess is also a reinforcement learning problem:

Problem	Win a chess game
Agent	Player
Environment	Opponent
Action	Chess move
State	Arrangement of chess pieces
Reward	The reward is obtained at the end of the game as a win, lose, or draw

Table 1.3: Chess as RL problem

Neural Architecture Search (NAS)

RL has been successfully applied to the domain of Neural network Architecture Search (NAS). The goal is to get the best performance on some datasets by selecting the number of layers or their parameters, adding extra connections, or making other changes to the architecture. The reward, in this case, is the performance of neural network architecture:

Problem	To find robust Neural Network Architecture
Agent	Architect
Environment	Nature of a process or dataset
Action	Generate new Neural Network Architecture
State	Test history and metrics
Reward	A positive reward is obtained if new architecture has better performance than preceding ones

Table 1.4: NAS as RL problem

As you can see, many practical problems can be solved using the reinforcement learning approach.

Conclusion

Reinforcement learning is a machine learning approach that aims to find optimal decision-making strategies. It differs from other machine learning approaches by emphasizing agent learning from direct interaction with its environment. It doesn't require traditional supervision or complete computational models of the environment. Reinforcement learning aims to find an appropriate long-term strategy that allows collecting maximum rewards to an agent. In the next chapter, we will study the theory of Markov decision processes that form the base of the entire reinforcement learning approach.

Points to remember

- A solution that has a quick effect can be fatal in the long run.

- RL doesn't assume any supervisor. Agent only receives a reward signal.

- RL produces a sequential decision-making strategy.

- Reinforcement learning is a dynamic model, and supervised learning is a static model.

Multiple choice questions

1. Let's consider a popular and simple computer game called Tetris, which has relatively simple mechanics. When the player builds one or more completed rows, the completed rows disappear, and the player gains some points. The game's goal is to prevent the blocks from stacking up to the top of the screen and collect as many points as possible.

Figure 1.6: Reinforcement learning

What do you think? Can Tetris be considered as an RL problem?

   a. Yes

   b. No

2. Considering Tetris as an RL problem, define an agent.

   a. Score

   b. Player

   c. Number of disappeared lines

3. Considering Tetris as an RL problem, define a state.

   a. Score

   b. Arrangement of bricks and score

   c. Arrangement of bricks, score, and the next element

Answers

1. a
2. b
3. c

Key terms

- **Agent**: A decision-maker who defines what action to take.
- **Action**: A concrete act in a surrounding environment that takes the agent.
- **Environment**: A problem context that the agent cooperates with.
- **State**: A position of an agent in the environment.
- **Reward**: A numerical value returned by an environment as the reaction of the agent's action.

## CHAPTER 2

Playing Monopoly and Markov Decision Process

In the last chapter, you got a general introduction to **reinforcement learning (RL)**. We saw different examples for different problems and highlighted the main characteristics of reinforcement learning. But before we start solving practical problems, we will formally describe how you can solve them using the RL approach. One of the RL cornerstones is the **Markov decision process (MDP)**. This concept is the foundation of the whole theory of reinforcement learning. We will dedicate this chapter to explaining what the Markov decision process is with the help of Monopoly game examples. We'll discuss MDPs in greater detail as we walk through the chapter. Markov chains and Markov decision processes are extensively used in many aspects of engineering and statistics. Reading this chapter will be useful for understanding the context of reinforcement learning and a much wider range of topics. If you're already familiar with MDPs, you can quickly get a grasp of this chapter, just by focusing on the terminology definitions that will be used later in the book.

Structure

In this chapter, we will discuss the following topics:

- What is the best strategy for playing Monopoly?
- Markov chain

- Markov reward process
- Markov decision process
- Policy
- Monopoly as Markov decision process

Objectives

The primary goal of this chapter is to provide the basics and fundamental concepts of reinforcement learning: Markov reward process and Policy. We will look at simple and straightforward examples that will allow us to understand what lies at the heart of these concepts. This chapter will give you a clear understanding of tasks that reinforcement learning deals with.

Choosing the best strategy for playing Monopoly

The formal mathematical explanation of Markov decision process often confuses the reader, although this concept is not as complicated as it might seem. In this chapter, we will explore what Markov decision process is by playing the popular game of Monopoly.

Let's create a list of simplified versions of the Monopoly game.

We will consider only simplified rules of the game here. This chapter does not need to go through a complete list of rules.

List of rules

Our custom simplified Monopoly game will follow the given set of rules:

1. Two players are playing. For the sake of simplicity, we will consider a game for two players only. We will denote the players by a square and a triangle:

Figure 2.1: *Monopoly players*

2. Each player rolls the dice and moves forward a certain number of cells:

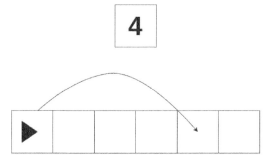

Figure 2.2: *Player 1 moves four steps forward*

3. Each cell can be purchased for the price indicated on it. When a player gets on a free cell, they have two options:

   • Buy a cell

   • Do not buy a cell

   It is not obligatory to buy a free cell:

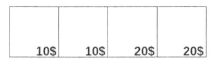

Figure 2.3: *Cell prices*

4. If a player lands on someone else's cell, then he must pay the other player 20% of the cost of the cell.

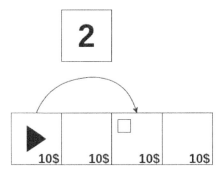

Figure 2.4: *Player 1 has to pay $2 to Player 2*

5. Each player starts the game with $100.

6. There are surprise cells on the board. They randomly give three results:

   - Player gets $10 from the bank

   - Player gives $5 to the bank

   - Player skips one turn

7. A player loses when they run out of money.

Let's take a look at the entire board:

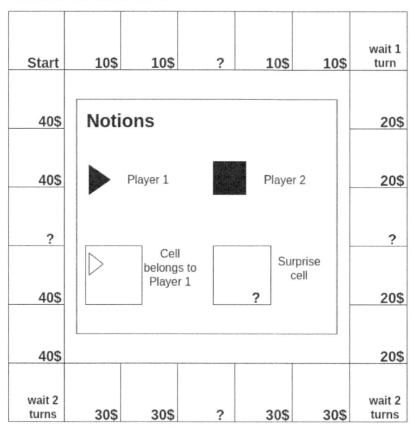

Figure 2.5: Monopoly playing board

Now that we have defined the rules, we have a more interesting question: *what strategy should we choose for the game?* It would seem that there is a reasonable and straightforward strategy: *buy everything you can!* Indeed, the more cells the player buys, the more rent he will receive when another player hits his cells. But everything is not so simple. Let's take a look at the example in *Figure 2.6*:

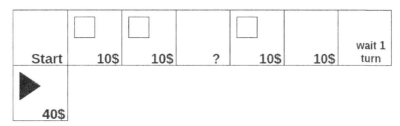

Figure 2.6: *To buy or not to buy?*

Suppose player 1 has only $40 left. And he just got on the cell that costs $40. Should they buy it? If player 1 buys it, then the probability of losing on the next move is extremely high. Because player 1 will have no money left, and they can get to the cells that have already been bought by player 2:

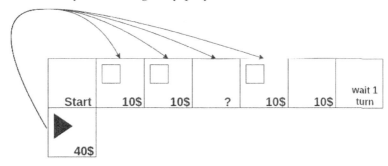

Figure 2.7: *Player 1 can lose on the next turn if he buys a cell*

As we can see, there is no primitive strategy in this game. A more advanced approach is needed to find the optimal strategy.

Markov chain

Assume that you have some process that you can only observe. At each moment, the process belongs to some state and can switch between states according to some transition probabilities. You cannot control the process but can only observe the states changing. All possible states of the process form a state space. For Markov chains, we require the state space to be finite. The sequence of process states forms a chain. That's why Markov chain is called as such. Markov chain requires that the probability of transition to the next state depend only on the current state. Markov chain processes do not have long-term memory. The probability distribution of the next state depends on the current state.

Let's consider a strictly mathematical definition of Markov chain. Markov chain is a random process defined by (**S, P**).

Where,

- **S** is a set of all possible states $\{S_1, S_2, ..., S_n\}$

- **P** is the state-transition probability. P_{ij} is the probability to reach state S_i directly from state S_j.

In simple cases, a Markov chain can be depicted using the state transition diagram. Let's consider vacation activities state transition diagram depicted in *Figure: 2.8*:

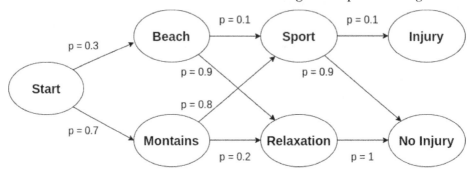

Figure 2.8: Vacation activities as Markov chain

The main question that the theory of Markov chains studies is as follows:

"What is the probability of reaching the state S' from the state S".

Example: What is the probability that a vacation will end with an injury?

The player's movement across the board in a monopoly game is a typical Markov chain. The probability of moving to each of the next six cells equals $1/6$.

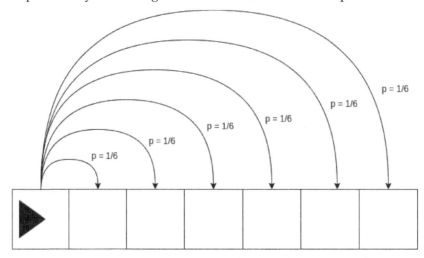

Figure 2.9: Monopoly as Markov Chain

Now let's add rewards to the Markov chain model to make it closer to reinforcement learning problems.

Markov reward process

Let's introduce a reward to the process that we have observed before. Imagine that each transition between states adds some positive or negative reward to the process' bank. Each transition has some influence that is expressed by some number. To make Markov reward process from Markov chain, we need to add value to each transition.

Let's consider a mathematical definition first. Markov reward process is a random process defined by (**S, P, R**), where:

- **S** is a set of all possible states $\{S_1, S_2, ..., S_n\}$

- **P** is the state-transition probability. P_{ij} is the probability of reaching state S_i directly from state S_j.

- **R** is the state-transition reward. R_{ij} is the reward gained by to state S_i directly from state S_j.

We can try to visualize Markov reward process adding rewards to transitions. Let's consider vacation activities observed earlier. *Figure 2.10* demonstrates a transition diagram with rewards:

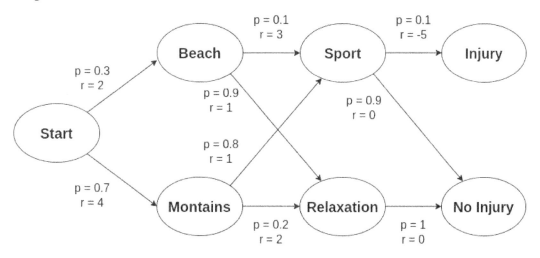

Figure 2.10: *Vacation activities as Markov reward process*

Positive emotions are the main thing on vacation. We can call these positive emotions rewards that we receive during the rest. In *Figure 2.10*, we have assigned the received positive emotions through *r*.

You may notice an interesting detail. The reward is assigned not only to the state but to the transition as well. And it makes sense. Will we get great enjoyment if we immediately go in for sports after a long walk in the mountains? We will be tired, and it is unlikely that we will have a lot of energy for sports. But after relaxing on the beach, we will have a lot of energy, and sports will give us much more pleasure.

That is why we have such rewards:

- $R_{mountains,sport} = 1$
- $R_{beach,sport} = 3$

The main question that the theory of Markov reward processes studies is as follows:

"What is the probability of gaining x scores after n number of steps".

Example: What is the probability that we will collect 5 scores during vacation?

As you can see, the theory of Markov reward processes is not as concerned about the state in the future as it is about the rewards received in the random process.

If we make a small change in rule 3 of our monopoly game, like *if the player has the required amount of money, then they must buy a free cell he gets in*, then our game will turn into a pure Markov reward process.

You can see that after each random transition, players receive a particular reward:

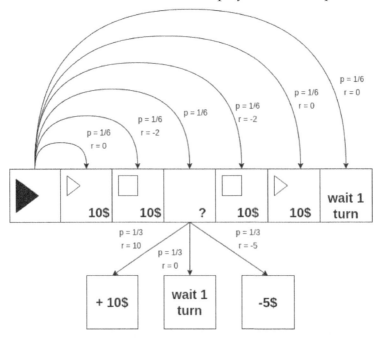

Figure 2.11: Monopoly as Markov reward process

We can elaborate on the information given in *Figure 2.11* in the following table:

Dice	Probability	Reward	Explanation
1	1/6	0	This cell already belongs to player 1.
2	1/6	-2	This cell belongs to player 2, so $2 should be paid (20% of cell price).
3 and Card 1	$1/6 \times 1/3 = 1/18$	10	Transitions to Surprise cell and Card1 is picked, which gives $10.
3 and Card 2	$1/6 \times 1/3 = 1/18$	0	Transitions to Surprise cell and Card2 is picked, and we need to skip 1 turn.
3 and Card 3	$1/6 \times 1/3 = 1/18$	-5	Transitions to Surprise cell and Card1 is picked, which takes $5.
4	1/6	-2	This cell belongs to player 2, so $2 should be paid (20% of cell price).
5	1/6	0	This cell already belongs to player 1.
6	1/6	0	We need to skip 1 turn.

Table 2.1: Probabilities and rewards of the next turn

Let's now answer the question: what is the probability of not losing money on the next turn? The answer to this question is pretty simple. We just need to sum up the probabilities of transitions that have non-negative rewards:

$$\frac{1}{6} + \frac{1}{18} + \frac{1}{18} + \frac{1}{6} + \frac{1}{6} = \frac{11}{18}$$

We are more likely not to lose money, but what is the probability of making money on the next move? Everything is much simpler here. To earn at least something, we need to get on the surprise cell and get **Card1**. The probability of this event is $1/18$.

The theory of Markov reward processes studies the probabilities of rewards to be received in the future.

Markov decision process

And now, we come to the most interesting part of this chapter. All the models that we have described till now do not imply the participation of the player. All of them represented a series of random events.

Let's take a look at the game of monopoly we described before with the original rule 3:

Each cell can be purchased for the price indicated on it. When a player gets on a free cell, they have two options:

- Buy a cell

- Do not buy a cell

It is not obligatory to buy a free cell.

So, now the player can make a decision *to buy or not to buy a cell.* Let's consider the situation presented in *Figure 2.12*:

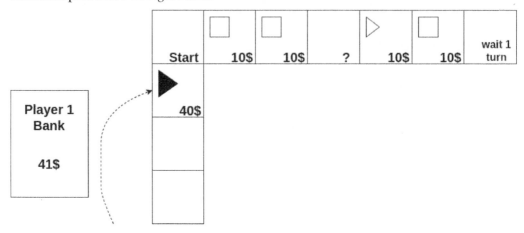

Figure 2.12: *To buy or not to buy?*

Player 1 has $41 in the bank and transits to a cell that costs $40. Would it be a good decision to buy it? Let's try to answer this question mathematically. If we buy this cell, then we only have $1 left. Will this dollar be enough for the next turn?

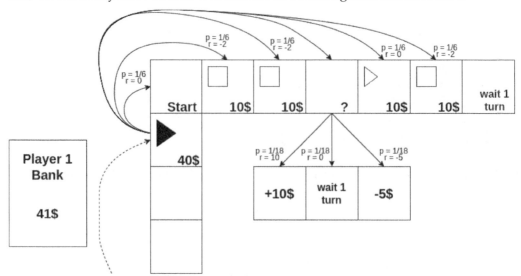

Figure 2.13: *Next turn probabilities and rewards*

Let's calculate the probability that we will not be bankrupt on the next turn, that is, let's calculate the probabilities of transitions that will not make us lose more than $1:

$$\frac{1}{6} + \frac{1}{18} + \frac{1}{18} + \frac{1}{6} = \frac{4}{9}$$

This means that with a probability of more than 50%, we will lose on the next turn if we buy a cell now.

The Markov decision process consists of states, a transition probability, a reward function, and actions: (**S, P, R, A**).

Where,

- **S** is a set of all possible states $\{S_1, S_2, ..., S_n\}$

- **P** is the state-transition probability. P_{ij} is the probability of reaching state S_i directly from state S_j.

- **R** is the state-transition reward. R_{ij} is the reward gained by to state S_i directly from state S_j.

- A is a set of all available actions.

The Markov decision process theory helps estimate the effectiveness and consequences of making a particular decision.

Let's look at the concepts of states, probabilities, rewards, and actions using the example of the monopoly game.

State

The state is the game board snapshot. It can be depicted as follows:

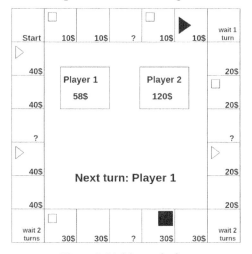

Figure 2.14: Monopoly State

The state depicted in *Figure 2.14* includes the following:

- Player positions
- Player balances
- Player assets (cells that were purchased)
- Who makes the next turn?

Probability

During the game, the state can change with a certain probability:

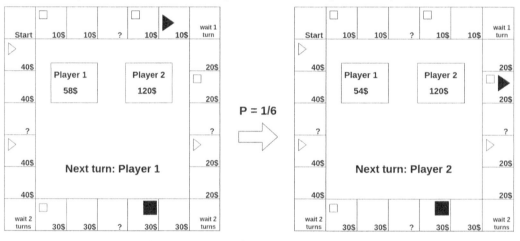

Figure 2.15: Monopoly state transition probability

It is worth mentioning that most state transitions are not possible. The probability of such transitions is equal to zero:

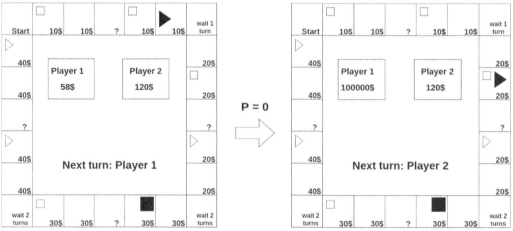

Figure 2.16: Monopoly impossible state transition

Figure 2.16 shows that player 1 can't raise their balance to $1,000,000 in one move. This transition is impossible.

Reward

Each state transition has its reward. In our case, the reward is player 1's balance change:

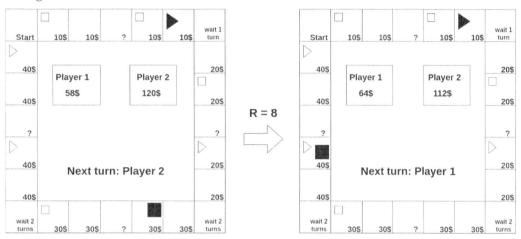

Figure 2.17: *Monopoly state transition reward*

Figure 2.17 shows that player 2 moves to the cell that belongs to player 1 and is obliged to pay them $8.

Actions

Each state defines a set of valid actions. There are only two actions for the game of monopoly:

- No action

- Buy a cell

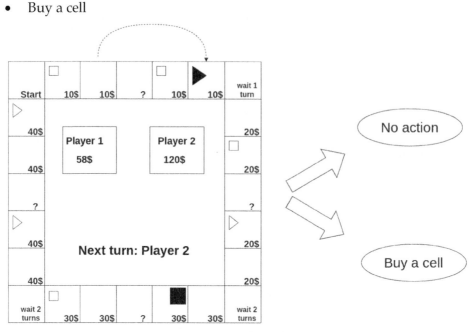

Figure 2.18: Actions allowed for player 1

As we can see in *Figure 2.18*, player 1, after completing the move to the cell, has 2 possible actions: No action or Buy a cell. But in most states of the game, player 1 will only have one formal action: No action.

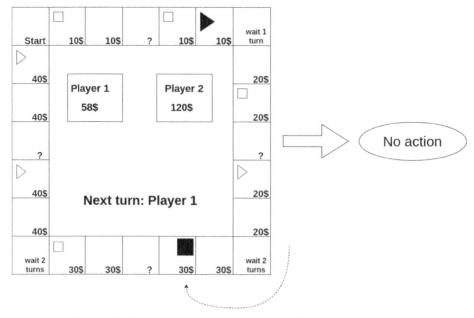

Figure 2.19: Player 1 cannot do anything when Player 2 makes their turn

Player 1 has two possible actions only when they get to a free cell. In all other cases, player 1 does not have any freedom of choice, and the game process behaves as a purely random process.

We do not consider rolling the dice as a separate game action. Of course, the player technically makes action by rolling the dice, but the result of this action is entirely random and in no way depends on the player's will.

Now that we have studied Markov decision process, we're ready to consider the critical thing for reinforcement learning: policy.

Policy

And so, we come to the key concept of this chapter. The result of applying reinforcement learning is a policy. Policy is some predefined set of rules that answers the question, *What action should be taken in a certain situation?*

In mathematical terms, a policy is a function from the set of all possible states to the set of all possible actions.

$$\pi: \{State\ set\} \rightarrow \{Action\ set\}$$

In reinforcement learning, policy completely defines the behavior of the agent. Let's give some examples of policies for reinforcement learning problems.

Blackjack

In blackjack, a policy can define a player's strategy. What actions should the agent take depending on the cards on the table?

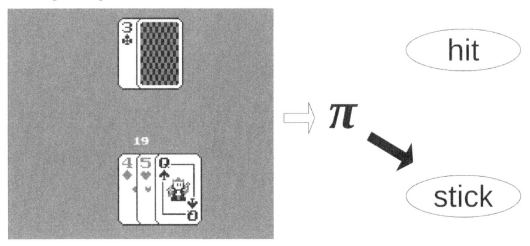

Figure 2.20: *Blackjack policy*

Figure 2.20 demonstrates how policy returns a decision to a stick action, which is quite reasonable since the player is already getting too close to the number 21.

Stock trading

In a stock trading, policy manages the investor's orders:

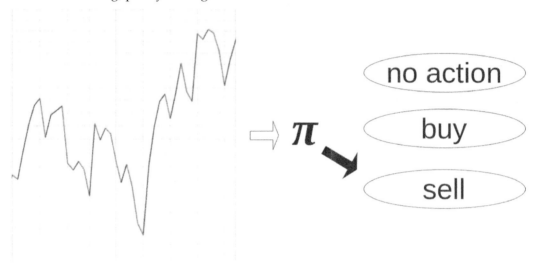

Figure 2.21: *Stock trading policy*

Figure 2.21 demonstrates how policy returns a decision to sell shares.

Video games

In video games, a policy can press the joystick buttons depending on what is happening on the screen.

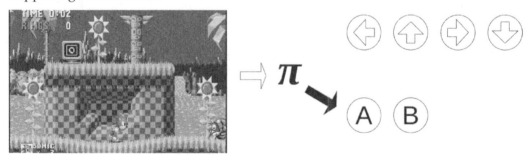

Figure 2.22: *Video game policy*

Figure 2.22 demonstrates how policy returns a decision to press A button, which means jump to avoid meeting with an enemy.

The main goal of the agent in reinforcement learning is to collect as much return as possible. Different policies can give us different amounts of rewards. Therefore, reinforcement learning aims to create a policy that is most likely to maximize rewards. And this is a fascinating challenge! We often don't know the internal mechanics of the environment. We usually don't see what lies behind the logic of the environment. But when interacting with the environment, we learn how to get the maximum rewards.

Monopoly as Markov decision process

Let's get back to our monopoly game. Suppose we play this game versus the robot. The robot plays this game with us according to the prescribed rules: *Buy everything you can.*

This game belongs to the class of Markov decision processes:

- Next state probability distribution depends on the current state only
- State-to-state transaction has predefined probability
- State-to-state transaction has predefined reward
- There is an action space to take

What policy do we need to choose in this game to most likely beat the robot? Despite the simplicity of this question, the answer can be complicated. Analytical and mathematical analysis of this model can take weeks or months of theoretical calculations, whereas reinforcement learning can automatically find the most optimal policy in this game. Even for environments whose laws and rules of behavior are well known to us, the answer to the question of optimal behavior can be very complex.

Conclusion

The MDP gives a mathematical core for solving the RL problems. Almost all RL problems can be modeled as an MDP. Many approaches to solving reinforcement learning problems are based on the theory of Markov processes. A good understanding of the principles described in this chapter will make it much easier to dive into RL.

That's it. We have finished the introduction part, and now we are ready to practice. In the next chapter, we will look at modeling various environments using the OpenAI GYM framework.

Points to remember

- The Markov chain theory studies the distribution probability of future states.

- The Markov reward processes theory studies the probabilities of rewards to be received in the future.

- Markov decision process is an extension of the Markov reward process with an action space.

- The goal of reinforcement learning is to find an optimal policy that controls agent behavior.

Multiple choice questions

1. Let's consider two states in monopoly game: State A (*Figure 2.23*) and State B (*Figure 2.24*). What is the probability that the system will move to state B from state A after two turns?

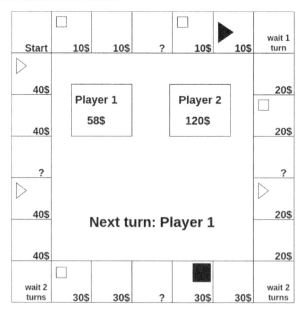

Figure 2.23: State A

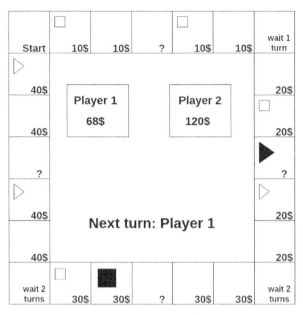

Figure 2.24: State B

   a. 1/36

   b. 1/3

   c. 1/108

   d. None of these

2. Let's take another look at the reward transition diagram (*Figure 2.25*). What is the probability that the vacation will end with $r = 0$?

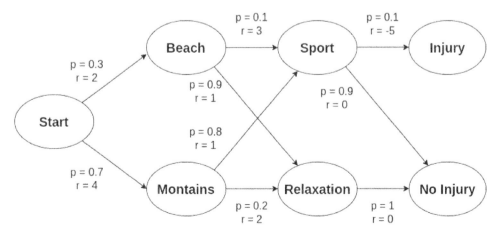

Figure 2.25: Vacation state-to-state transition diagram

    a. 0.003

    b. 0.5

    c. 0.01

3. Let's take a look at the blackjack game. Let's say we have two game policies:

π_1: *always hit*

π_2: *always stick*

Estimate the probabilities of these policies.

    a. $P(\pi_1) = P(\pi_2) = 0$ – both these policies lose the blackjack game in all cases.

    b. $P(\pi_1) = 0$ – policy π_1 loses the game in all cases. $P(\pi_2) > 0$ – policy π_2 has some chances of winning.

Answers

1. **c**

2. **a**

3. **b**

Key terms

- Markov chain is a random process in which the future state is dependent on the current state only.

- Markov reward process is a random process that extends Markov chain by adding a reward at state-to-state transition.

- Markov decision process is an extension of the Markov reward process with action space.

- Policy is a set of rules that defines a specific agent behavior in the Markov decision process.

CHAPTER 3
Training in Gym

In the first two chapters of this book, we saw the basics of reinforcement learning. The set of tasks that can be solved using the means of reinforcement learning tools is quite broad, and each of these tasks may have its own code implementation. At the same time, various RL techniques can be applied to any RL problem. But at this point, an applicability problem may arise since each task can have its own implementation, and it can be quite challenging to implement a specific RL algorithm in a particular situation. Gym solves this problem by unifying all reinforcement learning tasks, and we dedicate this chapter to exploring this useful toolkit.

Structure

In this chapter, we will look at the following topics:

- Why do we need Gym?
- Installation
- CartPole environment
- Interacting with Gym
- Gym environments
- Custom environment
- Custom environment with PyGame

Objectives

The primary goal of this chapter is to present the Gym library as the primary tool for reinforcement learning tasks. After completing this chapter, you will know how to use existing environments and develop custom ones.

Why do we need Gym?

Gym unifies the process of testing solutions to reinforcement learning problems. Each RL problem can have its own unique solution, which will allow the agent to maximize rewards. It is often helpful to test several pre-designed RL algorithms and see which one performs the best. Such brute force technique can provide a useful direction for developing your own solution or possibly applying an existing one. The Gym toolkit offers a standard interface for all RL problems, which allows you to test various solution production-ready algorithms.

The key Gym concept is an *environment*. Environment is an object that has all Markov reward process features. The entire process of constructing a solution to the RL problem can be illustrated as follows:

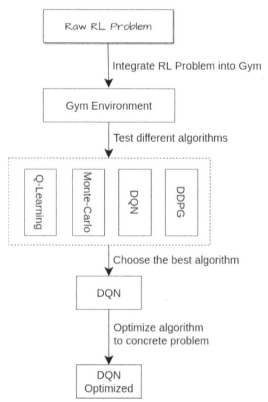

Figure 3.1: *Constructing a solution to the RL problem*

Figure 3.1 illustrates the process of constructing a solution to the RL problem:

- We integrate the problem into a Gym environment

- We test different RL algorithms

- We choose the best RL algorithm

- We optimize the chosen RL algorithm for our task

As you can see, to apply various solutions to reinforcement learning problems, we need to start by learning the Gym toolkit. So, let's get started!

Installation

Installation is straightforward, but there are minor differences in different versions. We are using version 0.19.0 in this book, and we strongly recommend that you install the same version because we will use this version further:

```
pip install gym==0.19.0
```

Additionally, install a separate package of Atari games:

```
pip install gym[atari]==0.19.0
```

And package for Box2D environments:

```
conda install swig
pip install box2d-py
pip install pyglet
```

CartPole environment

After installation, let's look at the classic example of reinforcement learning in robotics. The problem is as follows:

An un-actuated joint attaches a pole to a cart, which moves along a frictionless track. The pendulum starts moving, and the goal is to prevent it from falling over by moving the cart left and right.

***Figure 3.2**: CartPole environment*

Let's see how Gym simulates interaction with the CartPole environment **ch3/cart_pole/cart_pole_random.py**.

Importing necessary packages:

```
from time import sleep
import gym
import random
```

Initializing CartPole Environment:

```
env = gym.make('CartPole-v1')
```

Making the script reproducible:

```
seed = 0
random.seed(seed)
env.seed(seed)
print(f'Action Space: {env.action_space}')
```

```
>>> Action Space: Discrete(2)
```

Agent has two actions in this environment:

- 0 – move cart left
- 1 – move cart right

```
print(f'Observation Space: {env.observation_space}')
```

```
>>> Observation Space: Box([-4.8 -inf -.418 +inf], [4.8 +inf .418 +inf],
(4,))
```

The environment has the following state space:

Parameter	Min	Max
Cart Position	-4.8	4.8
Cart Velocity	$-\infty$	$+\infty$
Pole Angle	-0.418	0.418
Pole Anglular Velocity	$-\infty$	$+\infty$

Table 3.1: *CartPole State Space*

Let's run 10 episodes in a row:

```
episodes = 10
for i in range(episodes):
```

We reset environment state:

```
init_state = env.reset()
reward_sum = 0
```

We are trying to balance the pole **forever**:

```
while True:
```

The **render** method visualizes the process and is very helpful for the understanding:

```
env.render()
```

We generate random action: 0 (left) or 1 (right):

```
random_action = random.randint(0, 1)
```

The **step** method returns the reaction of the environment on the action we made:

Figure 3.3: *Environment transition after an action*

Table 3.2 describes the data returned by the environment after an action is taken:

State	Next state of the environment after the action we made
reward	1 if pole did not fall and 0 otherwise
done	False if pole did not fall and True otherwise
debug	Debug information: it should not be used in learning

Table 3.2: *env.step method result*

```
state, reward, done, debug = env.step(random_action)
```

Summing up all rewards:

```
reward_sum += reward
```

Artificially slowing down the process:

```
sleep(.01)
```

We quit an episode when the pole falls:

```
if done:
    print(f'Episode {i} reward: {reward_sum}')
    sleep(1)
    break
```

Closing the environment:

```
env.close()
```

Result

Episode	Reward
0	35
1	15
2	44
3	16
4	33
5	22
6	31
7	22
8	26
9	11

Obviously, random movements cannot keep the balance for a long time. Balancing is one of the most challenging tasks in robotics. Let's review exactly how we keep the balance. Often, we try to move in the same direction in which the center of gravity is shifted to prevent the object from falling. It means that we shift the cart to the right when the pole is shifted to the right, and we shift the cart to the left when the pole is shifted to the left. *Figure 3.4* illustrates this principle:

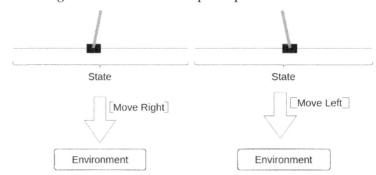

Figure 3.4: Balancing the pole

So, let's try to implement this idea. We move the cart to the left if the pole angle is negative, and we move the cart to the right if the pole angle is positive **ch3/cart_pole/cart_pole_angle.py**:

```
from time import sleep
import gym
import random

env = gym.make('CartPole-v1')

seed = 1
random.seed(seed)
env.seed(seed)

episodes = 10

for i in range(episodes):
    state = env.reset()
    reward_sum = 0
    while True:
        env.render()
        action = 1 if state[2] > 0 else 0
        state, reward, done, debug = env.step(action)
        reward_sum += reward
        sleep(.01)
        if done:
            print(f'Episode {i} reward: {reward_sum}')
            sleep(1)
            break

env.close()
```

Result

Episode	Reward
0	50
1	38
2	41
3	25

Episode	Reward
4	24
5	50
6	37
7	40
8	47
9	25

Well, this approach performs better than random actions, but it still drops the pole too quickly. The problem that we are trying to solve is quite complex, and the development of an analytical solution can take weeks of efforts and the involvement of highly qualified specialists. In contrast, reinforcement learning methods can solve similar problems without involving a human.

You can watch this exciting video on how reinforcement learning helps a robot balance a pole: https://www.youtube.com/watch?v=5Q14EjnOJZc

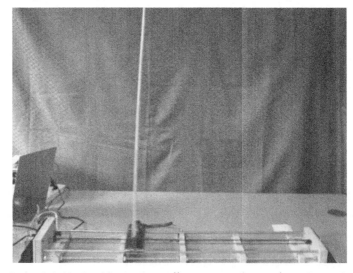

Figure 3.5: Real pole balancing (Source: https://www.youtube.com/watch?v=5Q14EjnOJZc)

This section has implemented a simple example of interacting with the CartPole environment using the Gym toolkit. Let's take a closer look at Gym's capabilities.

Interacting with Gym

Gym is a pretty simple framework. This section will list the main methods that you may need when working with the Gym.

List of environments

Each environment has its own unique id. You can get a list of all pre-installed environments the following way **ch3/gym_methods/env_list.py**:

```
from gym import envs


for e in envs.registry.all():
    print(e.id)
```

Environment initialization

The very first step is to initialize the environment **ch3/gym_methods/env_init.py**:

```
import gym


env = gym.make('Blackjack-v0')
```

Reproducible script

It is often necessary to reproduce the same script several times with the same random events. The random seed is set as follows **ch3/gym_methods/env_repr.py**:

```
import gym
import random


env = gym.make('Blackjack-v0')


seed = 1
random.seed(seed)
env.seed(seed)
```

Action space

Each environment has its own action space **ch3/gym_methods/env_act_space.py**:

```
import gym


env = gym.make('Blackjack-v0')
print(env.action_space)
```

Result

```
>>> Discrete(2)
```

Discrete(2) means that the **Blackjack-v0** environment assumes only two actions: 0 and 1. We'll take a closer look at this environment in the next chapter.

Reset environment

The **reset** method resets the environment to its original state:

```
init_state = env.reset()
```

Render environment

The **render** method renders the current state of the environment. This method makes the problem-solving process more enjoyable **ch3/gym_methods/env_render.py**:

```
from time import sleep
import gym


env = gym.make('CartPole-v1')
env.reset()
env.render()
sleep(10)
```

Send action to environment

The most critical method is the **step** method. This method simulates the action of the agent in the environment. The **step** method dispatches a specific action and receives four variables as a result:

- **state**: Next state of the environment after the action is made.

- **reward**: Reward received after the action.

- **done**: Whether it's time to reset the environment again. Most (but not all) tasks are divided into well-defined episodes and done being True indicates that the episode has terminated.

- **debug**: Diagnostic information useful for debugging. Official evaluations of your agent are not allowed to use this for learning.

  ch3/gym_methods/env_action.py:

  ```
  import gym
  ```

```
env = gym.make('CartPole-v1')

env.reset()

state, reward, done, debug = env.step(-1)
```

Close environment

The **close** method closes the environment. This method should be used so that the environment can shut down gracefully and release some processes and descriptors.

In this section, we covered the basic methods of operating with the Gym. Let's take a look at the variety of environments now.

Gym environments

Gym has many built-in and third-party environments. The solution of some problems can have great theoretical importance. The process of reinforcement learning in some environments is quite fun. In this section, we'll take a look at some of the popular environments.

Lunar Lander

The agent's goal is to land the lander between yellow flags. The landing pad is always at the coordinates (0,0). The reward for moving from the top of the screen to the landing pad and zero speed is about 100-140 points. If the lander moves away from the landing pad, it loses reward. The episode finishes if the lander crashes or comes to rest, receiving additional -100 or +100 points. Each leg ground contact is +10. Landing outside the landing pad is possible. Fuel is infinite, so an agent can learn to fly and then land on its first attempt. Four discrete actions are available:

- Do nothing
- Fire left orientation engine
- Fire main engine
- Fire right orientation engine

You can run Lunar Landar environment with random agent **ch3/gym_environments/ lunar_lander.py**:

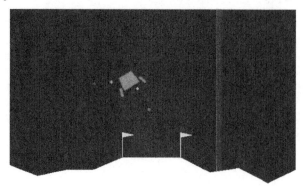

Figure 3.6: Lunar Lander

Mountain car

A car is positioned between two *mountains*. The goal is to reach the mountain on the right. The car's engine is not strong enough to ascend the mountain in a single pass. The only way to succeed is to drive back and forth to build up impulse.

Here is the script to test Mountain Car environment **ch3/gym_environments/ mountain_car.py**:

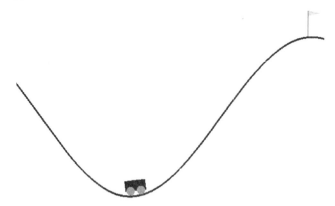

Figure 3.7: Mountain car

Phoenix

This environment is one of the legendary Atari video game series. In this game, you have to maximize your score. Developing agents who can play this game is as exciting as playing it **ch3/gym_environments/phoenix.py**:

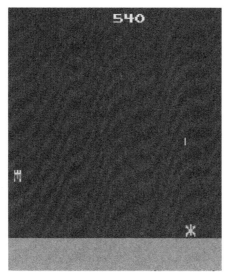

Figure 3.8: Atari Phoenix

Custom environment

We have already seen many ready-made environments for testing various reinforcement learning algorithms. But what if we need to implement a custom environment for a specific problem? Our goal is to solve practical, real-life issues, but not artificial ones. Let's study how to build your own custom Gym environment.

Let's try to create a simple computer game. We will call it a coin catcher. The plane is flying in the sky. There are many coins with different points: 1, 2, or 3 in the sky field. The plane intends to collect the maximum number of points moving left and right:

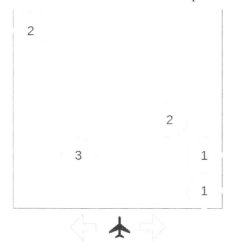

Figure 3.9: Coin catcher game design

Each timeframe, the coins are shifted one step lower, and the plane can perform one of the following three actions:

- Move to the left
- Stay in place
- Move to the right

The gameplay of this game can be represented as follows:

- **Timeframe #1**: The field contains 2 coins. The plane moves left to catch a 3-point coin.

Figure 3.10: *Timeframe #1*

- **Timeframe #2**: The plane catches a 3-point coin and moves right to catch a 2-point coin.

Figure 3.11: *Timeframe #2*

- **Timeframe #3**: The plane catches a 2-point coin. There are no more coins left on the field.

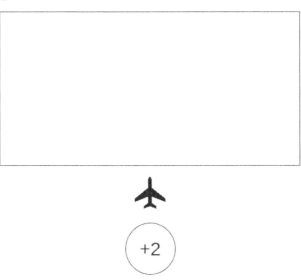

Figure 3.12: *Timeframe #3*

To implement our coin catcher environment in Gym, we need to define four methods: **__init__**, **step**, **reset**, and **render**. Let's study the implementation **ch3/custom_ env/catch_coins_env.py**:

Importing necessary packages:

```
from math import ceil
from random import random, randint
import gym
import sys
import collections
```

Initialization

The **CatchCoinsEnv** class inherits **gym.Env**:

```
class CatchCoinsEnv(gym.Env):
```

The first version of the environment will only have the **ascii render** mode:

```
    metadata = {"render.modes": ["ascii"]}
```

The environment has three parameters:

- **display_width**: Field width

- **display_height**: Field height

- **density**: Coin density. The higher this parameter is, the more coins will appear in the field

```python
def __init__(self, display_width = 10, display_height = 10,
density = .8):
    self.display_width = display_width
    self.display_height = display_height
    self.density = density
    self.display = collections.deque(maxlen = display_height)
    self.last_action = None
    self.last_reward = None
    self.total_score = 0
    self.v_position = 0
    self.game_scr = None
```

The **line_generator** method generates a new line with some coins:

```python
def line_generator(self):
    line = [0] * self.display_width
    if random() > (1 - self.density):
        r = random()
        if r < .6:
            v = 1
        elif r < .9:
            v = 2
        else:
            v = 3

        line[randint(0, self.display_width - 1)] = v
    return line
```

Step

The **step** method takes the agent's action and calculates the rewards:

```
def step(self, action):
    self.last_action = action
    self.v_position = min(max(self.v_position + action, 0), self.
display_width - 1)
    reward = self.display[0][self.v_position]
    self.last_reward = reward
    self.total_score += reward
    self.display.append(self.line_generator())
    state = self.display, self.v_position
    done = False
    info = {}
    return state, reward, done, info
```

Reset

The **reset** method generates a new environment:

```
def reset(self):
    for _ in range(self.display_height):
        self.display.append(self.line_generator())
    self.v_position = ceil(self.display_width / 2)
    state = self.display, self.v_position
    return state
```

Render

The **render** method renders the environment in ascii format:

```
def render(self, mode = "ascii"):
    if mode == "ascii":
        self._render_ascii()
    else:
        raise Exception('Not Implemented')

    def _render_ascii(self):
```

```
    outfile = sys.stdout


    area = []


    for i in range(self.display_height):
        line = self.display[self.display_height - 1 - i]
        row = []
        for j in range(len(line)):
            p = line[j]
            if p > 0:
                row.append(str(p))
                if i > 0 and area[-1][j] == ' ':
                    area[-1][j] = '|'
                if i > 1 and area[-2][j] == ' ':
                    area[-2][j] = '.'
            else:
                row.append(' ')
        area.append(row)


    pos_line = (['_'] * self.display_width)
    pos_line[self.v_position] = str(self.last_reward) if self.last_
reward else 'V'


    area.append(pos_line)
    outfile.write(f"\nTotal score: {self.total_score} \n")
    outfile.write("\n".join("  ".join(line) for line in area) + "\n")
```

Custom Coin Catcher Environment is ready! Now let's let the random agent play this game **ch3/custom_env/random_agent.py**:

```
import random
from time import sleep
from ch3.custom_env.catch_coins_env import CatchCoinsEnv


env = CatchCoinsEnv()
```

```
init_state = env.reset()
# -1: left
#  0: stay
# +1: right
action_space = [-1, 0, 1]


for _ in range(1000):
    env.render()
    action = random.choice(action_space)
    state, reward, done, debug = env.step(action)
    sleep(1)


env.close()
```

And you can see the gameplay process:

```
Total score: 7
1

            .

            |

            2

        .

        |  .

    1   |              .

    .   1              |

    |                  1

    3

_   _   _   _   _   _   _   V   _   _
```

Nice! We have constructed our first custom environment in Gym. But it would be better to have another environment rendering. We will study visual rendering approach in the next section.

Custom Environment with PyGame

Never underestimate the power of human intuition. Sometimes, a simple glance at the visualization of a dataset or a process can say about it more than hundreds of numbers and parameters. Therefore, in machine learning, primary visualization of datasets and their characteristics is essential. The same goes for reinforcement learning. A well-visualized environment can go a long way and leads to solving a problem and making the research process more enjoyable.

In the previous section, we used the ASCII environment rendering. In some cases, this rendering format may be acceptable, but let's look at a way to make the environment rendering more attractive.

To do this, we use the PyGame library, which allows us to draw various geometric objects on the screen. Studying the PyGame library is outside the scope of this book. To learn all the features of this library, you can refer to the official documentation: https://www.pygame.org.

The class responsible for drawing the game screen looks as follows **ch3/custom_env_pygame/catch_coins_screen.py**:

```python
import os

#Set up the colors
BLACK = (0, 0, 0)
RED = (255, 0, 0)
GREEN = (0, 255, 0)
BLUE = (0, 0, 255)
WHITE = (255, 255, 255)

class CatchCoinsScreen:
    img_path = os.path.dirname(os.path.realpath(__file__)) + '/airplane.png'
    rct_size = 50

    def __init__(self, h = 5, w = 5) -> None:
        import pygame
        pygame.init()
        self.h = h
        self.w = w
        scr_size = ((w + 2) * self.rct_size, (h + 3) * self.rct_size)
```

```python
        self.scr = pygame.display.set_mode(scr_size, 0, 32)
        self.img = pygame.image.load(CatchCoinsScreen.img_path)
        self.font = pygame.font.SysFont(None, 48)
        pygame.display.set_caption('Catch Coins Game')
        super().__init__()

    def plus(self):
        import pygame
        self.scr.fill(GREEN)
        pygame.display.update()

    def update(self, display, plane_pos, total_score):
        import pygame
        self.scr.fill(WHITE)
        for i in range(len(display)):
            line = display[len(display) - 1 - i]
            for j in range(len(line)):
                p = line[j]
                if p > 0:
                    coord = ((j + 1) * self.rct_size, (i + 1) * self.
rct_size)
                    self.scr.blit(self.font.render(str(p), True, BLACK),
coord)

        self.scr.blit(self.font.render(f'Total: {total_score}', True,
BLACK), (10, 10))
        self.scr.blit(self.img, (self.rct_size * plane_pos + 30, (self.h
+ 1) * self.rct_size))
        pygame.display.update()

    @classmethod
    def render(cls, display, plane_pos, total_score):
        scr = CatchCoinsScreen()
        scr.update(display, plane_pos, total_score)
```

Accordingly, we need to implement another rendering method in the Coin Catcher environment **ch3/custom_env_pygame/catch_coins_env.py**:

```python
def _render_human(self):
    from catch_coins_game import CatchCoinsScreen
    if not self.game_scr:
        self.game_scr = CatchCoinsScreen(
            h = self.display_height,
            w = self.display_width
        )

    if self.last_reward:
        self.game_scr.plus()
        sleep(.1)

    self.game_scr.update(
        self.display,
        self.v_position,
        self.total_score
    )
```

Now, let's see what it looks like running the following script **ch3/custom_env_ pygame/random_agent.py**:

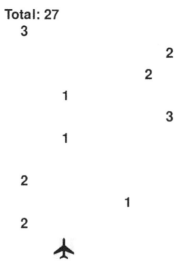

Figure 3.13: PyGame environment rendering

As you can see, this rendering format is much smoother and more enjoyable to observe. While developing your custom environments in the Gym toolkit, try to pay more attention to producing good-quality rendering.

Conclusion

That's it! In this chapter, we have taken the last important step. We introduced the Gym framework, which allows us to unify the work with various Markov reward processes. We are now ready to move on to examining various approaches that allow us to create RL agents. In the next chapter, we'll study an algorithm that trains an agent to play Blackjack, maximizing their chances of winning.

Points to Remember

- Gym unifies the process of testing solutions to reinforcement learning problems

- Gym allows creating a custom environment for a specific problem

Multiple choice questions

1. Finish the phrase: Gym environment simulates ...

    a. Random process

    b. Markov reward process

    c. Markov process

2. When we played with the CartPole environment, we suggested the following approach: "move the cart to the left if the pole angle is negative and move it to the right if the pole angle is positive". But what if we reverse this logic: "move the cart to the right if the pole angle is negative and move it to the left if the pole angle is positive". How can the results of this approach be characterized?

    a. Better than a random agent

    b. Same as a random agent

    c. Worse than a random agent

Answers

1. b

2. c

CHAPTER 4

Struggling with Multi-Armed Bandits

We already know what tasks reinforcement learning can solve and how to emulate the environment for those tasks. Now is the time to start solving real problems! This chapter will examine one of the classic reinforcement learning problems called the multi-armed bandit problem. Despite the simplicity of the formulation and solution, this problem has great practical value. In this chapter, we will study two policies for solving the multi-armed bandits problem: epsilon greedy policy and Thompson sampling policy. The concepts of the epsilon greedy policy influence many aspects of reinforcement learning, so learning about it will come in handy.

Structure

In this chapter, we will discuss the following topics:

- Gambling with Multi-Armed Bandits
- Emulating Multi-Armed Bandits in Gym
- Epsilon greedy policy
- Thomson sampling policy
- Epsilon greedy versus Thompson sampling

- Exploration versus Exploitation

Objectives

After reading this chapter, you will be able to know what the epsilon greedy policy and Thompson sampling policy are and how these techniques help solve multi-armed bandit problems. In addition to this, you will learn one of the fundamental problems in reinforcement learning: exploration vs exploitation.

Gambling with Multi-Armed Bandits

Let's pretend we are the heroes of the movie *Ocean's 11*, and we decided to make money in a casino in a not entirely fair way. At the casino, we have a team member who manages the one-armed bandit's machines. The principle of a one-armed bandit's action is quite simple: a person throws a 1$ coin into the machine, and with a certain probability p, they get back $2, and with a probability 1-p, they do not get anything. Obviously, if the casino wants to earn money using such machines, the probability p must be less than 0.5. But! Our team member changed the probability of winning p of one of the machines to 0.6 at night. Therefore, we have a good chance of earning a little extra money today! But unfortunately, in the morning, there was a re-arrangement in the row of one-armed bandit machines. The machine which our teammate reprogrammed has now changed its place. And we do not know exactly which one of the one-armed bandits is set to win with a probability of 0.6:

Figure 4.1: *A row of One-Armed Bandit machines*
(Source: https://en.wikipedia.org/wiki/Multi-armed_bandit)

So, we came to the casino. We have $1000 and five one-armed bandit machines in the row in front of us. Four of these machines have a winning probability of less than 0.5, and in the long term, we will lose money playing them. But one device has a probability of winning that is equal to 0.6, and in the long run, we will be able to make money on it. *Figure 4.2* illustrates this situation:

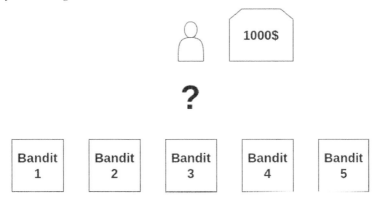

Figure 4.2: *Where is the most profitable machine?*

And we can do the following: We can spend $50 on the exploration process and find the most profitable slot machine. So, we run 10 rounds on each machine, like it is shown in *Figure 4.3*:

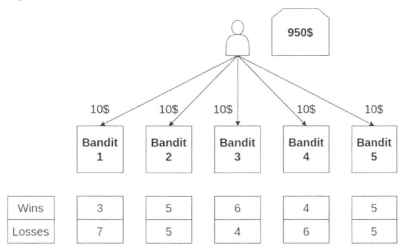

Figure 4.3: *Exploration process*

According to our statistics, the most profitable slot is One-Armed Bandit 3. Therefore, we will invest all the remaining money only in it:

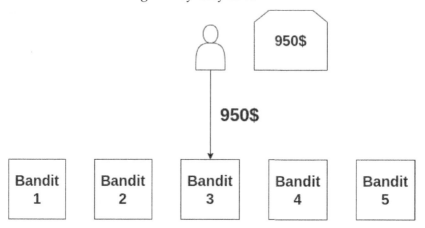

Figure 4.4: Exploitation process

Thanks to the law of large numbers from the probability theory, we can increase the number of trials in the exploration process to be more likely to determine the most profitable machine. For instance, we can spend $200 on the exploration process and run each one-armed bandit 40 times. But in this case, we will spend more money on testing unprofitable machines.

Now, we come to the formulation of our problem: what policy should we follow to maximize our profit by trying various options with different return probabilities.

This problem is called "multi-armed bandit" because we have many "arms" of one-armed bandits in the row.

The multi-armed bandit problem has significant practical applications. Let's list some of them.

Online advertising

Let's say we have several advertising campaigns that we run online. We test a campaign on a site visitor, and then we measure its conversion rate. But we don't know which of these ad campaigns is the most effective. We can only learn about the effectiveness of advertising by examining it on visitors. At the same time, we want to minimize our costs by showing ineffective ads. We can see that we have a classical multi-armed bandit problem here.

Clinical trials

Let's assume that we are managing clinical trials and testing new strategies for the treatment of complex diseases. We cannot afford to expose large numbers of volunteers to ineffective treatment, and we need to find the most effective treatment as soon as possible. This problem is also solved by the methods of the multi-armed bandit problem.

Well, we have already described in some detail the problem that we need to solve. Let's get to exploring ways to solve it.

Emulating Multi-Armed Bandits in Gym

The official release of Gym framework does not contain an environment that simulates the multi-armed problem. But this is not a problem for us. We can make our custom gym environment that emulates multi-armed problem **ch4/gym/ multiarmed_bandit_env.py**:

Import part:

```
import random
import gym
import numpy as np


class MultiArmedBanditEnv(gym.Env):
```

The **init** method receives **bandit** winning probabilities:

```
    def __init__(self, bandits):
        self.bandits = bandits


        self.state = {}
        self.reset()
```

After each action environment returns 1$ or -1$ to an agent:

```
    def step(self, action):
        p = self.bandits[action]
        r = random.random()
        reward = 1 if r <= p else -1
        self.state[action].append(reward)
        done = False
```

```
        debug = None
        return self.state, reward, done, debug


    def reset(self):
        self.state = {}
        for i in range(len(self.bandits)):
            self.state[i] = []
        return self.state
```

The **render** method shows the overall statistics of all rounds:

```
    def render(self, mode = "ascii"):
        returns = {}
        trials = {}
        for i in range(len(self.bandits)):
            returns[i] = sum(self.state[i])
            trials[i] = len(self.state[i])

        print(f'=====Total Trials: {sum(trials.values())}=====')
        for b, r in returns.items():
            t = trials[b]
            print(f'Bandit {b}| returns: {r}, trials: {t}')
        print(f'=====Total Returns: {sum(returns.values())}=====')
```

Here is the environment that simulates our casino problem with 5 one-armed bandits:

```
def get_bandit_env_5():
    bandits = [.45, .45, .4, .6, .4]
    return MultiArmedBanditEnv(bandits)
```

And so, let's run the environment with an agent that is guided by a random policy:

```
if __name__ == '__main__':
    seed = 1
    random.seed(seed)
    np.random.seed(1)

    balance = 1_000
```

```
env = get_bandit_env_5()

state = env.reset()
rewards = []

for i in range(balance):
    random_bandit = random.randint(0, 4)
    state, reward, done, debug = env.step(random_bandit)
    rewards.append(reward)

env.render()
env.close()
```

Result

Bandit	Returns	Trials
#0	-22$	196
#1	-22$	200
#2	-55$	201
#3	+37$	185
#4	-40$	218

```
Total Trials: 1000$

Total Returns: -102$
```

As expected, the random policy is unlikely to provide an opportunity to make money in the casino. The result shows that reprogrammed machine #3 allows us to earn some money, but other machines produce a loss in the long run.

Epsilon Greedy Policy

Let's talk about a more intelligent way that will allow us to make money in the casino. This section will study the Greedy Policy, a famous reinforcement learning principle. The way the Greedy Policy acts is relatively simple. We set an exploration action limit and make trials on each machine n times. After completing the exploration process, Greedy Policy switches to Exploitation mode and uses the accumulated experience only from the accumulated early experience. The Greedy Policy does not collect any new information after the completion of the Exploration process.

The implementation of the Greedy Policy **ch4/policy/greedy_policy.py** is as follows:

```python
import numpy as np


def greedy_policy(state, explore = 10):
    bandits = len(state)

    trials = sum([len(state[b]) for b in range(bandits)])
    total_explore_trials = bandits * explore

    # exploration
    if trials <= total_explore_trials:
        return trials % bandits

    # exploitation
    avg_rewards = [sum(state[b]) / len(state[b]) for b in
range(bandits)]
    best_bandit = np.argmax(avg_rewards)

    return best_bandit
```

We can depict exploration and exploitation in the Greedy Policy as follows:

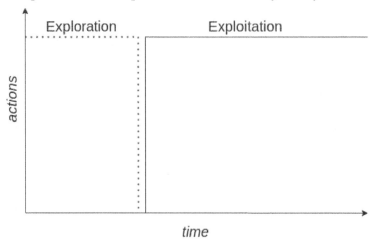

Figure 4.5: *Greedy Policy: exploration and exploitation*

Now, let's take a look at how this policy solves the multi-armed bandit problem **ch4/run/run_greedy_policy.py**:

Import Part

```
import random

from ch4.gym.multiarmed_bandit_env import get_bandit_env_5

from ch4.policy.greedy_policy import greedy_policy

import matplotlib.pyplot as plt

import numpy as np
```

Greedy Policy in Action

```
def run_greedy_policy(balance, env, exploration = 10):
    state = env.reset()
    rewards = []

    for i in range(balance):
        action = greedy_policy(state, exploration)
        state, reward, done, debug = env.step(action)
        rewards.append(reward)

    env.close()
    return env, rewards
```

Initialize Environment and Run Greedy Policy

```
if __name__ == '__main__':
    seed = 0
    random.seed(seed)

    balance = 1_000
    env = get_bandit_env_5()
    env, rewards = run_greedy_policy(balance, env)
    env.render()

    cum_rewards = np.cumsum(rewards)
    plt.plot(cum_rewards)
```

```
plt.title('Greedy Policy')
plt.xlabel('Trials')
plt.ylabel('Reward')
plt.show()
```

Result

Bandit	Returns	Trials
#0	-9$	41
#1	-6$	10
#2	-3$	11
#3	+186$	928
#4	-8$	10

```
Total Trials: 1000$
```

```
Total Returns: 160$
```

We see that Greedy Policy earned us $160. Keep in mind that $160 is the net income, which means we came with $1,000, and we will leave with $1,160. Let's examine the Greedy Policy flow:

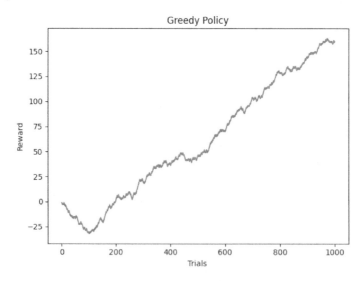

Figure 4.6: *Greedy Policy flow*

Figure 4.6 illustrates how Greedy Policy acts. It first loses money while completing the exploration process, but then the returns rise in the exploitation mode.

This policy is called "Greedy" because it regrets spending any resources on the additional investigation of the environment and relies solely on the accumulated experience.

Greedy Policy does a good job, but let's try modifying it. Let's add to the Greedy Policy the possibility of remaining to explore the environment. This policy is called the **Epsilon Greedy Policy**. Epsilon greedy policy chooses a random action with probability *e*, and relies solely on its experience with probability 1-*e*, that is, acts as a Greedy Policy **ch4/policy/e_greedy_policy.py**:

```python
import random

import numpy as np


def e_greedy_policy(state, explore = 10, epsilon = .1):
    bandits = len(state)


    trials = sum([len(state[b]) for b in range(bandits)])
    total_explore_trials = bandits * explore


    # exploration
    if trials <= total_explore_trials:
        return trials % bandits


    # random bandit
    if random.random() < epsilon:
        return random.randint(0, bandits - 1)


    # exploitation
    avg_rewards = [sum(state[b]) / len(state[b]) for b in
range(bandits)]
    best_bandit = np.argmax(avg_rewards)


    return best_bandit
```

The exploration and exploitation process for the epsilon greedy policy looks as follows:

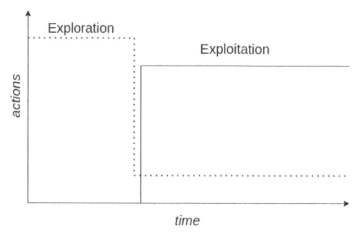

Figure 4.7: *Epsilon greedy policy: exploration and exploitation*

Let's take a look at how the epsilon greedy policy acts in the multi-armed bandit environment **ch4/run/run_e_greedy_policy.py**:

Import part

```
import random

from ch4.gym.multiarmed_bandit_env import get_bandit_env_5

from ch4.policy.e_greedy_policy import e_greedy_policy

import matplotlib.pyplot as plt

import numpy as np
```

Epsilon greedy policy in Action

```
def run_e_greedy_policy(balance, env, exploration = 10, epsilon = .1):
    state = env.reset()
    rewards = []


    for i in range(balance):
        action = e_greedy_policy(state, exploration, epsilon)
        state, reward, done, debug = env.step(action)
        rewards.append(reward)


    env.close()
```

```
    return env, rewards


Initialize Environment and Run epsilon greedy policy


if __name__ == '__main__':
    seed = 1
    random.seed(seed)

    balance = 1_000
    env = get_bandit_env_5()
    env, rewards = run_e_greedy_policy(balance, env)
    env.render()

    cum_rewards = np.cumsum(rewards)
    plt.plot(cum_rewards)
    plt.title('Epsilon Greedy Policy')
    plt.xlabel('Trials')
    plt.ylabel('Reward')
    plt.show()
```

Result

Bandit	Returns	Trials
#0	-9$	33
#1	-9$	29
#2	-20$	38
#3	+202$	870
#4	-6$	30

```
Total Trials: 1000$
Total Returns: 158$
```

In general, the epsilon greedy policy performs worse than the pure greedy policy for multi-armed bandit problem. But there is a reason for that: epsilon greedy policy works well in environments with an infinite or very large number of states. But in this case, collecting samples of information about the environment is quite simple, so there is no need to continue collecting additional information during the exploitation process. Let's examine the epsilon greedy policy flow:

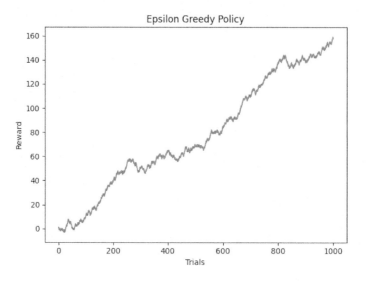

Figure 4.8: Epsilon greedy policy flow

In *Figure 4.8*, we can see that epsilon greedy policy starts well, but in the long run, it loses a lot of resources to continue the exploration process.

We have examined the agent's behavior for the first two policies to solve the reinforcement learning problem, but each of them assumes that we need to ensure balance between exploration and exploitation manually. It would be nice to have a policy that manages this balance automatically. We will cover this policy in the next section.

Thomson sampling policy

We will now look at a more complex method called Thompson sampling. Thompson sampling policy assigns a probability distribution to each action. Actions that were more rewarded in the past are more likely to be selected the next time, but there is always a chance to test some unsuccessful actions again.

The logical core of the Thompson sampling policy is based on the properties of beta distributions and the theory of random processes. This topic is far beyond the scope of this book, but we will look at how the technique works.

Let's say we have a history of trials for two one-armed bandits:

- **Bandit #1**: -1, +1, +1, +1, +1, -1. (4 wins from 6 trials)
- **Bandit #2**: +1, -1, -1, +1, -1, -1. (2 wins from 6 trials)

Thompson sampling builds beta distributions β(wins, total number of trials) for each bandit according to its history of trials. Beta distribution β(a,b) has one property: As the ratio increases, the beta distribution β (a, b) shifts to the right. The beta distributions β(4,6) for Bandit #1 and β(2,6) for Bandit #2 will look as follows:

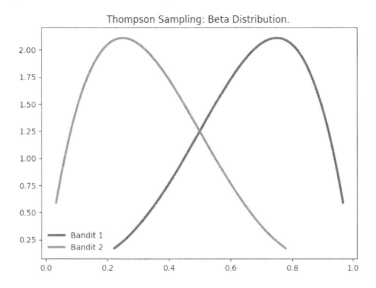

Figure 4.9: Beta distributions: β(4,6) and β(2,6)

The random number r_1 generated by distribution *β(4,6)* is more likely to be higher than the random number r_2 generated by distribution *β(2,6)*. Thompson sampling for each bandit generates a random number according to the beta distribution built on its history of trials. The bandit whose distribution generated the maximum random number is chosen for the next action. The essence of this method is that the better a bandit's history of trials, the more likely it will be chosen next time. However, there is always a possibility that a bandit with a bad history will be chosen for the next action.

Let's look at the Thompson sampling policy implementation **ch4/policy/ thompson_sampling.py**:

Import part

```
import numpy as np
from scipy.stats import beta
import matplotlib.pyplot as plt


def thompson_sampling_policy(state, visualize = False, plot_title = ''):
    action = None
    max_bound = 0
```

```
color_list = ['red', 'blue', 'green', 'black', 'yellow']
```

Iterating each bandit

```
for b, trials in state.items():
    w = len([r for r in trials if r == 1])
    l = len([r for r in trials if r == -1])

    if w + l == 0:
        avg = 0
    else:
        avg = round(w / (w + l), 2)
```

Generating random number for bandit's beta distribution:

```
random_beta = np.random.beta(w + 1, l + 1)
if random_beta > max_bound:
    max_bound = random_beta
    action = b
```

Visualization

```
    if visualize:
        color = color_list[b % len(color_list)]
        x = np.linspace(beta.ppf(0.01, w, l), beta.ppf(0.99, w, l),
100)
        plt.plot(
            x, beta.pdf(x, w, l),
            label = f'Bandit {b}| avg={avg}, v={round(random_
beta,2)}',
            color = color, linewidth = 3)
        plt.axvline(x = random_beta, color = color, linestyle = '--')


    if visualize:
        plt.title('Thompson Sampling: Beta Distribution. ' + plot_title)
        plt.legend()
        plt.show()


    return action
```

Now, we can examine Thompson sampling policy in action for Bandit #1 and Bandit #2 **ch4/run/demo_thompson_sampling.py**:

```python
from ch4.policy.thompson_sampling import thompson_sampling_policy

import random

import numpy as np


seed = 10

random.seed(seed)

np.random.seed(seed)


for i in range(3):
    action = thompson_sampling_policy(
        {
            1: [-1, 1, 1, 1, 1, -1],
            2: [1, 1, -1, -1, -1, -1]
        },
        visualize = True,
        plot_title = f'attempt: {i}'
    )
    print(f'Iteration {i}: {action}')
```

Result

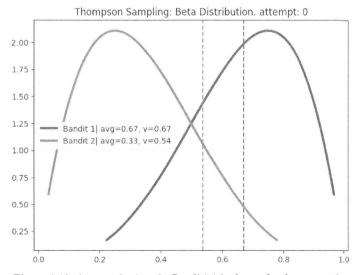

Figure 4.10: *Attempt 0. r1 > r2 . Bandit#1 is chosen for the next action*

The *Figure 4.10* illustrates that the random number *r1* generated by the distribution of β(4,6) is greater than the random number *r2* generated by β(2,6). Accordingly, the Bandit #1 is selected for the next action:

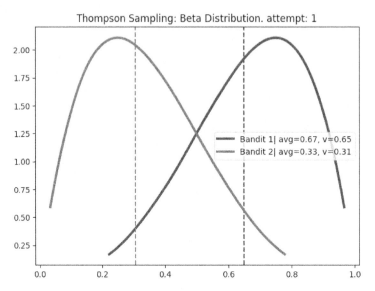

Figure 4.11: *Attempt 1. $r_1 > r_2$. Bandit#1 is chosen for the next action*

Figure 4.11 demonstrates the decision logic of attempt 1, and it is similar to attempt 0.

However, *Figure 4.12* shows that attempt 2 shows that Bandit 2 still has chances to be selected for the next action:

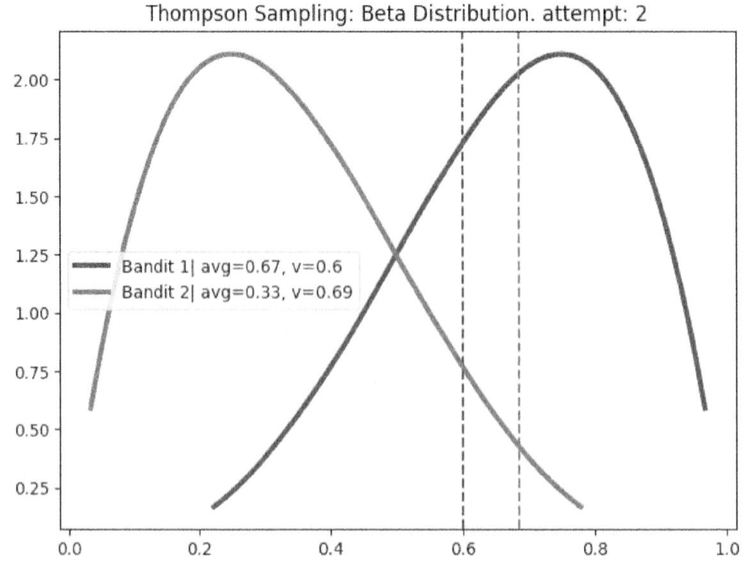

Figure 4.12: *Attempt 1. $r_1 < r_2$. Bandit#2 is chosen for the next action*

We can now see that Thompson sampling does not make an explicit separation between exploration and exploitation processed. In each trial, the Thompson sampling policy leaves the chance to recheck actions that have failed in the past.

Now, let's investigate the agent's performance that would follow the Thompson sampling policy in a casino **ch4/run/run_thompson_sampling.py**:

Import part

```
from ch4.policy.thompson_sampling import thompson_sampling_policy

import random

from ch4.gym.multiarmed_bandit_env import get_bandit_env_5

import matplotlib.pyplot as plt

import numpy as np
```

Thompson sampling policy in Action

```
def run_thompson_sampling(balance, env, visualize = False):

    state = env.reset()

    rewards = []


    for i in range(balance):

        if i % 50 == 0:

            action = thompson_sampling_policy(state, visualize, plot_
title = f'Iteration: {i}')

        else:

            action = thompson_sampling_policy(state, False, plot_title =
f'Iteration: {i}')


        state, reward, done, debug = env.step(action)

        rewards.append(reward)


    env.close()

    return env, rewards
```

Initialize Environment and Run Thompson sampling policy

```
if __name__ == '__main__':

    seed = 3

    random.seed(seed)
```

```
balance = 1_000
env = get_bandit_env_5()
env, rewards = run_thompson_sampling(balance, env, visualize = True)
env.render()


cum_rewards = np.cumsum(rewards)
plt.plot(cum_rewards)
plt.title('Thompson Sampling Policy')
plt.xlabel('Trials')
plt.ylabel('Reward')
plt.show()
```

Result

Bandit	Returns	Trials
#0	-8$	26
#1	-9$	17
#2	-8$	14
#3	+206$	912
#4	-5$	31

```
Total Trials: 1000$
Total Returns: 178$
```

Thompson's sampling policy results are close to those of the Greedy Policy. There is only one difference here: in the Thompson sampling policy, we did not explicitly define the exploitation and exploitation processes.

It is also interesting to look at the logic of Thompson sampling policy during the game:

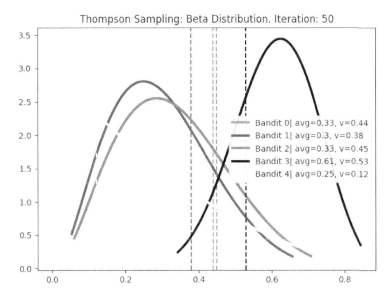

Figure 4.13: *After 50 trials*

Figure 4.13 shows that after 50 trials, our cheat one-armed bandit machine has the best chance of being selected for the next trial:

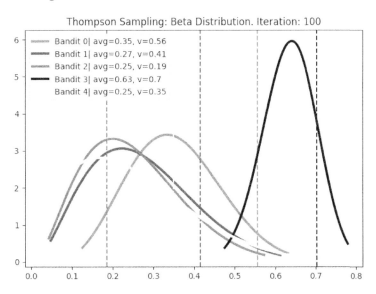

Figure 4.14: *After 100 trials*

Figure 4.14 illustrates that after 100 trials, the beta distribution of Bandit #3 shifts to the right significantly:

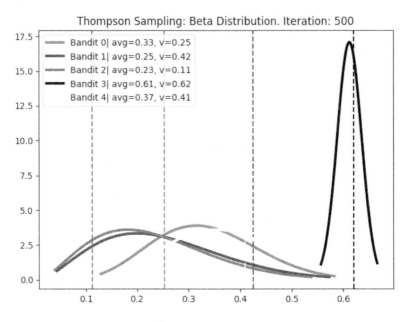

Figure 4.15: *After 500 trials*

And *Figure 4.15* shows that the most successful Bandit #3 will be chosen in most cases in the long run. Finally, let's examine the Thompson policy flow:

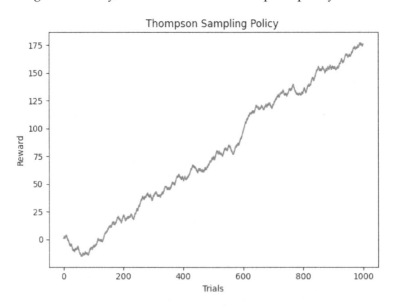

Figure 4.16: *Thompson policy flow*

Figure 4.16 predictably shows the presence of losses initially and the rise of rewards after the policy determined the most profitable machine.

Epsilon greedy versus Thompson sampling

In this chapter, we looked at two important approaches to solving one of the reinforcement learning problems. But which one is better? There is no answer to this question. Everything depends on the specific environment and its characteristics. epsilon greedy policy might be better for environment A, and for environment B, Thompson sampling policy might be better. Nevertheless, it is always useful to compare several policies to estimate the expectation of its application.

Let's run each of the policies 50 times and plot their average return **ch4/run/run_egreedy_vs_thompson.py**:

```
import matplotlib.pyplot as plt

import numpy as np

from ch4.gym.multiarmed_bandit_env import get_bandit_env_5

from ch4.run.run_e_greedy_policy import run_e_greedy_policy

from ch4.run.run_thompson_sampling import run_thompson_sampling


seed = 0

random.seed(seed)

np.random.seed(seed)


episodes = 50

balance = 1_000


env_gen = get_bandit_env_5

rewards = {

    'Epsilon Greedy':    [np.cumsum(run_e_greedy_policy(balance, env_
gen())[1]) for _ in range(episodes)],

    'Thompson Sampling': [np.cumsum(run_thompson_sampling(balance, env_
gen())[1]) for _ in range(episodes)],

}


for policy, r in rewards.items():

    plt.plot(np.average(r, axis = 0), label = policy)
```

```
plt.legend()
plt.xlabel("Rounds")
plt.ylabel("Average Returns")
plt.title('Battle')
plt.show()
```

Result

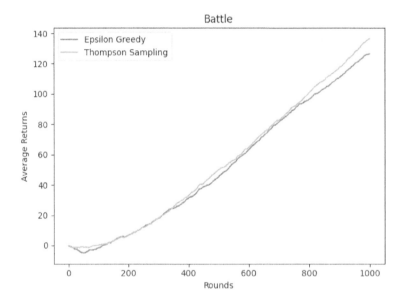

Figure 4.17: *Thompson policy flow*

In *Figure 4.17*, we can see that the average returns for each method are fairly close to each other. We may be able to tune epsilon greedy policy such that it will start to outperform Thompson sampling. However, it is always essential to emulate a method in a test environment before applying it.

Exploration versus exploitation

In this chapter, we have raised one of the most critical issues in reinforcement learning: how to ensure the right balance between exploration and exploitation? In general, in reinforcement learning, data collection for agent education is not free. You have to pay for each new sample of data. It is not necessarily a money payment; it can be paid with consumed resources or time. Successful policies try to minimize costs, thereby maximizing rewards. At the same time, each new sample of data can provide helpful information for an agent, which will significantly improve its behavior, which means the resources spent on obtaining new information will pay off many times in the future.

At the same time, we cannot waste our resources on constant data exploration. At some point, the collection of new data should be limited, and we must start exploiting the information we have observed. The more efficiently we can analyze the received data, and the earlier we move on to the exploitation of this data, the faster we can earn rewards.

In many cases, agent policy uses a logic similar to epsilon greedy policy and Thompson sampling policy. At first, the agent's behavior is aimed at collecting data. Then, we begin to take actions solely based on the analysis of the data that we have collected, combining this with the continuation of the exploration process. After that, the exploration process is minimal, and agent policy acts in exploitation mode. But agent sometimes takes experimental actions to collect new data samples:

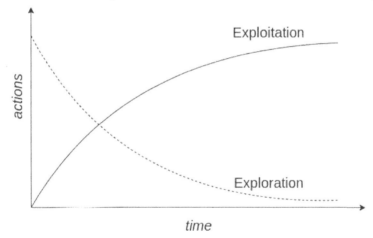

Figure 4.18: *Exploration vs exploitation*

There is no silver bullet to help you choose the right balance between exploration and exploitation. The answer to this question depends on the specific task. But understanding how to approach this problem's solution can significantly help solve a concrete reinforcement learning problem.

Conclusion

In this chapter, you studied your first reinforcement learning task: the multi-armed problem. You learned two problem-solving methods: epsilon greedy policy and Thompson sampling policy. This problem may seem a little funny, but it has vast practical applications: online advertising, medicine, marketing, etc.

In the next chapter, we will stay at our casino and play blackjack! Yes, gambling has been and remains an essential engine of mathematics. Probability theory, game theory, and reinforcement learning owe much to gambling. Therefore, it is natural to continue learning reinforcement learning in the casino.

Points to remember

- Multi-armed bandit problem has practical applications in advertising, clinical trials, marketing, etc.

- Greedy Policy doesn't allow any exploration actions after switching to exploitation mode.

- Epsilon greedy policy allows random exploration actions.

- Long-term exploration provokes a significant loss of resources, while short exploration threatens the lack of information about the environment.

- Thompson sampling policy does not have a strict border between exploration and exploitation modes.

Multiple choice questions

1. Let's say we want to develop the greediest policy and reduce the exploration process to a minimum by setting the parameter explore = 2 (that is, two exploration trials for each device). What can happen after applying this policy to the multi-armed problem?

    a. This policy will not differ from the Greedy Policy with the parameter explore = 10

    b. This policy is likely to fail because the probability of identifying a profitable machine in 2 trials is small

2. Take a look at the beta distributions in *Figure 4.14*. Is there any possibility for Bandit #0 to be selected for the next trial?

    a. Yes

    b. No

3. Let's say we have a multi-armed problem with the following probabilities:

    A = 0.6, B = 0.5, C = 0.4. Choose the correct statement below.

    a. The probability of selecting a machine is equal in the first trial in Thompson sampling: $P_0(A) = P_0(B) = P_0(C)$

b. The probability of selecting a machine is equal in the 100th trial in Thompson sampling: $P_0(A) = P_0(B) = P_0(C)$

Answers

1. b
2. a
3. a

Key terms

- **Multi-armed bandit problem**: What policy should we follow to maximize our reward by trying various options with different return probabilities.

- **Greedy Policy**: Agent constantly makes the action that is assumed to return the highest expected reward.

- **Thompson sampling policy**: Acts by constructing beta distribution on the average rewards of its arms.

- **Exploration**: Process that studies an environment by performing actions that may not be rewarding.

- **Exploitation**: Process that makes the most effective action from experience gained during the exploration process.

CHAPTER 5
Blackjack in Monte Carlo

In *Chapter 4, Struggling with Multi-Armed Bandits*, we explored the solution for multi-armed bandit problem. As mentioned in the previous chapters, the study of gambling was very useful in solving practical reinforcement problems. Therefore, we will continue studying gambling problems and stay in the casino for a while. We will move from the slot machine room to the blackjack room. First, we will try to develop an optimal strategy for playing blackjack and then challenge the dealer. In this chapter, you will be introduced to the significant concept of the Q(s, a) action-value function. The action-value function is one of the cornerstones of reinforcement learning and will appear in every chapter hereon. A good understanding of the Q(s, a) action-value function will lay a solid foundation for understanding reinforcement learning concepts.

Structure

In this chapter, we will discuss the following topics:

- Blackjack as a reinforcement learning problem
- Q(s,a) – action-value function
- Monte Carlo method

- Monte Carlo Policy Exploration and Greedy Policy Exploitation

- Optimal policy for unbalanced Blackjack

Objectives

After reading this chapter, you will be able to construct a Q(s, a) action-value function using the Monte Carlo method. You will also be able to create an agent that performs effective actions based on the values of Q(s, a) action-value function.

Blackjack as a Reinforcement Learning Problem

Let's first examine the Blackjack environment that we have to operate with. Blackjack is a popular card game played by two persons: a player and a dealer. The objective of the game is to win money by creating card totals higher than those of the dealer's hand but not exceeding 21 or by stopping at a total in the hope that the dealer will bust. If a person scores more than 21, they lose automatically.

Let's take a look at the process of playing blackjack. Each card gives a certain number of scores:

- *Ace*: gives 1 or 11 scores

- **2, 3, 4, ..., 10**: gives 2, 3, 4, ..., 10 scores, respectively

- **Jack, Queen, King**: gives 10 scores each

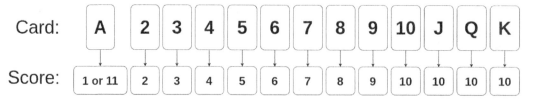

Figure 5.1: Blackjack card scores

Ace gives 1 or 11 points, depending on which score is more beneficial for the player:

- **Usable Ace**: Ace gives 11 points

- **No usable Ace**: Ace gives 1 point

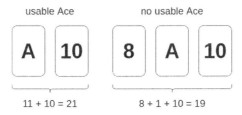

Figure 5.2: *"usable" Ace and "no usable" Ace*

We say that a player bust in blackjack if they have gained more than 21 points. Bust means the player's defeat:

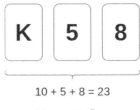

Figure 5.3: *Bust*

Professional blackjack includes more rules, such as Double down, Split and Surrender. We will not consider them in our environment.

Now that we have recalled the rules of blackjack, let's look at the blackjack game from a reinforcement learning context. The game starts with the dealer dealing two cards to the player and one to themselves. Let's examine the example of such a hand in *Figure 5.4*:

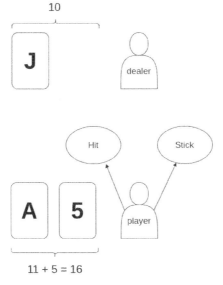

Figure 5.4: *Initial state*

The dealer gave the player cards: **Ace** and **5**, and a **Jack** to themselves. This is a good deal for the player as they have a usable ace, and a player can take one more card without being afraid to lose.

We can record the hand state shown in *Figure 5.4* as follows:

Player Sum	Dealer Sum	Usable Ace
16	10	True

Table 5.1: *Initial state of the game*

Now, the player needs to select their next action: *Hit* or *Stick*. The player chooses *Hit*, which means that the dealer deals one more card to the player. The dealer deals *Queen* to the player. The situation on the table looks like this now:

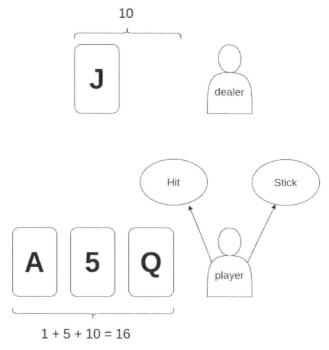

Figure 5.5: *First hit*

The sum of the player's points has not changed, but now the player has no usable Ace, which partly worsens the player's situation. We can record the hand state shown in *Figure 5.5* as follows:

Player Sum	Dealer Sum	Usable Ace
16	10	False

Table 5.2: *State after the first hit*

However, 16 points are a little far from 21, and the player makes the *Hit* action again. The dealer deals 4, and the player has 20 points now:

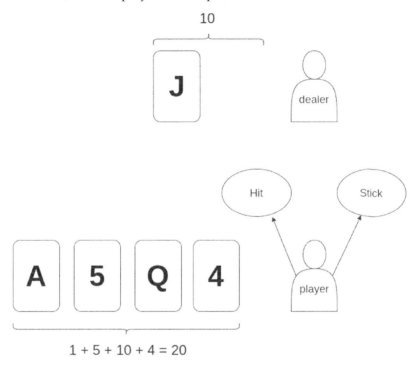

$$1 + 5 + 10 + 4 = 20$$

Figure 5.6: Second hit

And the state after the second hit can be recorded as follows:

Player Sum	Dealer Sum	Usable Ace
20	10	False

Table 5.3: State after the second hit

The player makes the *Stick* action, and the dealer deals the cards to themselves:

- **First card**: Dealer deals 4, and his sum is 14. 14 is less than the player's 20, so the dealer has to deal another card to himself.

- **Second card**: Dealer deals 9, and his sum is 23. That means the player won!

10 + 4 + 9 = 23

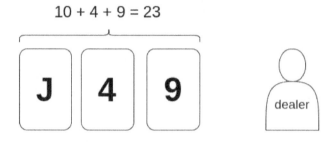

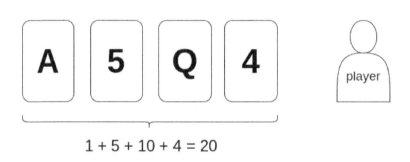

1 + 5 + 10 + 4 = 20

Figure 5.7: *Final state*

In case of a win, the player gets $1, and in case of a loss, the player loses $1. If the player and the dealer have the same number of points, then a draw is considered, and the reward is zero.

Now, let's convert the blackjack game into a reinforcement learning problem:

- **Agent**: player
- **Reward**: 1 if the player wins, -1 if the player loses, 0 in case of a draw
- **Action Space**: Hit or stick
- **State Space**: All possible combinations of values are shown below:

Player Sum	Dealer Sum	Usable Ace
[4, 30]	[4, 30]	{True, False}

Table 5.4: *Blackjack State Space*

In the context of reinforcement learning, the blackjack gameplay we made earlier looks like this:

- Agent gets the initial state: (16, 10, True)
- Agent performs the action: Hit
- Environment returns a new state (16, 10, False) and reward = 0
- Agent performs the action: Hit
- Environment returns a new state (20, 10, False) and reward = 0
- Agent performs the action: Stick
- Environment returns state: (20, 23, False) and reward = 1
- The episode is finished

And we can depict the gameplay as follows:

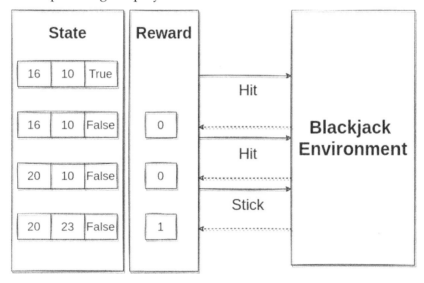

Figure 5.8: *Blackjack as a reinforcement learning problem*

Gym framework has a built-in environment for emulating Blackjack games. So, let's try to play several games following a simple policy:

- **Hit**: If the number of points is less than 18
- **Stick**: If the number of points is greater than or equal to 18

Let's examine the emulation of this policy in the blackjack environment **ch5/gym/ random_agent.py**:

Global parameters

```python
import gym

action_map = {
    1: 'Hit',
    0: 'Stick'
}
seed = 10
episodes = 100
```

Initializing the environment

```python
env = gym.make('Blackjack-v0')
env.seed(seed)

wins = 0
loss = 0
draws = 0
```

Running 100 episodes in a row

```python
for e in range(1, episodes + 1):
    state = env.reset()
    print(f'===== Episode: {e} =====')
    while True:
        agent_sum = state[0]
        dealer_sum = state[1]
```

Hit if player's sum is less than 18 and stick otherwise

```python
        if agent_sum < 18:
            # hit
            action = 1
        else:
            # stand
            action = 0

        next_state, reward, done, _ = env.step(action)
```

```
print(f'state: {state} | action: {action_map[action]} '
      f'| reward: {reward} | next state: {next_state}')

    if done:
        if reward > 0:
            wins += 1
        elif reward < 0:
            loss += 1
        else:
            draws += 1
        break

    state = next_state

print(f'Wins: {wins} | Loss: {loss} | Draws: {draws} ')
```

Result

Episode	State	Action	Reward	Next State
1	(13, 6, False)	Hit	-1	(23, 6, False)
2	(8, 10, False)	Hit	0	(11, 10, False)
	(11, 10, False)	Hit	0	(18, 10, False)
	(18, 10, False)	Stick	+1	(18, 10, False)
3	(8, 10, False)	Hit	0	(18, 10, False)
	(18, 10, False)	Stick	-1	(18, 10, False)
...				
Wins: 36	**Loss: 59**		**Draws: 5**	

Table 5.5: Blackjack random agent summary

Table 5.5 demonstrates a process that a simple *hit if the sum is less than 18 and stick otherwise* policy is not so effective. This policy won 36 games and lost 59. Let's see how we can use reinforcement learning techniques to improve the agent's performance dramatically.

Q(s,a) – action-value function

In the previous section, we covered the blackjack gameplay. Some of the player's decisions were obvious. For example, in a state (16, 10, true), *Hit* is better than *Stick*, and in a state (20, 10, false), *Stick* is better than *Hit*. But what about the state (16, 10, false)? In this situation, it is much more difficult to estimate the effectiveness of *Hit* and *Stick* actions.

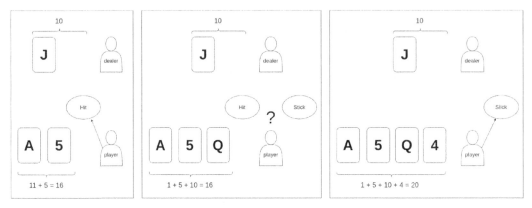

Figure 5.9: *Estimating Hit and Stick actions*

To build an effective policy, we need a function that would allow us to evaluate the effectiveness of action *a* in state *s*. And this is what the function *Q(s, a)* does:

- *Q(s, a)* returns long-term estimation of action *a* in state *s*.

- $Q(s, a_1) > Q(s, a_2)$ - means that action a_1 is more effective than action a_2 for state s.

> **Therefore, the function *Q(s, a)* is called the action-value function because it returns a value of an action *a* in state *s*. Q stands for Quality.**

But still, there is a challenge of constructing the function Q(s, a) somehow. In the next section, we will study how to create an action-value function using the Monte Carlo method.

Monte Carlo method

The Monte Carlo method is a broad algorithm class that generates repeated random sampling. The main property of this method is that after a sufficiently large number of random experiments of a particular process (or environment), it is possible to determine the characteristics and properties of this process (or environment). The Monte Carlo method is used in many computational problems, especially when it is difficult to express any conclusions about the environment analytically.

Let's try to investigate the effectiveness of various actions in the state (20, 8, False), that is, when the player has 20, the dealer has 8 and there is no usable ace. We will run an emulation of random actions 100 times in this state **ch5/monte_carlo/ action_value_single.py**:

Import part

```
import random
import gym
```

Reproducible script

```
seed = 56
random.seed(seed)


a_map = {
    1: 'Hit',
    0: 'Stick'
}
```

Total 100 trials

```
episodes = 100
```

Initializing Blackjack Environment

```
env = gym.make('Blackjack-v0')
env.seed(seed)


reward_sum = [0, 0]
a_number = [0, 0]


e = 0
while True:
```

Generating random states

```
    state = env.reset()
    agent_sum = state[0]
    dealer_sum = state[1]
    usable_ace = state[2]
```

Skipping all states but (20, 8, False)

```
if agent_sum != 20 or dealer_sum != 8 or usable_ace != False:
    continue
```

Piking random action

```
action = random.randint(0, 1)
next_state, reward, done, _ = env.step(action)

if done:
    a_number[action] += 1
    reward_sum[action] += reward
    e += 1
    print(f'{e}: {a_number[action]}, {state}, {a_map[action]},
{reward}')

    if e == episodes:
        break
```

Summary

```
print(f'Stick | rewards:{reward_sum[0]}, trials:{a_number[0]}')
print(f'Hit | rewards:{reward_sum[1]}, trials:{a_number[1]}')

print(f'Q({state}, {a_map[0]})={round(reward_sum[0] / a_number[0], 2)}')
print(f'Q({state}, {a_map[1]})={round(reward_sum[1] / a_number[1], 2)}')
```

Results

Episode	Action number	State	Action	Reward
1	1	(20, 8, False)	Stick	0
2	1	(20, 8, False)	Hit	-1
3	2	(20, 8, False)	Hit	-1
4	3	(20, 8, False)	Hit	-1
5	2	(20, 8, False)	Stick	1
6	3	(20, 8, False)	Stick	1
		...		

Table 5.6: Episodes of Monte Carlo simulation for (20, 8, False) state

Table 5.6 demonstrates all episodes of Monte Carlo simulation for (20, 8, False) state, and *Table 5.7* shows us the summary:

Action	Total reward	Total trials
Stick	56	65
Hit	-35	35

Table 5.7: *Summary of Monte Carlo simulation for (20, 8, False) state*

Let us introduce the G function. $G(s, a; n)$ is the return on n^{th} episode from our immediate action a in state s, plus all discounted future rewards that happened after.

We define:

- **G(s, a; n):** Reward received in episode n after action a in state s, plus all discounted future rewards

- **N(s, a):** Total number of trials of action a in state s

And now we come to one of the main formulas of this chapter:

$$Q(s, a) = \frac{\sum_n G(s, a; n)}{N(s, a)}$$

$Q(s, a)$ is the sum of all returns of action a in state s divided by the total number of actions a in state s.

For example, based on *Table 5.6* and *Table 5.7*, we can conclude that:

- **G((20, 8, False), Hit; 2)** = -1

- **N((20, 8, False), Hit)** = 35

Then, we can calculate the value of the *Hit* action in the state (20, 8, False) as the sum of all rewards $\sum_n G((20,8,False), Hit; n)$ divided by the number of all *Hit* actions $N((20, 8, False))$:

$Q((20, 8, False), Hit) = -35/35 = -1$

And $Q((20, 8, False), Stick)$ is calculated the same way:

$Q((20, 8, False), Stick) = 56/65 = 0.86$

So, in the state (20, 8, False), the expected reward of action *Hit* in is -1, and the expected reward of action *Stick* is 0.86:

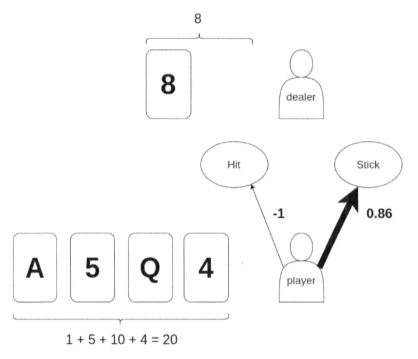

Figure 5.10: Hit and Stick action values

However, this information does not give us a lot of helpful knowledge. Any novice blackjack player would immediately understand that performing a *Hit* action with 20 points is pointless.

Okay, let's see how you can calculate the values of the function $Q(s, a)$ for other states and actions. Here, we will explore a little theory. Let's take a look at some of the chain of state transitions that led to the end of an episode of the game:

Current State	Action	Reward	Next State
s_0	a_0	r_0	s_1
s_1	a_1	r_1	s_2
s_2	a_2	r_2	s_{done}

Table 5.8: State transition table

And we calculate $G(s_k, a_k; n)$ the following way:

$$G(s_k, a_k; n) = \sum_{i=k}^{t} \gamma^{i-k} r_k$$

Where,

- γ is a discount factor in the $[0; 1]$
- **t** is a total number of transitions in the episode

For example,

- $G(s_0, a_0; n) = \gamma^0 r_0 + \gamma r_1 + \gamma^2 r_2$
- $G(s_1, a_1; n) = \gamma^0 r_1 + \gamma r_2$
- $G(s_2, a_2; n) = \gamma^0 r_2$

Remember that γ^0 is equal to 1 for any real γ.

Yes, all these formulas may not be apparent at first, but let's consider their meaning. Take a look at *Figure 5.11*:

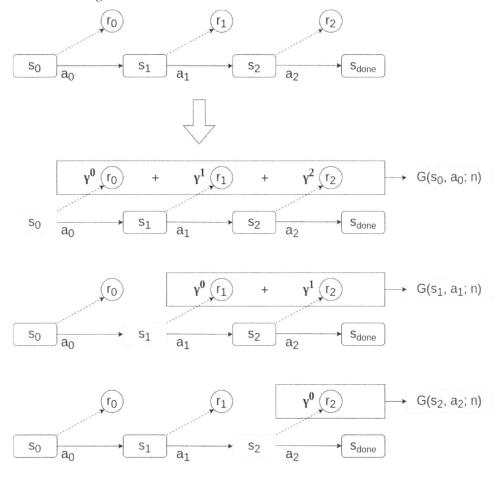

Figure 5.11: *Monte Carlo action-value function calculation*

The pair (s_0, a_0) generated a reward r_0, and obviously, reward r_0 should be added to the reward sum $G(s_0, a_0; n)$:

$$G(s_0, a_0; n) = r_0,$$

At the same time, the action a_0 had long-term consequences and led to the subsequent reward of r_1. A reward r_1 could have a random nature and strongly depend on the action of a_1. Nevertheless, in *Markov reward processes*, each action greatly influences the subsequent rewards, so the reward r_1 should also be added to the sum $G(s_0, a_0; n)$. But this would be an unfair addition since obtaining r_1 was less dependent on action a_0 than receiving r_1. Therefore, there is a discount factor γ in the formula, which reduces subsequent rewards:

$$G(s_0, a_0; n) = r_0 + \gamma r_1,$$

And finally, we can add the last reward that was in the transition chain:

$$G(s_0, a_0; n + 1) = r_0 + \gamma r_1 + \gamma^2 r_2$$

The main meaning of the formula $G(s_k, a_k; n+1) = \sum_{i=k}^{t} \gamma^{i-k} r_k$ is that $G(s_k, a_k; n+1)$ should consider all subsequent rewards that the agent received after the decision a_k was made.

We've covered enough formulas. Let's look at an example for calculating $G(s, a)$ for the blackjack environment.

First, let's examine the Monte Carlo policy that randomly plays blackjack. A completely random game can create too many irrelevant and unnecessary data samples, and we will make minor restrictions on the random behavior of the Monte Carlo Policy:

- If player sum is less than 12, then *Hit*

- If player sum is less than 18, then *Hit* with probability 0.8 and *Stick* with probability 0.2

- If player sum is greater or equal 18, then *Hit* with probability 0.2 and *Stick* with probability 0.8

Here, we provide the implementation of Monte Carlo Policy **ch5/monte_carlo/policy.py**:

```python
def monte_carlo_policy(env):
    state_history = []
    state = env.reset()
    actions = [0, 1]
    while True:
```

```
        player_sum = state[0]
        if player_sum < 12:
            action = 1
        else:
            probs = [0.8, 0.2] if player_sum > 17 else [0.2, 0.8]
            action = np.random.choice(actions, p = probs)


        next_state, reward, done, _ = env.step(action)
        state_history.append([state, action, reward, next_state])
        state = next_state
        if done:
            break


    return state_history
```

And now we can calculate the values of *G(s, a)* function using Monte Carlo Policy **ch5/monte_carlo/action_value_multiple.py**:

Import part

```
import random
import numpy as np
import gym
from ch5.monte_carlo.policy import monte_carlo_policy
```

Reproducible script

```
seed = 6
random.seed(seed)
```

Global parameters

```
a_map = {
    1: 'Hit',
    0: 'Stick'
}


episodes = 10
gamma = 0.8
```

```
env = gym.make('Blackjack-v0')
env.seed(seed)
```

Generating random plays

```
for e in range(1, episodes + 1):
    state_history = monte_carlo_policy(env)
    states, actions, rewards, next_states = zip(*state_history)
    discounts = np.array([gamma**i for i in range(len(rewards) + 1)])

    for i, state in enumerate(states):
        G = round(sum(rewards[i:] * discounts[:-(1 + i)]), 4)
        print(f'{e}: {state}, {a_map[actions[i]]} -> {G}')
```

Results

Episode	State	Action	G(s,a)
1	(8, 2, False)	Hit	0.64
1	(19, 2, True)	Hit	0.8
1	(19, 2, False)	Stick	1.0
2	(20, 9, False)	Stick	-1.0
3	(9, 9, False)	Hit	-0.8
3	(16, 9, False)	Hit	-1.0
...			

Table 5.9: *G(s, a) calculation*

Let's move on to describing the essence of the Monte Carlo method. The Monte Carlo method generates completely random sequences of actions, creating chains of transitions. After each episode, the $G(s, a; n)$ values are calculated and the action-value function $Q(s, a)$ is updated. After many tests, the function $Q(s, a)$ approximates the optimal behavior of the agent in the environment:

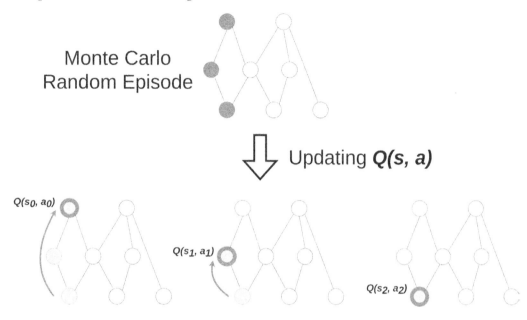

Figure 5.12: *Monte Carlo method*

Figure 5.12 shows how the Monte Carlo method works. It creates a random episode e, which is a particular chain of transitions: $[(s_0, a_0), (s_1, a_1), \ldots, (s_n, a_n)]$ in the space of all environment transitions. After the end of the episode, the action-value $Q(s, a)$ is updated, for each pair (s, a) from the episode e.

Now, we can put everything together and construct $Q(s, a)$ action-value function using the Monte Carlo method **ch5/monte_carlo/q_monte_carlo.py**:

Import part

```
import gym
import numpy as np
from collections import defaultdict
from ch5.monte_carlo.policy import monte_carlo_policy
```

Creating Q action-value function

```
def train_q_monte_carlo(env, train_episodes, gamma = 1):
    G = defaultdict(lambda: np.zeros(env.action_space.n))
    N = defaultdict(lambda: np.zeros(env.action_space.n))
```

```python
    Q = defaultdict(lambda: np.zeros(env.action_space.n))

    for e in range(1, train_episodes + 1):

        episode = monte_carlo_policy(env)

        states, actions, rewards, next_states = zip(*episode)

        discounts = np.array([gamma**i for i in range(len(rewards) + 1)])

        for i, state in enumerate(states):
            g = sum(rewards[i:] * discounts[:-(1 + i)])
            G[state][actions[i]] += g
            N[state][actions[i]] += 1.0
            Q[state][actions[i]] = G[state][actions[i]] / N[state]
[actions[i]]

        if e % 10_000 == 0:
            print(f'Episodes: {e}/{train_episodes}')

    return Q

if __name__ == '__main__':

    env = gym.make('Blackjack-v0')

    seed = 0
    random.seed(seed)
    env.seed(seed)

    Q = train_q_monte_carlo(env, 50_000)
```

Printing the results

```python
    # print several values
    i = 0
    for state in Q:

        if i == 10:
            break

        print(f'State: {state} | action-values: {Q[state]}')

        i += 1
```

Results

State	Hit-value	Stick-value
(18, 1, False)	-0.32	-0.68
(14, 10, False)	-0.55	-0.59
(20, 10, False)	0.43	-0.85
...		

Table 5.10: *Q(s, a) action-value function*

Great, we've built a $Q(s, a)$ action-value function for the Blackjack environment. We will use $Q(s, a)$ to play a real game in the next section.

Monte Carlo Policy Exploration and Greedy Policy Exploitation

Now is the time to move on to the real game. But before we proceed to test the Monte Carlo method, let's look at the global architecture of this technique. The Monte Carlo method is used as an exploitation method, and all the accumulated experience is collected in a $Q(s, a)$ action-value function. In the process of exploitation, a greedy policy π is used, which makes the most optimal decision according to $Q(s, a)$:

$$\pi(s) = max_a(Q(s, a))$$

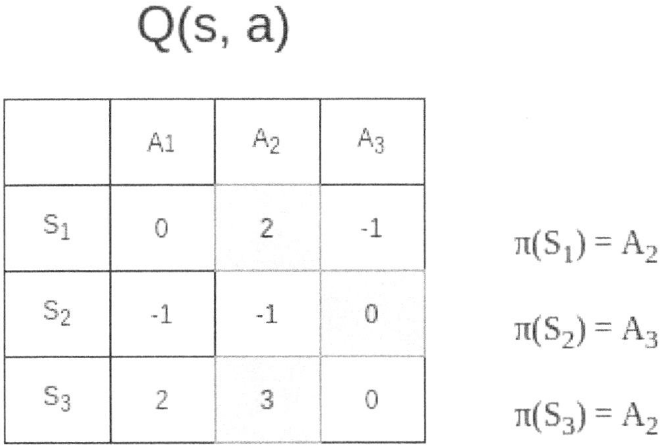

Q(s, a)

	A1	A2	A3
S_1	0	2	-1
S_2	-1	-1	0
S_3	2	3	0

$\pi(S_1) = A_2$

$\pi(S_2) = A_3$

$\pi(S_3) = A_2$

Figure 5.13: *Greedy policy based on Q*

And we can depict the whole process as follows:

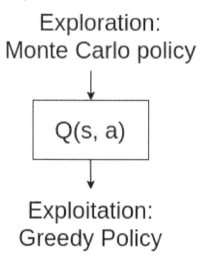

Figure 5.14: *Monte Carlo Exploration and Greed Exploitation*

Well, let's play blackjack for real **ch5/run/balanced_blackjack.py**:

Import part

```python
import random
import gym
from ch5.monte_carlo.policy import q_greedy_policy
from ch5.monte_carlo.q_monte_carlo import train_q_monte_carlo
from ch5.utils.plot_q import plot_q


env = gym.make('Blackjack-v0')


seed = 0
random.seed(seed)
np.random.seed(seed)
env.seed(seed)
```

Creating Q function

```python
Q = train_q_monte_carlo(env, 50_000)
```

Plotting action map

```
plot_q(Q)
```

Running 1000 real plays

```
episodes = 1000
wins = 0
loss = 0
draws = 0


for e in range(1, episodes + 1):
    reward = q_greedy_policy(env, Q)
    if reward > 0:
        wins += 1
    elif reward < 0:
        loss += 1
    else:
        draws += 1


print(f'Wins: {wins} | Loss: {loss} | Draws: {draws}')
```

Result:

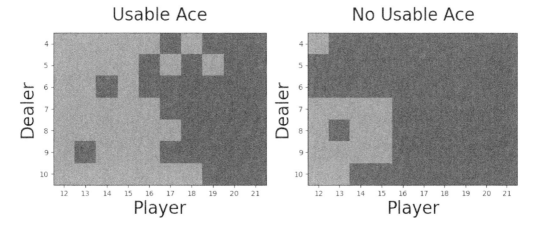

Figure 5.15: *Q(s, a) action map*

The *figure 5.15* shows action for each state: red – *Hit* and blue – *Stick*.

Wins: 455	Loss: 466	Draws: 79	Total: 1000

Table 5.11: Summary of real plays

We have very impressive results! Our agent won 455 games and lost 466. The question is, how can we consider our results impressive if we lost more than we won? Well, the harsh truth of life is that casinos don't really like to play games they lose. Like roulette and slot machines, blackjack is a losing game in the long run. The fact that our agent hasn't lost a lot of money is a pretty good result. But under certain conditions, you can win at blackjack. We'll talk about this in the next section.

Optimal policy for unbalanced Blackjack

From *Chapter 4, Struggling With Multi-Armed Bandits*, you should remember that we are the heroes of the movie *Ocean's 11*. And we have another partner in the casino. Our partner made a hidden card deck for the player. A regular blackjack card deck contains each card in equal proportions:

- *Ace*:   1
- 2:   1
- 3:   1
- …
- *Queen*:   1
- *King*:   1

But our hidden deck has too many low-valued cards:

- *Ace*:   10
- 2:   30
- 3:   30
- 4:   20
- 5:   10
- 6:   5
- 7:   3
- 8:   1

- 9:   1
- 10:   1
- *Jack*:   1
- *Queen*:   1
- *King*:   1

The dealer deals himself cards from a regular deck and deals the player cards from a hidden unbalanced deck. This fact significantly increases the player's chances of winning because now, it is much easier for the player to collect the number of scores close to 21:

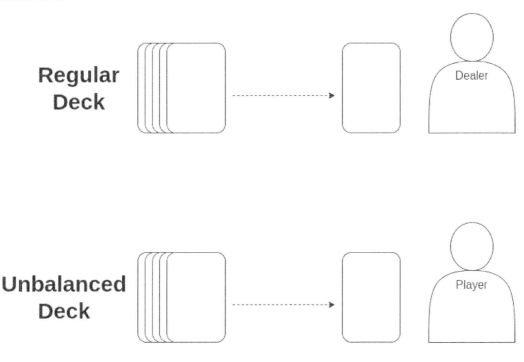

Figure 5.16: *Regular deck and Unbalanced deck*

Of course, you can make money under such conditions. Still, we want to maximize our profit by developing the most optimal game policy for an environment with an unbalanced deck of cards. The reader can examine the environment emulating the blackjack game with an unbalanced deck of cards: **ch5/gym/blackjack_hidden_deck_env.py**.

Let's develop the optimal game policy for an environment with an unbalanced deck of cards and play 1,000 times **ch5/run/unbalanced_blackjack.py**:

Import part

```
import random
import numpy as np
from ch5.gym.blackjack_hidden_deck_env import BlackjackHiddenDeckEnv
from ch5.monte_carlo.policy import q_greedy_policy
from ch5.monte_carlo.q_monte_carlo import train_q_monte_carlo
from ch5.utils.plot_q import plot_q
```

Hidden deck

```
hidden_deck = {
    1:  10,
    2:  30,
    3:  30,
    4:  20,
    5:  10,
    6:  5,
    7:  3,
    8:  1,
    9:  1,
    10: 1,
    10: 1,
    10: 1,
    10: 1
}
env = BlackjackHiddenDeckEnv(hidden_deck)
```

Reproducible script

```
seed = 6
random.seed(seed)
env.seed(seed)
np.random.seed(seed)
```

Creating Q function

```
Q = train_q_monte_carlo(env, 200_000)
```

Plotting Q

```
plot_q(Q)
```

Running 1000 plays

```
episodes = 1000
wins = 0
loss = 0
draws = 0

for e in range(1, episodes + 1):
    reward = q_greedy_policy(env, Q)
    if reward > 0:
        wins += 1
    elif reward < 0:
        loss += 1
    else:
        draws += 1

print(f'Wins: {wins} | Loss: {loss} | Draws: {draws}')
```

Result

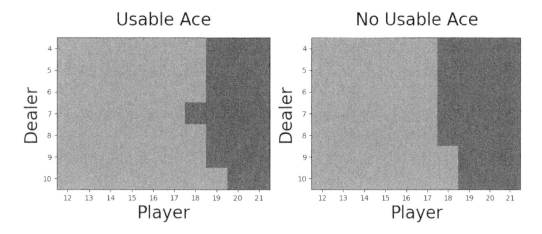

Figure 5.17: *Q(s, a) action map*

Figure 5.17 shows action for each state: red – *Hit* and blue – *Stick*.

Wins: 578	Loss: 288	Draws: 134

Table 5.12: *Summary of real plays*

Table 5.12 shows the result of our game. We see that the game policy we have developed for an unbalanced deck of cards leaves no chance for the dealer. Perhaps we would have won anyway, but the Monte Carlo method helped develop the game's most optimal rules in the given environment.

Conclusion

In this chapter, you studied the fundamental concepts of reinforcement learning. The idea of action-value function is one of the most important in reinforcement learning. All subsequent methods will construct the $Q(s,a)$ function for different tasks. You also learned the principles of building an effective policy for a multi-step game. The Monte Carlo method is well suited for simple environments with a not very large state space, but there are better and faster ways to generate $Q(s,a)$, which we will discuss in the next chapter.

Points to remember

- *G(s, a; n)* - reward received in episode n after action a in state s, plus all discounted future rewards.

- *Q(s, a)* is the sum of all returns of action a in state s divided by the total number of actions a in state s.

Multiple choice questions

1. Suppose we are playing chess, and at some point in the game, we take a computer hint. The computer displays the best moves in order of their value: *A, B, C, D*. What can we say about this statement in terms of reinforcement learning?

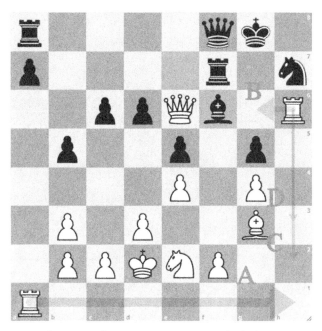

a. Action *A* has a maximum probability

b. $max_a Q(S,a) = A$ and $Q(S, A) > Q(S, B) > Q(S, C) > Q(S, D)$

c. Actions: *A, B, C, D* are the only possible actions in given state S

2. What would happen if we set $\gamma > 1$ in the return formula?

$$G(s_k, a_k; n) = \sum_{i=k}^{t} \gamma^{i-k} r_k$$

a. *Q(s, a)* will not reflect the real action value since the cost of immediate actions will be less than the subsequent ones.

b. That can increase the speed of *Q(s, a)* action-value function construction.

Answers

1. **b**

2. **a**

Key terms

- **Q(s, a):** Action-value function, which returns the value of action *a* in state *s*

- **Monte Carlo Method:** Constructs *Q(s, a) by* evaluating episodes by random policy

## CHAPTER 6

Escaping Maze with Q-Learning

In this chapter, we are going to finish our casino adventures. In *Chapter 4, Struggling With Multi-Armed Bandits*, we played slot machines, and in *Chapter 5, Blackjack in Monte Carlo*, we played blackjack. With the use of reinforcement learning techniques, we have developed effective agent policies for these games. We made some money, and now our task is to leave the casino as soon as possible. Most casinos have a maze inside, it is easy to enter a casino, but it is not easy to leave it. In this chapter, we will study a new method that produces an effective agent's policy, called Q-learning, and understand how this method helps find a way out of a maze.

Structure

In this chapter, we will discuss the following topics:

- Maze
- Q-learning
- Solving maze problem
- Q-learning vs. Monte-Carlo method
- Dense vs. Sparse rewards

Objectives

After going through this chapter, you will be able to operate the temporal-difference method, which is used to construct a Q(s, a) function efficiently. You will also have understood how to apply Q-learning technique to solve reinforcement learning problems.

Maze

Many machine learning methods solve the problem of finding a way out of the maze. In many children's books, it is suggested to draw a way out of the maze.

Figure 6.1: *Maze*

The maze problem can be considered as an artificial toy problem. But this task, like no other, illustrates the principles of Q-learning and demonstrates the problem of dense and sparse rewards. Solving the maze problem with Q-learning gives excellent intuition about the core principles of this method.

Let us convert the maze problem to a reinforcement learning context. Gym framework does not have a built-in maze environment, so we will create one by ourselves. A maze can be considered as a matrix of coordinates. This matrix contains wall coordinates and goal coordinates. The maze map can be implemented as follows **ch6/maze/map.py**:

```
def map1():
    x_coord = ['A', 'B', 'C', 'D']
```

```
y_coord = [1, 2, 3, 4, 5]
walls = ['B3', 'B4', 'C2', 'C4', 'D2']
goal = 'C3'
return x_coord, y_coord, walls, goal
```

The matrix of numbers is not so convenient to work with, so let's visualize our maze and add some helper methods **ch6/maze/core.py**:

Import part

```
import matplotlib.pyplot as plt

import random

from ch6.maze.map import map1

import numpy as np
```

Actions

In the maze, we have the following action set: Up, Right, Down, Left:

```
# Up, Right, Down, Left
actions = ['U', 'R', 'D', 'L']
```

Maze plot

```
def plot_maze_state(x_coord, y_coord, walls, current_state, goal, title
= ''):
    nrows = len(y_coord)
    ncols = len(x_coord)
    image = np.zeros(nrows * ncols)
    image = image.reshape((nrows, ncols))

    for x in range(ncols):
        for y in range(nrows):
            label = f'{x_coord[x]}{y_coord[y]}'
            if label in walls:
                image[y, x] = 0
            else:
                image[y, x] = 1

    plt.figure(figsize = (ncols, nrows), dpi = 240)
```

```
    plt.matshow(image, cmap = 'gray', fignum = 1)


    for x in range(ncols):
        for y in range(nrows):
            label = f'{x_coord[x]}{y_coord[y]}'
            if label == goal:
                plt.annotate('O', xy = (x - .2, y + .2), fontsize = 30,
weight = 'bold')
            if label == current_state:
                plt.annotate('X', xy = (x - .2, y + .2), fontsize = 30,
weight = 'bold')


    plt.xticks(range(ncols), x_coord)
    plt.yticks(range(nrows), y_coord)
    if title:
        plt.title(title)
    plt.show()
```

Move

This method moves the agent in the given direction:

```
def move(current_state, action, x_coord, y_coord, walls):
    x = current_state[0]
    y = int(current_state[1:])
    x_idx = x_coord.index(x)
    y_idx = y_coord.index(y)


    if action == 'U':
        next_state = x + str(y_coord[max([y_idx - 1, 0])])
    elif action == 'R':
        next_state = x_coord[min([x_idx + 1, len(x_coord) - 1])] + str(y)
    elif action == 'D':
        next_state = x + str(y_coord[min([y_idx + 1, len(y_coord) - 1])])
    elif action == 'L':
        next_state = x_coord[max([x_idx - 1, 0])] + str(y)
```

```
    else:
        raise Exception(f'Invalid action: {action}')


    if next_state in walls:
        return current_state


    return next_state
```

Random state

Returns random maze coordinate (except walls):

```
def random_state(x_coord, y_coord, walls):
    available_states = []
    for cell in maze_states(x_coord, y_coord):
        if cell in walls:
            continue
        available_states.append(cell)
    return random.choice(available_states)
```

Maze states

Returns all maze coordinates:

```
def maze_states(x_coord, y_coord):
    all_states = []
    for y in y_coord:
        for x in x_coord:
            cell = f'{x}{y}'
            all_states.append(cell)
    return all_states
```

Now, we put everything together and try to escape the maze:

```
if __name__ == '__main__':
```

Creating the map and setting initial state in A1:

```
    x_coord, y_coord, walls, goal = map1()
    state = 'A1'
```

Plotting maze:

```
plot_maze_state(x_coord, y_coord, walls, state, goal)
```

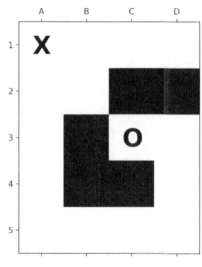

Figure 6.2: *Maze plot*

In *Figure 6.2,* **X** represents the agent's location and O exit from the maze. So, let's perform the following sequence of actions and escape the maze:

```
actions = ['D', 'D', 'D', 'D', 'R', 'R', 'R', 'U', 'U', 'L']
for action in actions:
    state = move(state, action, x_coord, y_coord, walls)
    plot_maze_state(x_coord, y_coord, walls, state, goal)
```

Here is the final state:

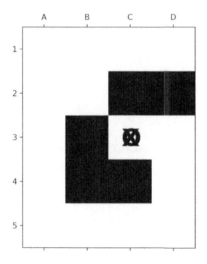

Figure 6.3: *Agent escaped the maze*

Now, let's consider a maze escaping as a reinforcement learning problem:

- **Agent**: It is an object inside a maze that is trying to escape it.
- **Action Space**:
  - *Up*
  - *Right*
  - *Down*
  - *Left*
- **State**: Coordinate of the agent
- **Reward**:
  - *-1 if agent makes a move.* We must force the agent to find a way out of the maze faster, so it is necessary to impose penalties for all actions so that the agent tries to get out by performing as few actions as possible.
  - *-10 if agent hits the wall.* The agent is blind and can crash into walls. It is better to protect the agent from hitting a wall.
  - *1000 if agent reaches the goal.* This is the main reward of the episode.

Agent transitions in the maze environment can be illustrated in the following way:

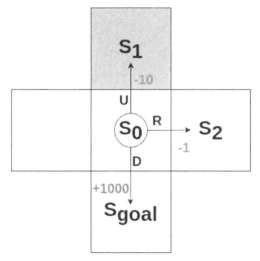

Figure 6.4: *Agent transition diagram*

Now, we are ready to create the Gym environment for the maze problem **ch6/gym_maze/maze_env.py**:

```
class MazeEnv(gym.Env):
```

Initializing environment

```python
def __init__(self, x_coord, y_coord, blocks, finish_state):

    self.x_coord = x_coord

    self.y_coord = y_coord

    self.blocks = blocks

    self.state = random_state(x_coord, y_coord, blocks)

    self.finish_state = finish_state


    # debug properties
    self._total_actions = 0

    self._total_reward = 0
```

Performing action

```python
def step(self, action):

    prev_state = self.state

    next_state = move(self.state, action, self.x_coord, self.y_coord, self.blocks)

    reward = 0

    done = False

    if next_state == self.finish_state:

        reward = 1000

        done = True

    elif prev_state == next_state:

        reward = -10

    elif prev_state != next_state:

        reward = -1

    self.state = next_state


    self._total_actions += 1

    self._total_reward += reward


    return self.state, reward, done, None
```

Reset Environment

```
def reset(self):

    self._total_actions = 0

    self._total_reward = 0

    not_allowed = self.blocks + [self.finish_state]

    self.state = random_state(self.x_coord, self.y_coord, not_
allowed)

    return self.state
```

Visualizing maze

```
def render(self, mode = "ascii"):

    plot_maze_state(

        self.x_coord,

        self.y_coord,

        self.blocks,

        self.state,

        self.finish_state,

        f'Total Reward: {self._total_reward} \n'

        f'Total Actions: {self._total_actions}'

    )
```

Similar to the previous chapters, we will give an example of an agent that follows a random policy, that is, performs a random action from Up, Right, Down and Left **ch6/gym_maze/random_policy.py**:

Import part

```
import random

from ch6.gym_maze.maze_env import MazeEnv

from ch6.maze.core import actions

from ch6.maze.map import map1
```

Loading map data

```
x_coord, y_coord, blocks, goal = map1()
```

Reproducible script

```
seed = 0
random.seed(seed)
env = MazeEnv(x_coord, y_coord, blocks, goal)
env.seed(seed)

env.reset()
action_history = []
```

Performing Random Policy

```
for i in range(1000):
    if i % 10 == 0:
        env.render()
    action = random.choice(actions)
    print(f'action: {action}')
    action_history.append(action)
    state, reward, done, debug = env.step(action)
    if done:
        env.render()
        break

env.close()

print(f'Moves: {len(action_history)}')
```

Result

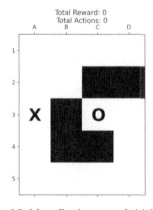

Figure 6.5: Maze Environment Initial State

Figure 6.5 displays the initial state of the environment. The environment places the agent at a random place on the map, where the agent must find a way out. In order to reach the goal, the agent needs to perform eight actions:

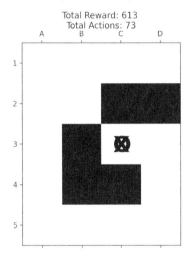

Figure 6.6: *Maze Environment Final State*

We see in *Figure 6.6* that, in reality, the random policy made 73 actions to get out, and the total reward is 613. In the next section, we will look at a much more efficient way of finding a way out of the maze.

Q-learning

The term "*Q-learning*" stands for "*quality learning*", referring to the term quality action-value function. Indeed, like the Monte Carlo method, Q-learning forms a Q(s, a) function. However, Q-learning is a much more efficient method than the Monte Carlo method. We will start with a bit of theory that will explain the essence of the q-learning method.

Let's examine the pseudocode of the Q-learning algorithm:

```
Set global parameters: α - learning rate, γ - discount rate
Initialize Q(s,a) to zeros
For each episode
    s ← random initial state
    For each step in episode
        Choose action a from state s using e-greedy policy
        Perform action a obtaining reward r
        and next state s'
```

```
Q(s,a) ← Q(s,a) + α[r + γ max_a.Q(s',a') - Q(s,a)]
s ← s'
break if s is final episode state
```

Yes, at the moment, you may not understand all the steps in our algorithm, but be patient. The meaning of each step can be explained as follows:

1. `Set global parameters: α - learning rate, γ - discount rate`

    The Q-learning method has two global hyper-parameters:

    - γ: Discount of all future rewards. $0 < \gamma \leq 1$
    - α: Weight of the new experience. $0 < \alpha \leq 1$

2. `Initialize Q(s,a) to zeros`

    We start with a no-experience matrix, where any action in any state is neutral, that is, the reward expectation of each action is 0.

3. `For each episode`

    This is a global loop that will iterate episodes.

4. `s ← random initial state`

    We get the initial state of the environment.

5. `For each step in episode`

    This is a local loop that will iterate actions in episode.

6. `Choose action a from state s using e-greedy policy`

    e-greedy policy returns the next action a for state **s** based on **Q(s, a)**:

    - random action with *e* probability
    - $max_a Q(s, a)$ with *1-e* probability

7. `Perform action a obtaining reward r and next state s'`

    Here, we execute action a, which we obtained in step 6, and the environment returns the reward r and the next state s'.

8. `Q(s,a) ← Q(s,a) + α[r + γ max_a.Q(s',a') - Q(s,a)]`

    And now we come to one of the most exciting concepts in this chapter: step 8 specifies the update rule of the $Q(s, a)$ function. Let us try to understand its meaning. The key to understanding the principles of Q-learning lies in this expression:

$$r + \gamma \, max_{a'} Q(s',a') - Q(s,a)$$

Q-learning uses the greedy policy in the exploitation process, so the variable $max_{a'} Q(s',a')$ denotes the sum of all expected rewards that the agent will receive if they apply greedy policy from the s' state. $max_{a'} Q(s',a')$ can be represented as $V(s')$, where $V(s')$ is the state value and means the total expected reward that the agent will receive in the future after visiting s state. Indeed, a greedy policy implies an unambiguous definition of action for each state. Therefore $V(s') = max_{a'} Q(s',a')$ is the total expected reward that an agent will receive following the greedy policy from state s. γ is a discount factor of estimated rewards after action a is made.

The variable $r + \gamma V(s')$ means the income received after action a in state s and the expected future income from state s'. And $Q(s, a)$ means the expected future income from state s.

If $r + \gamma V(s') > Q(s, a)$, it means the value of $Q(s, a)$ is underestimated, and actually, the value of action a in state s is higher than the current value of $Q(s, a)$.

If $r + \gamma V(s') < Q(s, a)$, then this means that the value of $Q(s, a)$ is overestimated, and actually, the value of action a in state s is lower than the current value of $Q(s, a)$.

Therefore, after receiving new experience when action a is made, we must increase or decrease $Q(s, a)$ depending on the value: $r + \gamma V(s') - Q(s, a)$.

Now, let's go back to step 8:

$$Q(s,a) \leftarrow Q(s,a) + \alpha[r + \gamma \ max_a Q(s',a') - Q(s,a)]$$

The value of $Q(s, a)$ is increased or decreased by $r + \gamma \ max_{a'} Q(s', a') - Q(s, a)$.

Figure 6.7 demonstrates the $Q(s, a)$ update rule:

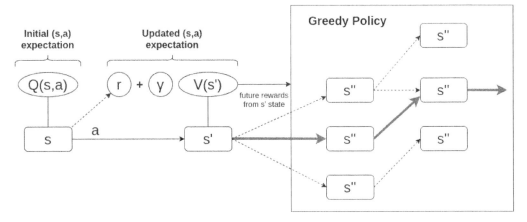

***Figure 6.7**: Q(s, a) update rule*

Let's summarize:

- $Q(s, a)$ means the initial total reward expectation from the action a in the state s.

- $r + \gamma\ V(s')$ or $r + \gamma\ max_{a'}\ Q(s', a')$ means the total reward expectation from the action a in the state s, taking into account the information about the performed action a.

- $r + \gamma\ max_{a'}\ Q(s',a') - Q(s,a)$ is the expectations difference at different moments of research or temporal difference.

- $Q(s, a)$ value is updated, considering the new experience gained with each subsequent action.

And the original update rule can be rewritten as follows:

$$Q(s, a) \leftarrow Q(s, a) + \alpha[r + \gamma\ max_{a'}\ Q(s', a') - Q(s, a)] \tag{1}$$

Transforms to

$$Q(s, a) \leftarrow Q(s, a) + \alpha[r + \gamma\ V(s') - Q(s, a)] \tag{2}$$

Transforms to

$$Q(s, a) \leftarrow Q(s, a) + \alpha(temporal\ difference) \tag{3}$$

Transforms to

$$Q(s, a)\ += \alpha\ (temporal\ difference) \tag{4}$$

It will become more apparent to you how this method works when we look at it in practice.

9. $s \leftarrow s'$

    We set *next state* as the *current state*.

10. `break if s is the final episode state`

    We exit the episode loop if we encounter the final episode state.

Usually, $V(s)$ state-value function denotes the mean value of all actions in s state, i.e., $V(s) = \dfrac{\sum_{i=1}^{n} Q(s, a_i)}{n}$, in this book, we will consider the $V(s)$ function as the maximum value of the function $Q(s, a)$ in the s state, i.e., $V(s) = max_a Q(s, a)$.

In this section, we covered the theoretical foundations of the Q-learning method, and in the next section, we will look at the practical implementation of this approach.

Solving maze problem

Now, let's get back to Python and apply the Q-learning algorithm we studied in the previous section. Here is the implementation of the e-greedy policy from step 6 **ch6/td/policy.py**:

```
def epsilon_greedy_policy(e, Q, s):
    r = random.random()
    if r > e:
        max_q = max(Q[s])
        candidates = [i for i in range(len(Q[s, :])) if Q[s, i] ==
max_q]
        return random.choice(candidates)
    else:
        return random.randint(0, len(Q[s]) - 1)
```

And here is the Q-learning update rule from step 8:

```
def q_learning(Q, current_s, next_s, a, r, gamma = .9, alpha = .5):
    # r + g*max[a](Q(S', a)) - Q(S, A)
    td = (r + gamma * max(Q[next_s]) - Q[current_s, a])
    Q[current_s, a] += alpha * round(td, 2)
    return Q
```

It is always useful to visualize a process or a function. There is a convenient way to visualize the maze problem's $Q(s, a)$ function. Each cell in the maze contains four arrows or four actions, and each of them has the $Q(s, a)$ value:

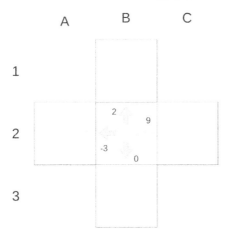

***Figure 6.8**: Q(s, a) visualization*

Figure 6.8 demonstrates the visualization of *Q(B2, a)* values:

- *Q(B2, Up)* = 2

- *Q(B2, Right)* = 9

- *Q(B2, Down)* = 0

- *Q(B2, Left)* = -3

Obviously, the greedy policy in state *B2* will choose the *Right* action.

Now, everything is ready to conduct the first Q-learning training session `ch6/td/q_learning_single_episode.py`:

Import part

```
import random
import numpy as np
from ch6.gym_maze.maze_env import MazeEnv
from ch6.maze.core import maze_states
from ch6.maze.map import map1
from ch6.td.policy import epsilon_greedy_policy
from ch6.td.td import q_learning
from ch6.td.utils import plot_q_map
```

Initializing environment

```
actions = ['U', 'R', 'D', 'L']
x_coord, y_coord, blocks, goal = map1()


seed = 10
random.seed(seed)
env = MazeEnv(x_coord, y_coord, blocks, goal)
env.seed(seed)


states = maze_states(x_coord, y_coord)
```

1. **Setting global parameters**

   ```
   epsilon = .2
   gamma = 0.9
   alpha = 0.8
   ```

2. **Initialize Q(s, a) to zeros**

```
Q = np.array(np.zeros([len(states), len(actions)]))
```

3. **Getting initial state**

We skip *step 3* here because we have only one training episode
```
state = env.reset()
```

4. For each step in episode
```
i = 1
while True:
```

5. Obtaining next action by e-greedy policy
```
    action_idx = epsilon_greedy_policy(epsilon, Q, states.
index(state))
    action = actions[action_idx]
```

6. Performing action
```
    next_state, reward, done, debug = env.step(action)
```

7. Updating Q
```
    Q = q_learning(
        Q,
        states.index(state),
        states.index(next_state),
        action_idx,
        reward,
        gamma,
        alpha
    )
```

8. Next step to current step
```
    state = next_state
```

9. Final step
```
    if done:
        plot_q_map(x_coord, y_coord, blocks, Q, goal,
                title = f'After Final Action')
        break
```

```
else:
    if i % 10 == 0 or i < 3:
        plot_q_map(x_coord, y_coord, blocks, Q, goal,
                   title = f'After Action: {i}')
    i += 1
```

Let us go through the analysis of the Q-learning process.

The agent starts the episode in square *A1*. In the beginning, *Q(s, a)* is a zero matrix, and for the e-greedy policy all actions are equally probable, so a random action is selected: *Up*.

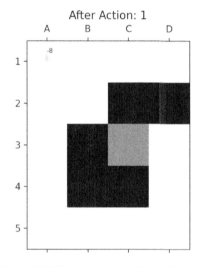

Figure 6.9: *Q(s, a) function after Action: 1*

The agent hits a wall and receives a reward of -10. *Figure 6.9* shows the *Q(s, a)* matrix after updating the value of *Q(A1, Up)*:

$$Q(A1, Up) = 0 + 0.8\,(-10 + 0.9 \times 0 - 0) = -8$$

The agent is still in square *A1*. In the second iteration, e-greedy policy selects the action: *Down*:

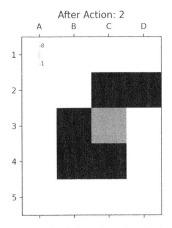

Figure 6.10: $Q(s, a)$ *function after Action: 2*

The agent makes a successful move and receives a reward of -1. *Figure 6.10* shows the $Q(s, a)$ matrix after updating the value of $Q(A1, Down)$:

$$Q(A1, Up) = 0 + 0.8 \ (-1 + 0.9 \times 0 - 0) = -0.8$$

For ease of perception, the visualization of $Q(s, a)$ action-value function rounds the values to the nearest integer. That's why in *Figure 6.10*, you see that $Q(A1, Down) = -1$, not -0.8.

Let's speed up the process a bit and see what the $Q(s, a)$ function looks like after 50 actions:

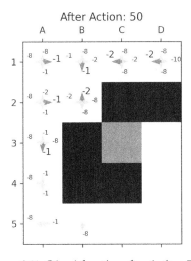

Figure 6.11: $Q(s, a)$ *function after Action: 50*

Figure 6.11 shows us that all $Q(s, a)$ values are either zero or negative. After 50 actions, there is no experience of receiving positive rewards. And that makes sense since you can get a positive reward only by finding a way out of the maze. Okay, let's examine the $Q(s, a)$ function after the agent finds a way out of the maze:

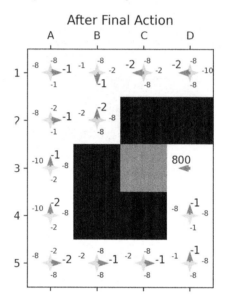

Figure 6.12: *Q(s, a) function after Final Action*

Do you see anything special in *Figure 6.12*? Yes, in square *D3*, we see that $Q(s, a)$ unambiguously recommends the action: Left promising very high reward after this action.

Now, let's look at a complete Q-learning exploration process through multiple episodes **ch6/td/q_learning_explore.py**:

Import part

```
import random

import numpy as np

from ch6.gym_maze.maze_env import MazeEnv

from ch6.maze.core import maze_states

from ch6.maze.map import map1

from ch6.td.policy import epsilon_greedy_policy

from ch6.td.td import q_learning

from ch6.td.utils import plot_q_map
```

Initializing environment

```
actions = ['U', 'R', 'D', 'L']
x_coord, y_coord, blocks, goal = map1()


seed = 1
random.seed(seed)
env = MazeEnv(x_coord, y_coord, blocks, goal)
env.seed(seed)


states = maze_states(x_coord, y_coord)
Q = np.array(np.zeros([len(states), len(actions)]))
```

Global Q-learning parameters

```
epsilon = .2
gamma = 0.9
alpha = 0.8
episodes = 50
```

Iterating episodes

```
for e in range(episodes):
    state = env.reset()
    i = 0
    while True:
        i += 1

        action_idx = epsilon_greedy_policy(epsilon, Q, states.
index(state))
        action = actions[action_idx]

        next_state, reward, done, debug = env.step(action)

        Q = q_learning(
            Q,
            states.index(state),
            states.index(next_state),
```

```
        action_idx,
        reward,
        gamma,
        alpha
    )

    state = next_state

    if done:
Visualizing final states
        if e < 5 or e % 10 == 9 or e == episodes - 1:
            plot_q_map(x_coord, y_coord, blocks, Q, goal,
                title = f'After Episode {e+1}')
        break

env.close()
```

This is what the function *Q(s, a)* looks like after the first episode:

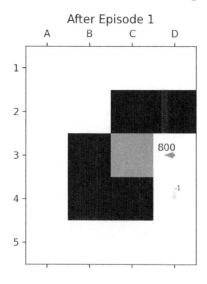

Figure 6.13: *Q(s, a) after Episode 1*

Figure 6.13 shows the *Q(s,a)* function after *Episode 1*. We see a familiar situation where *Q(D3, Left)* = 800. Let's see what happens next:

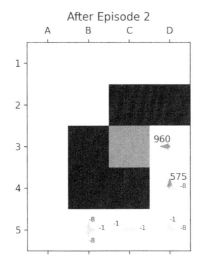

Figure 6.14: *Q(s, a) after Episode 2*

After *Episode 2* in *Figure 6.14*, we see that the value of *Q(D4, Up)* is 575. Let's see how this happened. During the movement towards the exit, the agent moved from square *D4* to square *D3*, and after this move, the value *Q(D3, Up)* was recalculated:

$$Q(D3, Up) = Q(D3, Up) + 0.8(-1 + 0.9 \times 800 - Q(D3, Up))$$

And the positive state value *V(D4)* = 800 significantly increased the *Q(D3, Up)* action value.

Perhaps you already know what will happen after *Episode 3*?

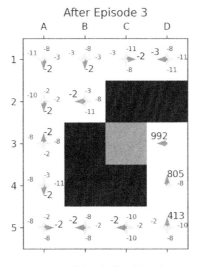

Figure 6.15: *Q(s, a) after Episode 3*

Yes, we see in *Figure 6.15*, that after *Episode 3* in square *D5*, the function *Q(s, a)* explicitly decides to perform the action *Up*. We see how reward is propagated back to previous states. After each new episode, the path to the exit becomes more and more apparent:

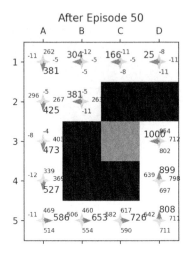

Figure 6.16: *Q(s, a) after Episode 50*

And after *Episode 50*, the *Q(s, a)* action-value function depicted in *Figure 6.16* gives us the shortest path out of the maze. Let's try to get out of the maze starting from square *D1*:

- *Q(D1, Left) = 25* is the maximum value in *D1*: *move Left*

- *Q(C1, Left) = 166* is the maximum value in *C1*: *move Left*

- *Q(B1, Left) = 304* is the maximum value in *B1*: *move Left*

- ...

- *Q(D4, Up) = 899* is the maximum value in *D4*: *move Up*

- *Q(D3, Left) = 1000* is the maximum value in *D3*: *move Left*

- *Exit!*

We have observed a fundamental principle of the Q-learning method. Q-learning back-propagates rewards across previous states. Thus, a particular route of action is created, which will lead to the greatest total reward in various situations. This principle is most clearly seen when solving the maze problem. In *Figure 6.16*, we can see how each square has an action that guides us towards a maximum reward. We remind you that the agent does not receive any positive reward during the movement but, on the contrary, receives -1 for each movement or -10 for hitting a wall, *Q(s, a)* shows only the total expected reward:

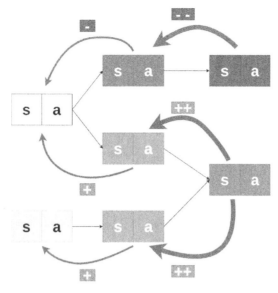

Figure 6.17: *Q-learning reward backpropagation*

Figure 6.17 shows the reward backpropagation process during a Q-learning exploration. Each new exploration episode will produce a reverse rewards propagation for states and actions. Thus, the more states and actions we have, the more exploration episodes need to be executed. After a sufficient number of episodes, $Q(s, a)$ contains the optimal rules for the agent's policy in exploitation.

Great! We studied the principles of Q-learning and learned how to create a $Q(s, a)$ function. Let's see how the agent finds a way out of the maze **ch6/td/q_learning_explore_and_exploit.py**:

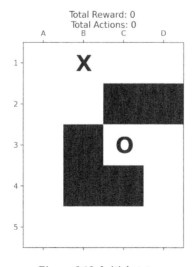

Figure 6.18: *Initial state*

The agent finds himself in square *B1* at the beginning of the episode.

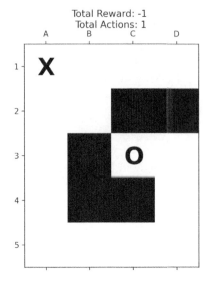

Figure 6.19: State after first action

The agent begins to move strictly according to the *Q(s, a)* function that we observed in the *Figure 6.16*:

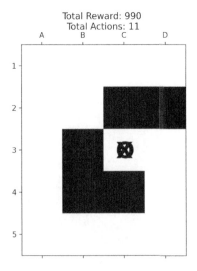

Figure 6.20: Final state

We see in *Figure 6.20* that the agent finds a way out in 11 actions, which is the minimum number of actions to leave the maze, starting from square *B1*.

Congratulations! We have just finished exploring the most significant reinforcement learning approach. All subsequent chapters will use the concepts of Q-Learning and *Q(s, a)* action-value functions. These principles are universal for all types of reinforcement learning problems and will immensely help you in the future.

Q-learning vs. Monte Carlo method

You may wonder: why is the Monte Carlo method worse than the Q-learning method? And this is a fair question that needs to be answered. Let us take a look at a more extensive maze **ch6/maze/map.py**:

```python
def map2():
    x_coord = ['A', 'B', 'C', 'D', 'E', 'F',
               'G', 'H', 'I', 'J', 'K', 'L']
    y_coord = [1, 2, 3, 4, 5, 6, 7, 8, 9, 10, 11, 12]
    walls = [
        'B3', 'B4', 'B6', 'B7', 'B8', 'B9', 'B11',
        'C2', 'C4', 'C11',
        'D2', 'D6', 'D7', 'D8', 'D11',
        'E3', 'E7', 'E8', 'E10', 'E11',
        'F4', 'F5', 'F6', 'F9', 'F10',
        'G7', 'G10', 'G12',
        'H4', 'H7', 'H8', 'H11',
        'I3', 'I5', 'I8', 'I11',
        'J1', 'J5', 'J6', 'J8',
        'K1', 'K3', 'K6', 'K7', 'K12',
    ]
    goal = 'G6'
    return x_coord, y_coord, walls, goal
```

And here is its visualization:

```python
if __name__ == '__main__':
    from ch6.maze.core import plot_maze_state

    x_coord, y_coord, walls, goal = map2()
    state = 'A1'
```

```
plot_maze_state(x_coord, y_coord, walls, state, goal)
```

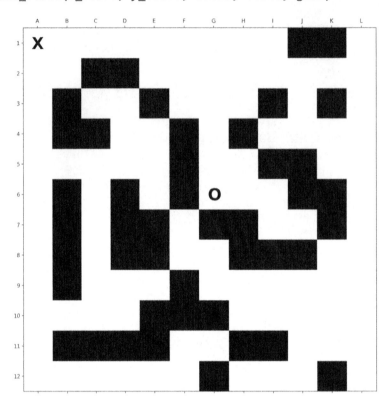

Figure 6.21: *Big Maze*

Figure 6.21 demonstrates that we are dealing with a serious maze problem. Of course, it is not a problem for someone who observes the maze from the top, but it is a problem for a blind agent inside.

Now, let us run one exploration episode for Q-learning and one for the Monte Carlo method **ch6/td/q_vs_mc_single_episode.py**:

Import part

```
import random
import numpy as np
from ch6.gym_maze.maze_env import MazeEnv
from ch6.maze.core import maze_states
from ch6.maze.map import map2
from ch6.td.policy import epsilon_greedy_policy
```

```python
from ch6.td.td import q_learning
```

Initializing environment

```python
actions = ['U', 'R', 'D', 'L']
x_coord, y_coord, blocks, goal = map2()


seed = 1
random.seed(seed)
env = MazeEnv(x_coord, y_coord, blocks, goal)
env.seed(seed)
states = maze_states(x_coord, y_coord)
```

Setting the same initial state for Q-learning and Monte Carlo methods

```python
initial_state = 'A1'
```

Q-learning episode

```python
epsilon = .2
gamma = 0.9
alpha = 0.8


Q = np.array(np.zeros([len(states), len(actions)]))
env.reset()
env.state = initial_state
state = initial_state
env.render()
while True:

    action_idx = epsilon_greedy_policy(epsilon, Q, states.index(state))
    action = actions[action_idx]
    next_state, reward, done, debug = env.step(action)
    Q = q_learning(
        Q,
        states.index(state),
```

```
            states.index(next_state),
            action_idx,
            reward,
            gamma,
            alpha
        )
        state = next_state

        if done:
            env.render()
            break

print(f'Q-learning total actions: {env._total_actions}')
```

Monte Carlo Episode

```
env.reset()
env.state = initial_state
state = initial_state
while True:

    action_idx = epsilon_greedy_policy(epsilon, Q, states.index(state))
    action = actions[action_idx]
    next_state, reward, done, debug = env.step(action)
    state = next_state

    if done:
        env.render()
        break

print(f'Monte Carlo total actions: {env._total_actions}')
```

Result

Q-learning total actions	597
Monte Carlo total actions	10135376

Table 6.1: *Q-learning vs Monte Carlo Exploration*

Wow! The Q-learning method found the exit after 597 actions in the first exploration episode, but Monte Carlo made more than 10 million actions to escape the maze with random policy. How does this happen?

Remember, Q-learning starts learning after the very first step. Q-learning immediately remembers the experience of hitting the walls and, already in the very first episode, tries to avoid unnecessary actions. During the first exploration of the maze, Q-learning begins to come out of dead ends faster because it only provokes negative rewards. In this way, Q-learning is much more efficient at learning various actions and states of the environment.

On the other hand, the Monte Carlo method calculates the Q(s, a) action-value function only after the exploration episode ends. No experience is accumulated during the episode, so the Monte Carlo method can extremely generate many useless data samples for analysis and have much less efficiency than Q-learning.

Does this mean that the Monte Carlo method is worse than the Q-learning method? The answer is: *it depends.*

The Monte Carlo method works well for directed states. That means that each new action transfers the agent closer to the final state, and it is impossible to return from the current state to the previous one. The blackjack environment we studied in *Chapter 4, Struggling With Multi-Armed Bandits,* has directed states.

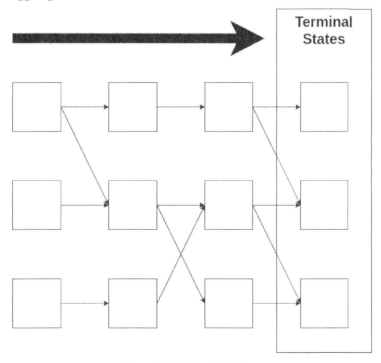

Figure 6.22: Directed states

On the other hand, the Q-learning method works well for undirected states. That means an agent can find itself in the same state several times in the same episode. Moreover, an action can both bring an agent closer to the final state and move further from it:

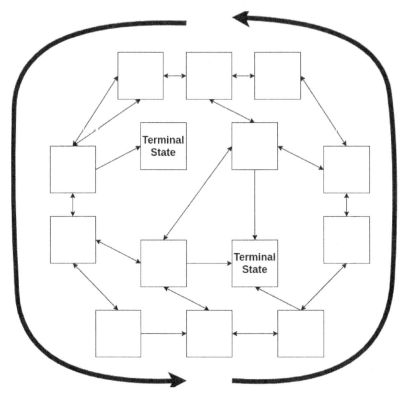

Figure 6.23: *Undirected states*

In any case, Q-learning is a more efficient and accurate method of creating a $Q(s, a)$ function than the Monte Carlo method.

Dense vs. Sparse rewards

In this chapter, we have handled another critical problem of reinforcement learning: the problem of sparse rewards. The essence of this problem is that there are only a few combinations (s, a) in the entire space of states and actions that bring positive rewards. In this case, the Q-learning algorithm needs too many exploration episodes to back propagate rewards to other states and actions:

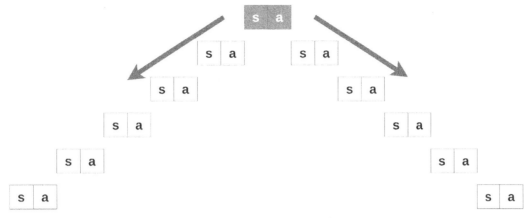

Figure 6.24: *Sparse rewards*

Examples of problems with sparse rewards:

- **Maze**: Agent receives a positive reward only after escaping a maze

- **Chess**: Agent receives a positive reward only after winning a game

- **Blackjack**: Agent receives a positive reward only after winning a game

On the other hand, tasks with dense rewards usually require fewer exploration episodes because rewards spread faster across all state-action pairs.

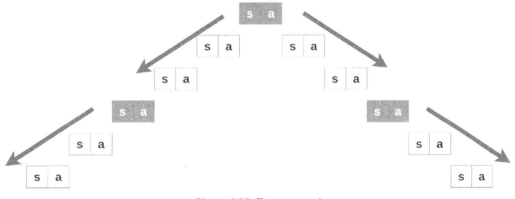

Figure 6.25: *Dense rewards*

Examples of problems with dense rewards:

- **Stock trading**: Agent can receive a positive reward after each action

- **CartPole**: A reward of +1 is provided for every timestep that the pole remains upright

The sparse reward problem is a serious computational problem in reinforcement learning that must be considered to solve a specific problem.

Conclusion

This chapter has covered perhaps one of the most important concepts of reinforcement learning. All further approaches will be based on the Q-learning method. We have studied the Q-learning algorithm's principles of constructing the $Q(s, a)$ action-value function. We have examined the principle of reward backpropagation and the problem of sparse rewards. These principles are fundamental for reinforcement learning so that the following chapters will seem more apparent to a you. In the next chapter, we will study one useful trick, called **discretization**, that lets a reader solve physics problems in infinite-dimensional state space.

Points to remember

- Q-learning algorithm updates $Q(s, a)$ value, considering the new experience gained with each subsequent action.

- Q-learning algorithm uses e-greedy policy during exploration process and greedy policy during exploitation process.

- Q-learning backpropagates rewards to previous state-action pairs.

- Monte Carlo method suites well for directed states environments.

Multiple choice questions

1. Let us take a look at two different environments for the same maze:

    A. Each sideways movement gives a -1reward

    B. Each sideways movement gives a 0 reward

    We have constructed a $Q(s, a)$ function for each of these environments. *Q1(s, a) function visualization*:

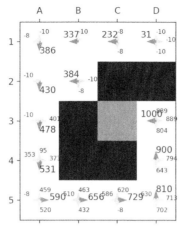

Figure 6.26: $Q_1(s, a)$

$Q_2(s, a)$ *function visualization:*

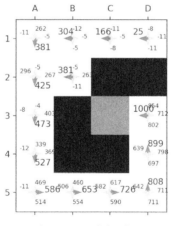

Figure 6.27: $Q_2(s, a)$

Can you determine which $Q(s, a)$ function belongs to which environment?

    a. $Q_1(s, a)$ belongs to A environment and $Q_2(s, a)$ belongs to B environment

    b. $Q_1(s, a)$ belongs to B environment and $Q_2(s, a)$ belongs to A environment

    c.   It is impossible to answer this question

2. Does chess have the property of the directed states?

    a.   Yes, each subsequent move in chess brings the game closer to the end, and no arrangement of pieces is repeated anymore.

    b.   No, technically, if the number of moves does not limit the game, then chess play can continue indefinitely.

Answers

1. b
2. b

Key terms

- **Q-learning algorithm**: Updates its value functions based on temporal difference equations after each action in the exploration episode.

- **Directed states**: Each new action transfers the agent closer to the final state, and it is impossible to return from the current state to the previous one.

- **Undirected states**: Can find itself in the same state several times in the same episode.

- **Dense rewards**: A lot of state-action pairs give a positive reward.

- **Sparse rewards**: Few state-action pairs give a positive reward.

CHAPTER 7
Discretization

In *Chapter 6, Escaping Maze with Q-learning*, we studied how to use the Q-learning method to create an action-value function $Q(s, a)$. Indeed, Q-learning is the core of most reinforcement learning approaches. And it would be natural to apply this technique to many practical problems. But here, we are faced with a problem: many environments have continuous state spaces; how to interact with continuous state space environments? Indeed, physical reinforcement learning problems often operate with speed, weight, and length variables, which are continuous in nature. In the previous chapters, we only examined discrete state space environments. This chapter will explore applying the discrete Q-learning technique to continuous state spaces.

Structure

In this chapter, we will discuss the following topics:

- Discretization of continuous variables
- Discretization of mountain car state space
- Decayed epsilon greedy policy
- Discrete Q-learning Agent

- Applying discrete Q-learning agent to mountain car problem
- Coarse versus Fine discretization
- Q-learning alpha parameter
- Hyperparameters in reinforcement learning
- From limits of discretization to deep reinforcement learning

Objectives

After going through this chapter, you will be able to apply the Q-learning method to a wide variety of continuous state reinforcement learning problems. Also, in this chapter, we will examine the impact of Q-learning hyperparameters on the exploitation process. This chapter will move you through a bridge from classical reinforcement learning to deep reinforcement learning.

Discretization of continuous variables

Let's define what a **continuous variable** is: we say that a variable x is continuous if, for any numbers $a < b$, x can take a value c such that $a < c < b$. An example of such variable is *speed*. A car can move at a speed of 60 km/h as well as at a speed of 61 km/h, 60.5 km/h, 60.0001 km/h, and so on. It is intuitively clear that speed has a continuous nature.

On the other hand, the values of a **discrete variable** can be separated from each other. An example of such a variable is the number of people in a city. There can be 0 people in a city, 1 person, 2 people, 3, 4, ... etc. But a discrete variable is not always is an integer value. For example, the variable s, which is the sum of two consecutive Fibonacci numbers divided by 2, is discrete, but it doesn't always take integer values:

Fibonacci number	Sum divided by two	R
1		
1	(1 + 1) / 2	1
2	(2 + 1) / 2	1.5
3	(3 + 2) / 2	2.5
5	(5 + 3) / 2	4
8	(8 + 5) / 2	6.5
13	(13 + 8) / 2	10.5
21	(21 + 13) / 2	17
...		

Table 7.1: Fibonacci average

In real life, we always round the values of continuous variables for convenience. For example, a car's speedometer shows 78 km/h, not 78.3425 km/h. In practice, it is much more convenient to work with integer values. Rounding continuous variables is the simplest way to discretize them.

Another way of discretization is **binning**. Binning method discretizes values of a continuous variable into a specified bins. Each bin has an equal range. Let's consider the following example: Say a car has the speed range from 0 km/h to 200 km/h; then, we can discretize car speed by four bins:

- **bin #0**: car speed belongs to $[0, 50)$ interval

- **bin #1**: car speed belongs to $[50, 100)$ interval

- **bin #2**: car speed belongs to $[100, 150)$ interval

- **bin #3**: car speed belongs to $[150, 200]$ interval

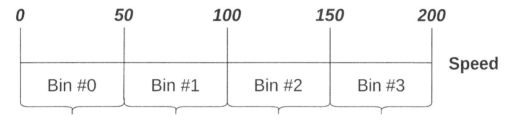

Figure 7.1: *Binning discretization*

In this chapter, we will only use binning discretization. Therefore, we will omit the term binning further.

We can apply the discretization technique if we deal with multiple continuous variables. For example, consider the following pair of continuous variables: car speed, s (from 0 km/h to 200 km/h) and engine temperature, t (from 0° to 150°). We can discretize them into 4 and 3 bins, respectively. The discretization result of the value (87.02 km/h, 105.61°) is (1, 2). *Figure 7.2* illustrates this approach:

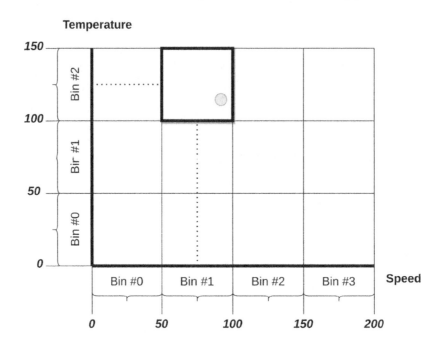

Figure 7.2: *2D discretization*

Let's implement discretization methods **ch7/utils.py**:

```
import numpy as np
```

Grid creation method

```
def create_grid(low, high, bins = (10, 10)):
    g = [
        np.linspace(low[dim], high[dim], bins[dim] + 1)[1:-1]
        for dim in range(len(bins))
    ]
    return g
```

Discretization method

```
def discretize(v, grid):
    return list(int(np.digitize(s, g)) for s, g in zip(v, grid))
```

Check how they act **ch7/discretize.py**:

```
from ch7.utils import discretize, create_grid


if __name__ == '__main__':
    g = create_grid([0, 0], [200, 150], bins = [4, 3])
    v = [87.02, 105.61]
    dv = discretize(v, g)
    print(dv)
```

Result

```
[1, 2]
```

Now, let's examine how the discretization method can help to solve a continuous state space problem.

Discretization of Mountain Car state space

We already mentioned the Mountain Car problem (**MountainCar-v0**) in *Chapter 3, Training in Gym*. Let's remember the basics of this problem. There is a car between the two mountains. An agent has to reach the top of the mountain on the right. For each action that does not lead to the final state, a reward of -1 is returned. Reaching the final state returns a zero reward. The episode ends after 200 actions. The essence of this problem is to reach the top of the right mountain as soon as possible.

There are three different actions available:

- Accelerate to the left

- Do nothing

- Accelerate to the right

Two continuous values characterize the agent's state:

- **Car position**: Value in range [-1.2 , 0.6]

- **Car velocity (or speed)**: Value in range [-0.07, 0.07]

If the car's velocity is negative, it means that the car is moving to the left, and if the speed is positive, it is moving to the right.

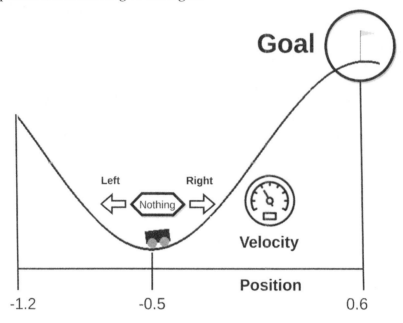

Figure 7.3: *Mountain Car problem*

Let's run a random policy and analyze the agent's states in Mountain Car environment **ch7/random_policy.py**:

```python
import gym

env = gym.make('MountainCar-v0')
seed = 0
env.seed(seed)

state = env.reset()
while True:
    env.render()
    random_action = env.action_space.sample()
    state, reward, done, debug = env.step(random_action)
    print(state)
    if done:
        break
env.close()
```

Result

#	Position	Velocity
1	-0.58763968	0.00148831
2	-0.58567401	0.00196567
3	-0.58324547	0.00242855
4	-0.58137196	0.00187351
...		

Table 7.2: Mountain Car states produced by random policy

We see that it is impossible to apply the Q-learning method to Mountain Car environment states in this form. It is impossible to iterate over an infinite number of states in order to match the most effective action for each one.

As you can guess, discretization is the solution to this problem. We can discretize each continuous variable into 10 bins. This will be a very coarse discretization, but probably it will allow us to solve the Mountain Car problem. Let's apply discretization to random policy **ch7/random_policy_on_discrete.py**:

Import part

```
import random
import gym
import numpy as np
from ch7.utils import discretize, create_grid, plot_route
```

Initializing environment

```
env = gym.make('MountainCar-v0')
seed = 0
env.seed(seed)
random.seed(seed)
np.random.seed(seed)

s_space = env.observation_space
```

Creating discretization grid

```
bins = (10, 10)
grid = create_grid(s_space.low, s_space.high, bins)
```

```
state_history = []

d_state = discretize(env.reset(), grid)
state_history.append(d_state)
while True:
    env.render()
    random_action = env.action_space.sample()
    state, reward, done, debug = env.step(random_action)
    d_state = discretize(state, grid)
    state_history.append(d_state)
    print(d_state)
    if done:
        break
env.close()

plot_route(bins, state_history, ['Position', 'Velocity'])
```

Result

#	Position	Velocity
1	3	5
2	3	5
...		
199	3	4
200	3	4

Table 7.3: Mountain Car discretized states produced by random policy

Figure 7.4 marks the states the agent went through in the episode. The darker the square is, the more time the agent spent in this state during the episode:

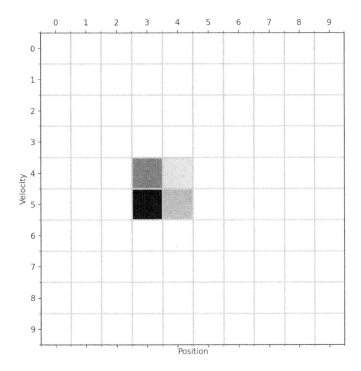

Figure 7.4: *Mountain Car discrete states*

Figure 7.4 demonstrates that the agent was in only four states during the episode: (3, 5), (4, 5), (4, 4), (4, 5), which is quite natural for a random policy. The car simply cannot accelerate to visit other states.

Decayed epsilon greedy policy

Let's look at one useful technique before we start implementing the Q-learning method for the Mountain Car problem. It is called the **decayed epsilon greedy policy**. The decayed epsilon greedy policy implies that the epsilon value will decrease as the number of exploration episodes increase until the epsilon value reaches the minimum threshold. The decaying of epsilon value is controlled by the decayed epsilon rate variable and is usually expressed by the following formula:

$$\xi_i = max(\xi_0 d^i, t)$$

Where:

- ○ ξ_0: initial epsilon value

- ○ *d*: decay rate

- ○ *i*: exploration episode number

    o   *t:* epsilon threshold

    o ξ_i: epsilon value for i^{th} episode

Let's take a look at the implementation of decayed epsilon values calculation **ch7/ decayed_epsilon.py**:

```python
import matplotlib.pyplot as plt


epsilon_original = .3
decay_rate = .9995
train_episodes = 5000
min_threshold = .05


epsilon_history = []
for i in range(0, train_episodes):
    epsilon = max(round(epsilon_original * pow(decay_rate, i), 10), min_threshold)
    epsilon_history.append(epsilon)
    print(f'Episode: {i + 1}| Epsilon: {epsilon}')


plt.plot(epsilon_history)
plt.xlabel('Episodes')
plt.ylabel('Epsilon')
plt.show()
```

Result

Episode	Epsilon
1	0.3
2	0.29985
...	
999	0.1821185198
1000	0.1820274606
...	
5000	0.05

Table 7.4: Decayed epsilon values

The decaying sequence is illustrated in *Figure 7.5*:

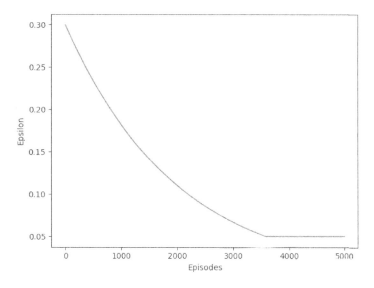

Figure 7.5: *Decayed epsilon sequence*

The point of the decayed epsilon policy is to reduce random actions with the accumulation of experience. This can improve the efficiency of the exploration process. Let's remember the maze problem we solved in *Chapter 5, Escaping Maze with Q-learning*. After a certain number of episodes $Q(s, a)$, the function had sufficient experience not to continue hitting walls in certain states:

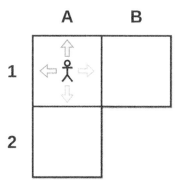

Figure 7.6: *A1 state in maze problem*

Figure 7.6 shows that it didn't make sense to continue performing *Left* and *Up* actions in state *A1*. However, random actions often provoked unnecessary calculation steps, and this was not critical for the Maze problem but could be critical for the Mountain Car problem because the number of actions is limited in each episode (agent has only

200 actions to reach the goal), and unnecessary random actions at the last moment can prevent the car from reaching the top:

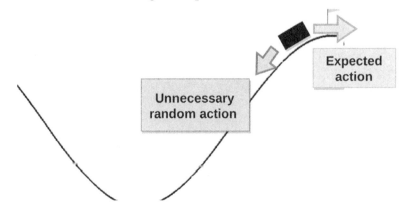

Figure 7.7: Critical random action that fails episode

The decayed epsilon greedy policy solves this problem and is usually a more effective exploration policy than the original epsilon greedy policy in an environment with limited actions per episode. We will be using the decayed epsilon greedy policy to solve the Mountain Car Problem.

Discrete Q-learning agent

As the tasks become more complex, the logic of the reinforcement learning agents' work becomes more complicated. Therefore, it is convenient to encapsulate all the logic of the agents' work in a specific class. This is what we will do in this section. Let's make a **DiscreteQLearningAgent** that will use a Q-learning method based on discretizing the environment's continuous state **ch7/discrete_q_learning_ agent.py**.

First, we define an **__init__** method on the **DiscreteQLearningAgent** class that accepts the hyperparameters of the Q-learning method and the decayed epsilon greedy policy:

```
class DiscreteQLearningAgent:

    def __init__(
            self,
            env,  # Environment
            state_grid,  # Discretization state grid
            # Q-learning alpha  parameters:
```

```
            q_alpha = 0.02,
            q_gamma = 0.99,
            # Decayed e-greedy policy parameters:
            degp_epsilon = 1.0,
            degp_decay_rate = 0.9995,
            degp_min_epsilon = .01
    ):

        self.env = env
        self.state_grid = state_grid

        # total number of states
        self.state_size = tuple(len(splits) + 1 for splits in self.
state_grid)

        # total number of actions
        self.action_size = self.env.action_space.n

        self.q_alpha = q_alpha
        self.q_gamma = q_gamma

        self.degp_epsilon = self.degp_initial_epsilon = degp_epsilon
        self.degp_decay_rate = degp_decay_rate
        self.degp_min_epsilon = degp_min_epsilon

        self.last_state = None
        self.last_action = None
        self.action_history = []

        # Initial Q-map
        self.q = np.zeros(shape = (self.state_size + (self.action_
size,)))
```

Then, we define a specific method that makes our agent discrete. The **transform_ state** method discretizes continuous state:

```
def transform_state(self, state):

    """State discretization"""

    return tuple(discretize(state, self.state_grid))
```

According to the decayed greedy policy, we adjust the epsilon parameter before each new episode:

```
def before_episode(self, state):

    """Adjusting Decayed Epsilon Greedy Policy Parameters before new
episode"""


    # Decaying epsilon
    self.degp_epsilon *= self.degp_decay_rate
    self.degp_epsilon = max(self.degp_epsilon, self.degp_min_
epsilon)


    # Register last actions
    self.last_state = self.transform_state(state)
    self.last_action = np.argmax(self.q[self.last_state])
    self.action_history = []


    return self.last_action
```

The **act** method returns the action to be taken according to the passed state.

- If the act method runs in train (exploration) mode, the logic of the Q-learning method is executed.

- If the act method runs in test (exploitation) mode, the Greedy Policy logic is executed based on the experience of the $Q(s, a)$ function (**selq.q**):

```
    def act(self, c_state, reward = None, done = None, mode =
'train'):

        """Returns actions for the given state"""


        d_state = self.transform_state(c_state)  # Discrete state


        if mode == 'test':
            # greedy decision for 'test' mode
            action = self.greedy_decision(d_state)
```

```
        else:
            # Q-learning process for 'train' mode
            last_sa = self.last_state + (self.last_action,)
            td = reward + self.q_gamma * max(self.q[d_state]) -
    self.q[last_sa]
            self.q[last_sa] += self.q_alpha * td


            action = self.e_greedy_decision(d_state)

        self.last_state = d_state
        self.last_action = action
        self.action_history.append(action)
        return action
```

The **e_greedy_decision** and **greedy_decision** are classical implementations of epsilon greedy and greedy policies:

```
    def e_greedy_decision(self, state):
        """Epsilon Greedy Policy Decision"""
        r = np.random.uniform(0, 1)
        if r < self.degp_epsilon:
            action = np.random.randint(0, self.action_size)
        else:
            action = self.greedy_decision(state)
        return action


    def greedy_decision(self, state):
        action = np.argmax(self.q[state])
        return action
```

The **direction_changes** method counts how many times the agent changed its direction. For example, there are two direction changes in the sequence: **[Right, Left, Left, Right]**. In the next section, we'll examine how this method can be used to measure the effectiveness of the exploration process:

```
    def direction_changes(self):
        """

        Counting Car direction changes (only 0-Left and 2-Right):
        [0, 1, 2, 1, 0, 0] -> 2
```

```
"""
prev_a = None
count = 0
no_ones = [a for a in self.action_history if a != 1]
for a in no_ones:
    if a != prev_a:
        count += 1
    prev_a = a
return count
```

And the **run** method runs the agent on a certain number of episodes in train (exploration) or test (exploitation) mode:

```
def run(self, env, episodes, mode = 'train'):
    """
    Runs episodes:
    - mode = train - Exploration process
    - mode = test - Exploitation process
    """
    total_rewards = []
    d_changes = []

    for e in range(1, episodes + 1):

        state = env.reset()
        action = self.before_episode(state)
        total_reward = 0
        done = False

        while not done:
            state, reward, done, info = env.step(action)
            total_reward += reward
            action = self.act(state, reward, done, mode)

        total_rewards.append(total_reward)
```

```
    d_changes.append(self.direction_changes())


    # Printing statistics
    if e % 100 == 0:
        avg_reward = np.mean(total_rewards[-100:])
        avg_dir_changes = np.mean(d_changes[-100:])
        print(
            f'Episode: {e}/{episodes} | '
            f'Last 100 Avg TotalReward: {avg_reward} | '
            f'Last 100 Avg DirChanges: {avg_dir_changes}'
        )


return total_rewards, d_changes
```

Now, we are ready to apply the **DiscreteQLearningAgent** to solve the Mountain Car problem.

As you may have noticed, the terms *train* and *exploration*, as well as *test* and *exploitation*, are used interchangeably. Usually, the terms *exploitation* and *exploration* are used in a *theoretical* context of reinforcement learning problems, and the terms *train* and *test* are used in an *application* context.

Applying discrete Q-learning agent to Mountain Car problem

When I first applied this technique, I was very excited that such a simple approach could really help solve such non-trivial problems. Let's try to start with the coarsest discretization:

- **Speed (Velocity)**: 10 bins
- **Position**: 10 bins

Let's examine the following script **ch7/run/run_10x10.py**:

Import part

```
import random
import gym
import numpy as np
```

```
from ch7.discrete_q_learning_agent import DiscreteQLearningAgent
from ch7.utils import create_grid, plot_rolling, plot_q_map, plot_route
```

Initializing Environment

```
env = gym.make('MountainCar-v0')
```

Setting random seed

```
seed = 0
env.seed(seed)
random.seed(seed)
np.random.seed(seed)
```

Discretization parameters

```
s_space = env.observation_space
bins = (10, 10)
labels = ['Position', 'Velocity']
grid = create_grid(s_space.low, s_space.high, bins)
```

Q-Learning Hyperparameters

```
# Q-Learning Hyperparamters
train_episodes = 10_000
alpha = .02


# Testing Parameters
test_episodes = 500
live_episodes = 10
```

Discrete Q-Learning agent

```
agent = DiscreteQLearningAgent(env, grid, q_alpha = alpha)
```

Training

Here, we begin the training process. After completing the training process, we visualize its progress:

- Average of total rewards for the last 100 episodes
- Average number of direction changes over the last 100 episodes

- Visualization of $Q(s, a)$ function

```
train_rewards, d_changes = agent.run(env, episodes = train_
episodes)


# Training Results

plot_rolling(train_rewards, title = 'Train Total Rewards')

plot_rolling(d_changes, title = 'Train Direction Changes')


# Q(s,a) visualization

plot_q_map(agent.q, labels, title = 'Q Map')
```

Testing

To estimate the efficiency of the discretization approach, we must run the agent in test mode:

```
test_rewards, _ = agent.run(env, episodes = test_episodes, mode =
'test')
# Testing Results
avg_reward = np.mean(test_rewards)
print(f"Exploitation Average Reward: {avg_reward}")
plot_rolling(test_rewards, title = 'Test Total Rewards')
```

Running live

And finally, let's see how our agent performs:

```
# Running Live
for e in range(1, live_episodes + 1):
    state = env.reset()
    score = 0
    state_history = []
    while True:
        action = agent.act(state, mode = 'test')
        state_history.append(agent.last_state)
        env.render()
        state, reward, done, _ = env.step(action)
```

```
        score += reward
        if done:
            plot_route(
                bins, state_history, labels,
                title = f'Live Episode: {e}'
            )
            break
    print('Final score:', score)


env.close()
```

Result

Figure 7.8 demonstrates that the discretization method works! If the car cannot reach the goal, then its episode ends with a total reward of -200. The fact that the total reward average is higher than -200 indicates that the car has been reaching the top of the right mountain in the last episodes:

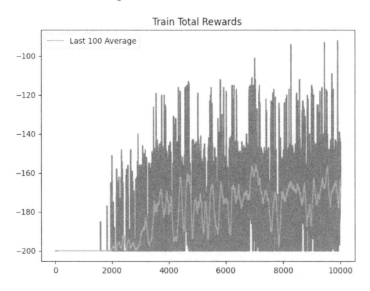

Figure 7.8: Train total rewards

In *Figure 7.9*, we see the number of car direction changes. At the beginning of the exploration process, the agent made too many random and erratic movements. But with the gaining experience, car direction changes number decreased significantly:

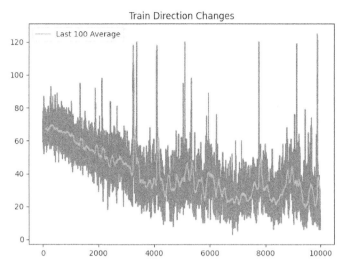

Figure 7.9: *Train direction changes*

Figure 7.10 renders the $Q(s, a)$ function:

- *left arrow*: Denotes left action
- *up arrow*: Means do nothing
- **right arrow**: Denotes right action

The average of Test Total Rewards is:

```
Exploitation Average Reward: -160.1
```

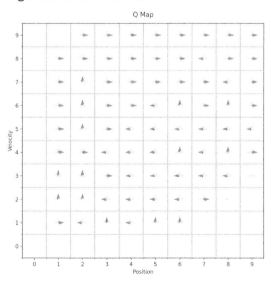

Figure 7.10: *Q(s, a) function visualization*

Figure 7.11 displays that all episodes have a total reward higher than -200, that is, the car reached its goal in all test episodes:

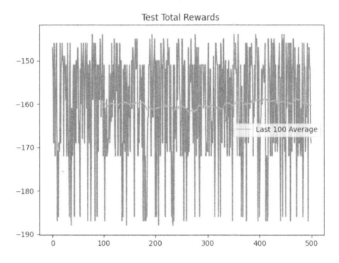

Figure 7.11: *Q(s,a) function visualization*

Finally, you can see the **DiscreteQLearningAgent** in action. And here you can see one interesting feature: all live episodes look very similar to each other. The car first accelerates to the left and then accelerates to the right and reaches its goal. But if we analyze the state heatmap of each episode, we will see that they are slightly different for all episodes.

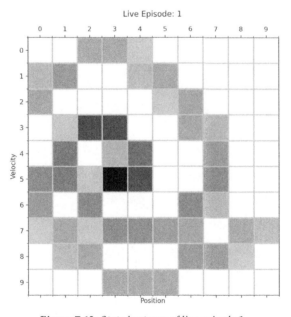

Figure 7.12: *State heatmap of live episode 1*

Let's take a look at the heatmaps for *Episode 1* (*Figure 7.12*) and *Episode 10* (*Figure 7.13*). They differ from each other.

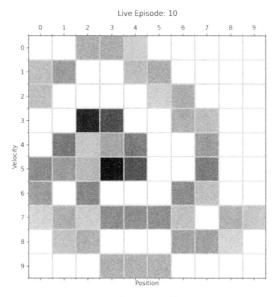

Figure 7.13: *State heatmap of live episode 10*

`DiscreteQLearningAgent` uses a greedy policy during exploitation, so it has no random behavior. Then why are the heatmaps for Episode 1 and Episode 10 different? This is because the Mountain Car environment does not behave in a deterministic manner. The environment's reaction to the same action in the same state may differ. This is very close to what we often see in the real world. In a complex environment, there are many random parameters that we cannot consider, so the sequence of actions for each episode may differ in reinforcement learning.

Coarse versus Fine discretization

In the previous section, we demonstrated the practical applicability of the discretization approach. Yes, the discretization method really helps solve problems with continuous states. However, we used a rather coarse discretization (10×10): Speed: 10 bins, Position: 10 bins. It will be interesting to compare 10×10 discretization with 20×20 discretization **ch7/run/run_10x10_vs_20x20.py**:

Import part

```
import random

import gym

import numpy as np

from ch7.discrete_q_learning_agent import DiscreteQLearningAgent
```

```
from ch7.utils import create_grid, plot_rolling
import matplotlib.pyplot as plt
```

Initializing Environment and Hyperparameters

```
# Initializing Environment
env = gym.make('MountainCar-v0')

# Setting Random Seed
seed = 10
env.seed(seed)
random.seed(seed)
np.random.seed(seed)

s_space = env.observation_space
labels = ['Position', 'Velocity']

# Q-Learning Hyperparamters
train_episodes = 10_000
test_episodes = 1_000
```

Defining two types of Discretization: (10×10 and 20×20)

```
# Discretization Types
bin_map = {
    'Coarse 10x10': (10, 10),
    'Fine 20x20':   (20, 20)
}
# Test Results
test_results = {}
```

Evaluating two discretization experiments

```
# Evaluating Discretization Type
for discretization_name, bins in bin_map.items():
    grid = create_grid(s_space.low, s_space.high, bins)
    # Agent
    agent = DiscreteQLearningAgent(env, grid)

    # Training
```

```
        train_rewards, d_changes = agent.run(env, episodes = train_episodes)
        plot_rolling(
            train_rewards,
            title = f'{discretization_name}: Train Total Rewards')

        # Testing
        test_rewards, _ = agent.run(env, episodes = test_episodes, mode = 'test')
        test_results[discretization_name] = test_rewards

env.close()

# Comparing Test Results
fig, ax = plt.subplots()
ax.boxplot(test_results.values())
ax.set_xticklabels(test_results.keys())
ax.set_title('Test Results')
plt.show()

for k, data in test_results.items():
    print(f'{k}. Avg: {round(sum(data) / len(data), 2)}')
```

Results

Figure 7.14 shows 10×10 training performance:

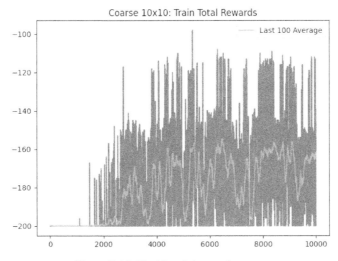

Figure 7.14: *10×10 training performance*

And it will be interesting to compare *Figure 7.14* with *Figure 7.15*:

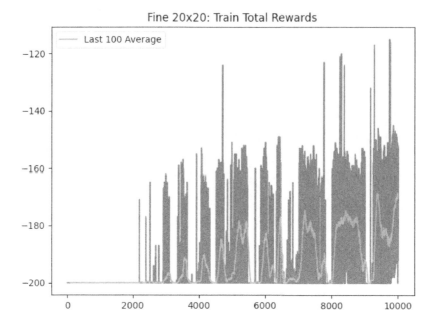

Figure 7.15: *20×20 training performance*

We can see that 20×20 training progress looks significantly worse than 10×10 training. 20×20 train total rewards often drop to -200, which means the agent fails train episodes. But in any case, the most significant indicator is the test results:

Discretization Type	Test Average
Coarse 10×10	-157.87
Fine 20×20	-178.4

Table 7.5: *Average results*

The result shown in *Table 7.5* may seem quite surprising. 20×20 discretization is more refined, which means it can provide a more flexible policy:

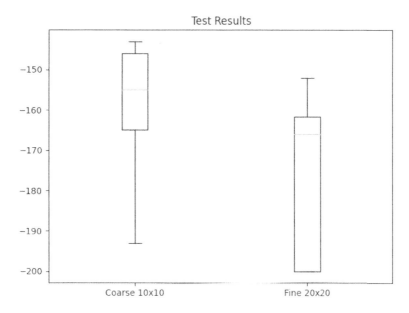

Figure 7.16: *10×10 versus 20×20*

In reality, the resolution increase of the state space dimensions only worsens the performance for a given task. *Figure 7.16* demonstrates a notable superiority of 10×10 resolution over 20×20 resolution. But how do you choose the best resolution for your task? This is a very interesting question, and we will come back to it at the end of this chapter.

Q-learning Alpha parameter

You may have noticed that we used different hyperparameters in different cases of the Q-learning method usage. For example, in *Chapter 6, Escaping Maze With Q-learning*, we used **alpha = 0.9**, and in this chapter, we used **alpha = 0.02**. The alpha hyperparameter determines the weight of the new experience's influence. The higher the alpha is, the more important the new experience is. Now, let's compare the performance of a Q-learning method with different alpha parameters `[0.02,` `0.2, 0.5, 0.9]` `ch7/run/run_10x10_alpha_comparison.py`.

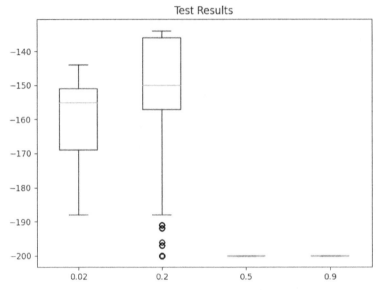

Figure 7.17: *α-hyperparameter comparison*

Wow! The `0.5` and `0.9` alpha parameters turned out to be completely unsuitable for this task. None of the agents trained with these hyperparameters could achieve their goal. But why? Typically, hyperparameters will speed up or slow down the search, sometimes degrade performance, but in this case, some alpha parameter values are not suitable at all. Let's take a look at why this is happening.

As we saw earlier, the algorithm for solving the Mountain Car problem looks as follows:

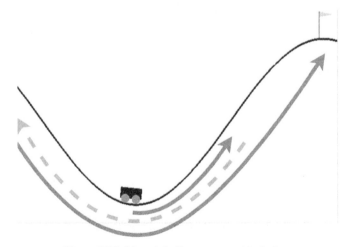

Figure 7.18: *Mountain Car movement trajectory*

As shown in *Figure 7.18*, the machine performs the following actions:

- Acceleration to the right (solid red arrow)

- Acceleration to the left (dashed greed arrow)

- Final acceleration to the right (solid red arrow)

Successful episode completion does not require many car movement direction changes. Let's consider the dynamics of direction changes with **alpha = 0.02** training (*Figure 7.19*):

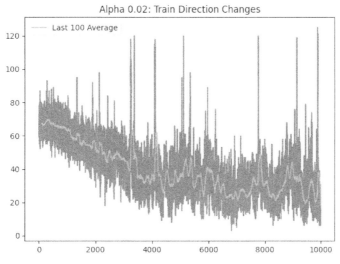

Figure 7.19: *Alpha = 0.02 direction changes*

And let's compare it with **alpha = 0.9** training (*Figure 7.20*):

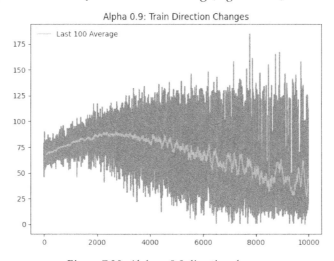

Figure 7.20: *Alpha = 0.9 direction changes*

We see that training with **alpha = 0.9** behaves much more chaotic than training with **alpha = 0.02**. Therefore, we can conclude that many direction changes during an episode damage training performance. And it makes sense; we saw, in *Figure 7.18*, that you don't have to change directions very often to complete an episode successfully.

And here we came to another question: Why does **alpha = 0.9** provoke many direction changes? Remember that we are dealing with a discrete space, and in most cases, we will remain in the same state after the action. Indeed, after a certain action, the car's position changes slightly, and the car's speed changes slightly, but the agent will likely stay in the same position bin and the same speed bin:

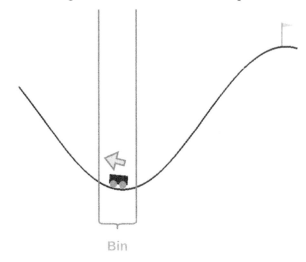

Figure 7.21: *Position bin*

Let's say we have *Table 7.6* of Q(s, a) values for state s:

Q(s, Left)	-5
Q(s, None)	-5.5
Q(s, Right)	-5.3

Table 7.6: *Q(s, a) values; step 0*

Being in state s, it is highly likely that decayed greedy policy selects the *Left* action, but the agent will probably stay in the same state s after action Left is performed, and then the value of Q(s, Left) will be updated as follows:

$$Q(s, Left) = Q(s, Left) + \alpha(r + \gamma\ V(s) - Q(s, Left)) =$$

$$= -5 + 0.9\ (-1 + 0.99\ (-5) - (-5)) = -5.855$$

Therefore, after the previous action, we get *Table 7.7* of Q(s, a) values:

Q(s, Left)	-5.855
Q(s, None)	-5.5
Q(s, Right)	-5.3

Table 7.7: *Q(s, a) values; step 1*

Since we are still in state s, we need to choose the most optimal action again, but the action *Q(s, Right)* turns out to be the most optimal for this step. And we update Q(s, Right) value as follows:

$$Q(s, Right) = Q(s, Right) + \alpha(r + \gamma\ V(s) - Q(s, Right)) =$$

$$= -5.3 + 0.9\ (-1 + 0.99\ (-5.3) - (-5.3)) = -6.1523$$

Now, let's take a look at the table of Q(s, a) function values:

Q(s, Left)	-5.855
Q(s, None)	-5.5
Q(s, Right)	−6.1523

Table 7.8: *Q(s, a) values; step 2*

You can notice the following pattern in *Table 7.6*, *Table 7.7*, and *Table 7.8*:

- After each action a, the value of this action in state s decreases too much
- In the next step, a different action a' is more likely to be chosen

This happens because a high α-hyperparameter lowers the Q(s, a) value drastically after receiving a reward of -1. And that is why a car makes too many direction changes:

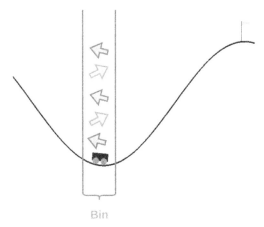

Figure 7.22: *Direction changes in the same state bin*

Therefore, the training process shown in *Figure 7.20* has so many direction changes that dramatically damage the process of constructing an effective *Q (s, a)* action-value function.

This section gave an example of how sensitive reinforcement learning is to hyperparameter selection. Of course, you don't have to study the effect of each hyperparameter on the Q-learning training process in detail, as we did in this section. It is nevertheless advantageous to understand that the value of one hyperparameter can drastically change the performance of a whole method. We'll examine the problem of choosing appropriate hyperparameters in the next section.

Hyperparameters in reinforcement learning

Now, we come to the harsh truth of life. As we saw in the previous section, the Q-learning method is very sensitive to hyperparameter choice. Almost all machine learning methods are sensitive to hyperparameter choice, but in the case of the Q-learning method, choosing the right hyperparameters can be critical. The Q-learning method worked fine with `alpha = 0.9` for the Maze Problem from *Chapter 5: Blackjack in Monte Carlo*, but it was entirely useless for the Mountain Car problem, which required a much lower alpha hyperparameter value. Yes, in the case of Mountain Car problem, you can intuitively choose the appropriate alpha hyperparameter value because we approximately understand the logic of the agent's training environment. But in most cases, we have no idea of how the reinforcement learning environment functions. And it is simply impossible to choose the best hyperparameters in advance. Therefore, you have to test the same approach with different hyperparameters. If some experiment with the Q-learning method has failed, it does not mean that the method is not suitable for this task. It is necessary to test the operation of the Q-learning method with various hyperparameters.

From limits of discretization to deep reinforcement learning

The discretization method allows you to overcome some difficulties when working with a continuous state space. But there are state spaces that are too large, and any attempt to discretize them will be too coarse and will not help solve the problem. In many cases, state spaces have a non-linear structure, and trivial binning discretization will not help in any way.

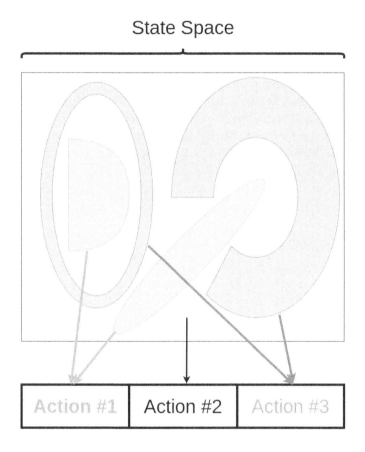

Figure 7.23: *Non-linear continuous state space*

Additionally, the exploitation process of some problems offers states that did not occur during the exploration process. However, it is necessary to adapt the already accumulated experience to the existing unique state that an agent faces for the first time. This is exactly how it happens in real life. Indeed, no life situation is repeated twice precisely in the same way, but a human knows how to extract patterns of previous experience and apply them to the existing situation. And for these problems, deep reinforcement learning comes to the rescue. Deep reinforcement learning combines two machine learning areas: deep learning and reinforcement learning. And we will see, in the upcoming chapters, how deep reinforcement learning will help us solve much more complex problems.

Conclusion

This chapter investigated a discretization approach that allows us to significantly expand the range of reinforcement learning problems that can be solved using the classical Q-learning method. You can try using the **DiscreteQLearningAgent** implementation to solve classic control theory problems from Gym environments: **https://www.gymlibrary.ml/environments/classic_control/**.

This chapter finishes the first part of this book, which was dedicated to the classical reinforcement learning methods. You learned the essence of reinforcement learning problems (*Chapter 1, Introduction to Reinforcement Learning*) and Markov reward processes' theoretical foundations (*Chapter 2, Playing Monopoly and Markov Decision Process*). We studied the Gym toolkit, which allows emulating interaction with the environment (*Chapter 3, Training in Gym*), and we studied the theory and practical application of various methods for solving reinforcement learning problems:

- Thompson sampling (*Chapter 4, Struggling With Multi-Armed Bandits*)

- Monte-Carlo method (*Chapter 5, Blackjack in Monte Carlo*)

- Q-learning method (*Chapter 6, Escaping Maze With Q-learning*)

- Discretization (*Chapter 7, Discretization*)

These approaches may be sufficient for solving many practical problems, but we need to strengthen our classical techniques with deep learning to solve the most challenging tasks. The mixture of reinforcement learning and deep learning produces fantastic results, and we are going to dive into deep reinforcement learning in the second part of the book.

Points to remember

- Decayed epsilon greedy policy prevents unnecessary random actions in the exploration process.

- The terms train and exploration, as well as test and exploitation, are used interchangeably.

- Fine discretization is not always better than coarse discretization.

- Reinforcement learning is very sensitive to hyperparameter choice.

Multiple choice questions

1. In *Table 7.9*, we examined the variable s, which is calculated using Fibonacci numbers: $s_n = \frac{f_n + f_{n+1}}{2}$. Now consider the following variable: $r_n = r_n = \frac{f_{n+1}}{f_n}$, which is the Fibonacci ratio, and the r_n sequence converges to the golden ratio ϕ.

Fibonacci number	Divided by the one before	R
1		
1	1 / 1	1
2	2 / 1	2
3	3 /2	1.5
5	5 / 3	1.6667
8	8 / 5	1.6
13	13 / 8	1.625
21	21 / 13	1.6154...
	...	
∞		ϕ = 1.6180...

Table 7.9: *Fibonacci ratio*

Is r a discrete variable?

    a.   Yes

    b.   No, because r_n sequence converges to ϕ and the values of r_n cannot be separated from ϕ

    c.   No, because r has infinite number of values

2. *Figure 7.24* shows a state heatmap of the completed episode.

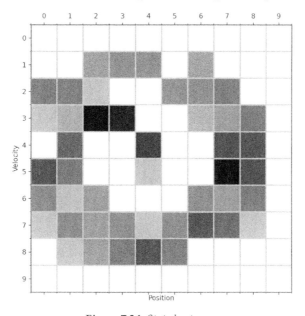

Figure 7.24: *State heatmap*

Determine, from *Figure 7.24*, whether the car has reached its goal in this episode.

    a.   It is impossible to answer this question.

    b.   No, the car hasn't reached its goal because it didn't visit any final state on position = 9.

    c.   No, the car hasn't reached its goal because it didn't visit all states.

3.   Take look at the script **ch7/run/run_10x10.py** from the *Applying Discrete Q-learning Agent to Mountain Car Problem* section. How many training hyperparameters are there in this script?

    a.   4: train_episodes, alpha, test_episodes, live episodes

    b.   2: train_episodes, alpha

    c.   6: train_episodes, DiscreteQLearningAgent params: q_alpha, q_gamma, degp_epsilon, degp_decay_rate, degp_min_epsilon

Answers

    1. **b**

    2. **b**

    3. **c**

Key terms

- **Continuous variable**: If, for any numbers $a < b$, variable can take a value c such that $a < c < b$.

- **Binning discretization**: Discretizes values of a continuous variable into a specified number of bins.

- **Decayed epsilon greedy policy**: It is epsilon greedy policy with a decreasing epsilon value.

Part - II

Deep Reinforcement Learning

The second part of the book is dedicated to deep reinforcement learning, which combines two vast areas of machine learning: reinforcement learning and deep learning. Deep reinforcement learning allows classic reinforcement learning methods to be applied to much more complex environments. These environments contain a very large or even infinite state space where classical reinforcement learning approaches cannot create an effective agent policy.

The second part of the book starts with *Chapter 8, TensorFlow, PyTorch, and Your first Neural Network*. TensorFlow and PyTorch are the most popular deep learning frameworks, and it was hard to pick one for this book. TensorFlow users would be disappointed to meet implementations using PyTorch. The same is true for PyTorch users. So, the second part of the book contains both implementations using PyTorch and TensorFlow. *Chapter 8, TensorFlow, PyTorch, and Your First Neural Network*, describes the basics of working with TensorFlow and PyTorch.

Deep learning itself and its methods are the subjects of a particular book. But in this book, we will not use complex neural network models, so the reader will be able to familiarize themselves with the application of deep learning to solving real-life reinforcement learning problems. This can be a good start for both deep reinforcement learning and deep learning.

## CHAPTER 8

TensorFlow, PyTorch, and Your First Neural Network

As we already mentioned earlier, complex reinforcement learning problems need new approaches, and deep learning is the solution. This chapter will cover TensorFlow and PyTorch basics, which are the most popular deep learning frameworks. This chapter explains the main deep learning concepts and their implementation with TensorFlow. The basics of working with TensorFlow and PyTorch are close to each other. Of course, there are fundamental differences between these frameworks. Still, this book will not use complex deep learning models, so the main methods for constructing neural networks will be presented here. You can skip this chapter if you are familiar with TensorFlow and/or PyTorch. If you are not familiar with TensorFlow or PyTorch, now is a great time to pick one of these frameworks. This chapter will explain the basic deep learning techniques and their implementation using each framework. Framework-specific implementation will be framed by the following blocks:

```
TensorFlow >>>>>>>>>>>>>>>>>>

…

TensorFlow implementation

…

>>>>>>>>>>>>>>>>>> TensorFlow
```

Or

```
PyTorch >>>>>>>>>>>>>>>>
...
PyTorch implementation
...
>>>>>>>>>>>>>>>> PyTorch
```

It is not necessary to walk through all implementations. Therefore, you can skip all PyTorch implementation blocks if you decide to stick with TensorFlow. On the other hand, you can skip all TensorFlow implementation blocks if you stick with the PyTorch framework.

Structure

In this chapter, we will discuss the following topics:

- Installation
- Derivative calculators
- Deep learning basics
- Deep learning layers
- Neural network architecture
- Supervised learning and loss function
- Training and optimizer
- Handwritten digit recognition model

Objectives

After completing this chapter, you will have mastered the basics of deep learning and its implementation with TensorFlow and PyTorch. You will also have understood how a neural network is designed, trained, and applied to real-world problems.

Installation

TensorFlow is available as a Python package, and you can install it as follows:

```
$ pip install tensorflow
```

This book uses 2.7.0 version of TensorFlow framework. Full installation guide can be found on official site: https://www.tensorflow.org/.

PyTorch also can be installed as follows:

```
$ pip install torch torchvision torchaudio
```

This book uses 1.9.0 version of PyTorch framework. Full installation guide can be found on the official site: https://pytorch.org/.

Also, we will use additional dataset library in this chapter:

```
$ pip install tensorflow-datasets
```

Derivative calculators

Let's explore what's special about deep learning frameworks. All deep learning models perform basic operations from calculus to linear algebra. But we already have excellent tools in Python, like NumPy or SciPy. So why do we need another tool, especially for deep learning?

In the context of deep learning, it is helpful to think about neural networks as computational graphs. One of the essential operations during neural network training is backpropagation. The backpropagation algorithm is based on the gradient descent concept, and it is impossible to perform gradient descent without the calculation of derivatives. The main feature of TensorFlow and PyTorch is the ability to calculate derivatives of composite multivariable functions. This feature is crucial in neural network training.

Let's see how TensorFlow and PyTorch operate with functions and calculate their derivatives. Say we have the following multivariate function:

$$f(x_1, x_2, x_3, x_4) = x_1^3 x_2 + x_3 x_4$$

Let us take a look at how f function can be implemented:

TensorFlow >>>>>>>>>> ch8/tf/dfdx/function.py

Function creation

```
import tensorflow as tf

def get_function(x1_val = 0, x2_val = 0, x3_val = 0, x4_val = 0):
    # variables
    x1 = tf.Variable(x1_val, dtype = tf.float32)
    x2 = tf.Variable(x2_val, dtype = tf.float32)
    x3 = tf.Variable(x3_val, dtype = tf.float32)
    x4 = tf.Variable(x4_val, dtype = tf.float32)

    # function
```

```
p1 = tf.math.pow(x1, 3)

m1 = tf.math.multiply(p1, x2)

m2 = tf.math.multiply(x3, x4)

f = tf.math.add(m1, m2)


vars = {'x1': x1, 'x2': x2, 'x3': x3, 'x4': x4}


return f, vars
```

Computing function value

```
if __name__ == '__main__':
    f, _ = get_function(2, 4, 3, 5)
    print(f.numpy())
```

Result

```
47.0
>>>>>>>>>> TensorFlow


PyTorch >>>>>>>>>> ch8/pt/dfdx/function.py
```

Function creation

```
import torch


def get_function(x1_val = 0, x2_val = 0, x3_val = 0, x4_val = 0):
    # variables
    x1 = torch.tensor(x1_val, requires_grad = True, dtype = torch.
float32)
    x2 = torch.tensor(x2_val, requires_grad = True, dtype = torch.
float32)
    x3 = torch.tensor(x3_val, requires_grad = True, dtype = torch.
float32)
    x4 = torch.tensor(x4_val, requires_grad = True, dtype = torch.
float32)


    # function
    p1 = x1.pow(3)
```

```
m1 = p1 * x2
m2 = x3 * x4
f = m1 + m2


vars = {'x1': x1, 'x2': x2, 'x3': x3, 'x4': x4}


return f, vars
```

Computing function value

```
if __name__ == '__main__':
    f, _ = get_function(2, 4, 3, 5)
    print(f.item())
```

Result

```
47.0

>>>>>>>>>> PyTorch
```

We see here that the defined function f has following value $f(2, 4, 3, 5) = 47$. Well, that is an absolutely trivial case, and there's nothing special about it... yet.

Each neural network is a function. This function can be very complicated, it could be a complex composition of other functions, but anyway, a neural network is a function. Let's take a look at the neural network in *Figure 8.1*:

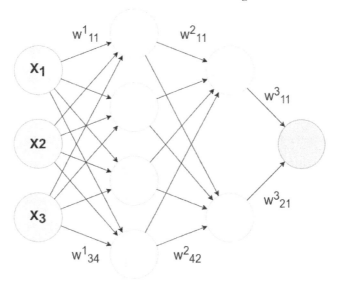

Figure 8.1: *Neural network example*

The neural network represented in *Figure 8.1* can be expressed as a function:

$$F(x_1, x_2, x_3 ; w^1_{11}, \dots, w^1_{34}, w^2_{11}, \dots, w^2_{42}, w^3_{11}, w^3_{21}),$$

Where x_1, x_2, x_3 is input and w^l_{ij} is neural network weights.

During the backpropagation process, we find derivative $\frac{\partial F}{\partial w}$ for each weight. And that's what TensorFlow and PyTorch do. They compute partial derivatives of any multivariable function. As we know from the calculus the derivative of the composite function is calculated using the chain rule: $[f(g(x))]' = f'(g(x)) \cdot g'(x)$. To apply the chain rule to derivative calculation, we need to treat the neural network function as a computational graph. A computational graph is a directed graph where the nodes correspond to mathematical operations. In *Figure 8.2*, we see the computational graph of function: $a \times sin(x) + b$:

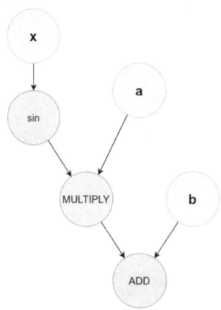

Figure 8.2: *a × sin(x) + b as computational graph*

And we come to the main TensorFlow and PyTorch feature, the ability to calculate partial derivatives. Let's find the partial derivative $\frac{\partial f}{\partial x1}$ (2, 4, 3, 5):

$$f'_{x1}(x_1, x_2, x_3, x_4) = (x_1^3 x_2 + x_3 x_4)' = (x_1^3 x_2)' = 3x_1^2 x_2$$

then f'_{x1} at point (2, 4, 3, 5) is: $3 \cdot 2^2 \cdot 4 = 48$

TensorFlow >>>>>>>>>>>>>>>>>>

Let's take a look at how TensorFlow calculates derivatives **ch8/tf/dfdx/ derivatives.py**:

```
import tensorflow as tf
from ch8.tf.dfdx.function import get_function


args = [2, 4, 3, 5]


with tf.GradientTape() as tape:
    y, params = get_function(*args)


dy_dx1 = tape.gradient(y, params['x1'])


print(dy_dx1.numpy())
```

Result

```
48.0
```

```
>>>>>>>>>> TensorFlow


PyTorch >>>>>>>>>>
```

Let's take a look at how PyTorch calculates derivatives **ch8/pt/dfdx/derivatives. py**:

```
from torch.autograd import grad
from ch8.pt.dfdx.function import get_function


f, params = get_function(2, 4, 3, 5)


df_dx1 = grad(outputs = f, inputs = [params['x1']])[0]


print(df_dx1.item())
```

Result

```
48.0


>>>>>>>>>> PyTorch
```

The result is the same as we calculated manually. Partial derivatives are calculated to find the function gradient:

$$\nabla f = [\frac{\partial f}{\partial x1}, \frac{\partial f}{\partial x2}, \frac{\partial f}{\partial x3}, \frac{\partial f}{\partial 4}]$$

And, of course, if a deep learning tool can calculate the partial derivative, it will not be difficult to calculate the function's gradient at a particular point.

TensorFlow >>>>>>>>>>>>>>>>

Let's examine how $\nabla f(2, 4, 3, 5)$ is calculated using TensorFlow **ch8/tf/dfdx/gradient.py**:

```
import tensorflow as tf
from ch8.tf.dfdx.function import get_function


args = [2, 4, 3, 5]


with tf.GradientTape() as tape:
    y, params = get_function(*args)


# Gradient as Tensor List
dy_dx = tape.gradient(y, params.values())


# Converting to Numpy List
g = [d.numpy() for d in dy_dx]


print(g)
```

Result

```
[48.0, 8.0, 5.0, 3.0]
```

>>>>>>>>>> TensorFlow

PyTorch >>>>>>>>>>

Let's examine how $\nabla f(2, 4, 3, 5)$ is calculated using PyTorch **ch8/pt/dfdx/gradient.py**:

```
from torch.autograd import grad

from ch8.pt.dfdx.function import get_function

f, params = get_function(2, 4, 3, 5)

# Gradient as Tensor List
dy_dx = grad(outputs = f, inputs = params.values())

# Converting to Numpy List
g = [d.item() for d in dy_dx]

print(g)
```

Result

```
[48.0, 8.0, 5.0, 3.0]
```

>>>>>>>>>> PyTorch

Creating a computational graph and calculating partial derivatives is critical for neural network training, and that's why we need a deep learning framework. Of course, this is not the only useful TensorFlow and PyTorch feature. They provide an easy and seamless way of deep learning model construction.

We will not use the differentiation functions listed above directly, so you may not remember how to work with them. They are provided to show how deep learning frameworks can work with partial derivatives.

Deep learning basics

This section will cover the basic concepts and methods of deep learning. Their TensorFlow and PyTorch implementations will be close to each other.

Tensors

The main deep learning objects are **tensors**. Tensor is a multidimensional matrix. Usually, deep learning models are using tensors up to five dimensions. Most methods of deep learning library accept tensors as input and return tensors as output. The name TensorFlow means the flow of tensors.

Tensor creation

The creation of a tensor is a simple action. You can create a vector or 1D tensor with a predefined list of values:

TensorFlow >>>>>>>>>>>>>>>

```
import tensorflow as tf

x = tf.constant([1, 2, 3])
print(x)

>>>
tf.Tensor([1 2 3], shape=(3,), dtype=int32)
```

>>>>>>>>> TensorFlow

PyTorch >>>>>>>>>>

```
import torch

x = torch.tensor(data = [1, 2, 3])
print(x)

>>>
tensor([1, 2, 3])
```

>>>>>>>>>> PyTorch

And the same can be done to create a matrix or 2D tensor:

TensorFlow >>>>>>>>>>>>>>>>>

```
import tensorflow as tf

x = tf.constant([[1, 2, 3], [4, 5, 6]])
print(x)

>>>
tf.Tensor(
[[1 2 3]
 [4 5 6]], shape=(2, 3), dtype=int32)
```

>>>>>>>>>> TensorFlow

```
PyTorch >>>>>>>>>>

import torch
x = torch.tensor(data = [[1, 2, 3], [4, 5, 6]])
print(x)

>>>
tensor([[1, 2, 3],
        [4, 5, 6]])
>>>>>>>>>> PyTorch
```

Usually, you must explicitly set the tensor type to make some mathematical operations available with the tensor you create:

```
TensorFlow >>>>>>>>>>>>>>>>>>

import tensorflow as tf

x = tf.constant([1.3, .5], dtype = tf.float32)

>>>>>>>>>> TensorFlow

PyTorch >>>>>>>>>>

import torch
x = torch.tensor(data = [1.3, .5], dtype = torch.float32)

PyTorch >>>>>>>>>>
```

In deep learning, we can distinguish two types of tensors:

- Constant tensors
- Variable tensors

Constant tensors represent a dataset, and they do not change their value. Let's look at an example from *Chapter 6, Escaping Maze With Q-Learning*. The reward received from the Up action in state *A1* is -10. This value is a data sample, and it will stay the same during the whole training process.

Variable tensors represent neural network weights, and they are adjusted during the training process. The $Q(s, a)$ function can be regarded as the typical 2D variable tensor.

```
TensorFlow >>>>>>>>>>>>>>>>>>>>
```

In TensorFlow, we have two different methods to create constant tensors and variable tensors:

```
# Constant Tensor
const = tf.constant([1, 2])


# Variable Tensor
var = tf.Variable([1, 2])


>>>>>>>>>> TensorFlow


PyTorch >>>>>>>>>>
```

PyTorch does not explicitly separate constant and variable tensors. It only sets whether the tensor should participate in calculating partial derivatives. In fact, the tensors by which partial derivatives are calculated are the neural network's weights:

```
const = torch.tensor(data = [1, 2])


var = torch.tensor(data = [1, 2], dtype = torch.float32, requires_grad =
True)


>>>>>>>>>> PyTorch
```

We will consider the most common ways to create constant tensors as follows.

Random tensor

Random tensors are an essential part of deep learning models. Usually, a deep learning model initiates with random sets of weights.

```
TensorFlow >>>>>>>>>>>>>>>>>>


# Random 2x2x2 Tensor
x = tf.random.uniform((2, 2, 2))
print(x)

>>>
tf.Tensor(
[[[0.47990894 0.17787063]
  [0.20623684 0.1585375 ]]


 [[0.37415576 0.613119  ]
```

```
  [0.14792264 0.05779374]]], shape=(2, 2, 2), dtype=float32)
```

```
>>>>>>>>>> TensorFlow
```

```
PyTorch >>>>>>>>>>
```

```
# Random 2x2x2 tensor
x = torch.rand((2, 2, 2))
print(x)
```

```
>>>
tensor([[[0.8553, 0.9385],
         [0.4108, 0.6903]],
        [[0.6604, 0.2956],
         [0.9576, 0.5071]]])
```

```
>>>>>>>>>> PyTorch
```

Reproducibility

Random tensors and random variables in common sense are essential for deep learning calculations. But of course, in some cases, it is very convenient to get reproducible results for further investigation. Completely reproducible results are not guaranteed across TensorFlow and PyTorch releases. Roughly speaking, there is no way to get a 100% guarantee that your script will get the same results in another environment. However, there is a measure you can take to limit the number of sources of nondeterministic behavior.

```
TensorFlow >>>>>>>>>>
```

```
tf.random.set_seed(0)
```

```
TensorFlow >>>>>>>>>>
```

```
PyTorch >>>>>>>>>>
```

```
torch.manual_seed(0)
```

```
>>>>>>>>>> PyTorch
```

Common tensor types

Some of the tensor types below are commonly used in math computations:

- **zeros**: Creates a tensor of zeros.

  TensorFlow >>>>>>>>>>

  ```
  x = tf.zeros((2, 2))
  print(x)
  ```

  ```
  >>>
  tf.Tensor(
  [[0. 0.]
   [0. 0.]], shape=(2, 2), dtype=float32)
  ```

  >>>>>>>>>> TensorFlow

  PyTorch >>>>>>>>>>

  ```
  x = torch.zeros((2, 2))
  print(x)
  ```

  ```
  >>>
  tensor([[0., 0.],
          [0., 0.]])
  ```

  >>>>>>>>>> PyTorch

- **ones**: Creates a tensor of ones.

  TensorFlow >>>>>>>>>>

  ```
  x = tf.ones((2, 2))
  print(x)
  ```

  ```
  >>>
  tf.Tensor(
  [[1. 1.]
   [1. 1.]], shape=(2, 2), dtype=float32)
  ```

  >>>>>>>>>> TensorFlow

  PyTorch >>>>>>>>>>

```
x = torch.ones((2, 2)))
print(x)

>>>
tensor([[1., 1.],
        [1., 1.]])

>>>>>>>>>> PyTorch
```

- **eye**: Creates an identity tensor.

```
TensorFlow >>>>>>>>>>

x = tf.eye(3)
print(x)

>>>
tf.Tensor(
[[1. 0. 0.]
 [0. 1. 0.]
 [0. 0. 1.]], shape=(3, 3), dtype=float32)

>>>>>>>>>> TensorFlow

PyTorch >>>>>>>>>>

x = torch.eye(3)
print(x)

>>>
tensor([[1., 0., 0.],
        [0., 1., 0.],
        [0., 0., 1.]])

>>>>>>>>>> PyTorch
```

Tensor methods and attributes

- **shape**: Returns tensor shape.

```
TensorFlow >>>>>>>>>>

x = tf.random.uniform((2, 3, 2))
```

```
print(x.shape)

>>>
(2, 3, 2)

>>>>>>>>>> TensorFlow

PyTorch >>>>>>>>>>

x = torch.rand((2, 3, 2))
print(x.shape)
>>>
torch.Size([2, 3, 2])

>>>>>>>>>> PyTorch
```

- **reshape**: Changes a tensor shape.
  ```
  TensorFlow >>>>>>>>>>

  x = tf.constant([1, 2, 3, 4])

  print(x)

  >>>
  tf.Tensor([1 2 3 4], shape=(4,), dtype=int32)

  y = tf.reshape(x, (2, 2))

  print(y)

  >>>
  tf.Tensor(
  [[1 2]
   [3 4]], shape=(2, 2), dtype=int32)

  >>>>>>>>>> TensorFlow

  PyTorch >>>>>>>>>>

  x = torch.tensor([1, 2, 3, 4])
  ```

```
print(x)

>>>
tensor([1, 2, 3, 4])

y = x.reshape((2, 2))

print(y)

>>>
tensor([[1, 2],
        [3, 4]])

>>>>>>>>>> PyTorch
```

- **transpose / permute**: Permutes tensor dimensions.

```
TensorFlow >>>>>>>>>>

x = tf.random.uniform((2, 3, 4))

print(x.shape)

>>>
(2, 3, 4)

# Permutes tensor dimensions from (0, 1, 2) to (2, 0, 1)
y = tf.transpose(x, perm = (2, 0, 1))

print(y.shape)

>>>
(4, 2, 3)
>>>>>>>>>> TensorFlow

PyTorch >>>>>>>>>>

x = torch.rand((2, 3, 4))

print(x.shape)

>>>
```

```
torch.Size([2, 3, 4])

# Permutes tensor dimensions from (0, 1, 2) to (2, 0, 1)
y = x.permute((2, 0, 1))

print(y.shape)

>>>
torch.Size([4, 2, 3])

>>>>>>>>>> PyTorch
```

- **numpy**: Extracts pure values from tensor.

```
TensorFlow >>>>>>>>>>

# Returning values
x = tf.ones((2, 3))

print(x.numpy())

>>>
[[1. 1. 1.]
 [1. 1. 1.]]

>>>>>>>>>> TensorFlow

PyTorch >>>>>>>>>>

# Returning values
l = torch.ones((2, 2))

print(l.numpy())

>>>
[[1., 1.], [1., 1.]]

>>>>>>>>>> PyTorch
```

Math functions

Mathematical operations with tensors are trivial and can be easily understood from the context. The following scripts are examples of basic mathematical operations on tensors:

```
TensorFlow >>>>>>>>>> ch8/tf/tf_math.py

import tensorflow as tf

x = tf.ones((1, 2), dtype = tf.float32)  # (1, 1)

y = tf.range(0, 2, dtype = tf.float32)  # (0, 1)

# implicit addition
z = x + y  # (1, 2)

# explicit addition
w = tf.add(z, y)  # (1, 3)

# implicit multiplication
k = w * -1  # (-1, -3)

# absolute value
a = tf.abs(k)  # (1, 3)

# implicit division
b = a / 2  # (0.5, 1.5)

# Rounding to nearest integer lower than
c = tf.floor(b)  # (0, 1)

# Rounding to nearest integer greater than
d = tf.math.ceil(b)  # (1, 2)

# Computes element-wise equality
eq = tf.equal(c, d)  # (False, False)

# Mean tensor value
avg = tf.reduce_mean(d)  # 1.5

# Max tensor value
mx = tf.math.reduce_max(d)  # 2

# Min tensor value
mn = tf.math.reduce_max(d)  # 1

# Sum of all tensor values
sm = tf.math.reduce_sum(d)  # 3
```

```
>>>>>>>>>> TensorFlow

PyTorch >>>>>>>>>> ch8/pt/pt_math.py

import torch

x = torch.ones((1, 2))  # (1, 1)

y = torch.range(0, 1)  # (0, 1)

# implicit addition
z = x + y  # (1, 2)

# explicit addition
w = z.add(y)  # (1, 3)

# implicit multiplication
k = w * -1  # (-1, -3)

# absolute value
a = k.abs()  # (1, 3)

# implicit division
b = a / 2  # (0.5, 1.5)

# Rounding to nearest integer lower than
c = b.floor()  # (0, 1)

# Rounding to nearest integer greater than
d = b.ceil()  # (1, 2)

# Computes element-wise equality
eq = c.eq(d)  # (False, False)

# Mean tensor value
avg = d.mean()  # 1.5

# Max tensor value
mx = d.max()  # 2

# Min tensor value
mn = d.min()  # 1
```

```
# Sum of all tensor values
sm = d.sum()  # 3
```

```
>>>>>>>>>> PyTorch
```

We've covered basic operations with tensors, and it doesn't seem like anything extraordinary so far. Next, we will examine special deep learning techniques that will allow us to create complex neural networks.

Deep learning layers

Deep learning neural networks have special. Each of these layers is a rather trivial mathematical function, but the composition of these layers creates sophisticated neural networks that can extract the most complex patterns from datasets.

Linear layer

The linear layer is the most straightforward functional approximation method. Linear layer is the classical linear transformation based on matrix product:

$$f(x) = Ax + b$$

Linear layer is a function with the following parameters:

- **weight**: matrix A
- **bias**: vector b

A linear layer is usually initialized with random weight and bias. It often makes sense because weight and bias will be used in neural network training and will be adjusted after:

```
TensorFlow >>>>>>>>>>
```

TensorFlow incorporates the functionality of Keras, which is another deep learning framework. Keras framework is built on top of TensorFlow, which allows developing the high-level neural network design in the simplest possible way. Let's examine the implementation of a linear layer in TensorFlow using the Keras API:

```
import tensorflow as tf
from tensorflow.keras.layers import Dense

tf.random.set_seed(0)

x = tf.constant([[1.0, 2.0, 3.0]])

linear = Dense(units = 2)
```

```
y = linear(x)

# Weight
print(linear.weights[0].numpy())
>>>
[[-0.45575964 -0.6428807 ]
 [ 0.07753718  0.13420844]
 [-0.18255705  0.67441726]]

# Bias
print(linear.weights[1].numpy())
>>>
[0. 0.]

print(y.numpy())
>>>
[[-0.8483564  1.648788 ]]


>>>>>>>>>> TensorFlow

PyTorch >>>>>>>>>>
```

Let's examine the implementation of a linear layer in PyTorch:

```
import torch

torch.manual_seed(0)

x = torch.Tensor([1, 2, 3])

linear = torch.nn.Linear(3, 2)

y = linear(x)

# Weight
print(linear.weight.tolist())
>>>
[[-0.00432, 0.30971, -0.47518], [-0.42489, -0.22236, 0.15482]]

# Bias
```

```
print(linear.bias.tolist())
>>>
[-0.01143, 0.45777]
```

```
print(y.tolist())
>>>
[-0.82188, 0.052604]
```

`>>>>>>>>>> PyTorch`

As we mentioned, all deep learning layers with trainable parameters are initialized with random values. Usually, it is not necessary to set parameters manually, but it can be helpful to study how each layer acts to see in practice how a particular layer performs calculations:

`TensorFlow >>>>>>>>>>`

Linear layer parameters can be set manually, as follows **ch8/tf/layers/linear. py**:

```
import tensorflow as tf
from tensorflow.keras.layers import Dense

x = tf.constant([[1.0, 2.0, 3.0]])

linear = Dense(units = 2)

# We have to `build` layer to initialize it
linear.build(input_shape = x.shape)

# set weights
linear.set_weights([
    tf.Variable([[0, 1], [2, 0], [5, 2]]),  # weights
    tf.Variable([1, 1])  # bias
])

y = linear(x)

print(y.numpy())
```

Result

```
[[20.  8.]]
```

```
>>>>>>>>> TensorFlow
```

```
PyTorch >>>>>>>>>
```

Linear layer parameters can be set manually, as follows **ch8/pt/layers/linear. py**:

```
import torch

x = torch.tensor(data = [1, 2, 3]).float()

linear = torch.nn.Linear(3, 2)

linear.weight = torch.nn.Parameter(
    torch.tensor([[0, 2, 5], [1, 0, 2]]).float()
)
linear.bias = torch.nn.Parameter(
    torch.tensor([1, 1]).float()
)

y = linear(x)

print(y.tolist())
```

Result

```
[20.0, 8.0]
```

```
>>>>>>>>> TensorFlow
```

Convolution

Convolution is a powerful technique to extract features and complex patterns from a dataset. The convolution layer is one of the most used deep learning layers. The idea of convolutions was borrowed from nature. Different neurons in the brain respond to different features. Convolution layers show outstanding results in image classification, pattern detection, speech recognition, natural language processing, etc.

There are three types of convolution layers:

- **1-D convolution**: It is mainly used for sequential data, like time series or audio data streams.

- **2-D convolution**: It is mainly used for image processing.

- **3-D convolution**: It is mainly used for 3D images of video streams.

Sometimes convolution is called as **filter**. In this section, we will cover only 1D and 2D convolutions.

It is easier to understand the idea of the convolution action by an example. The convolution layer needs two tensors to calculate convolution: input tensor and kernel tensor. Here, we will examine 2D Convolution. Say we have 4×4 matrix as the input tensor:

1	2	0	1
-1	0	3	2
1	3	0	1
2	-2	1	0

And 2×2 matrix as the kernel tensor:

1	-1
-1	1

The convolution result is the sum of element-wise multiplication of each "*box*" in the input tensor by the kernel tensor. First step: we take the upper right box in the input matrix and apply kernel to tensor to it: $1·1 + 2·(-1) + (-1)·(-1) + 0·1 = 0$, as shown in *Figure 8.3*:

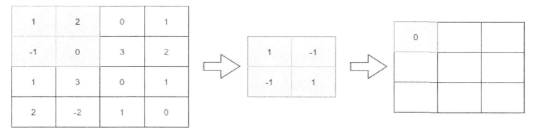

***Figure 8.3**: Convolution: 1ˢᵗ step*

Then, we move to another *box* and again calculate convolution:

$2·1 + 0·(-1) + 0·(-1) + 3·1 = 5$:

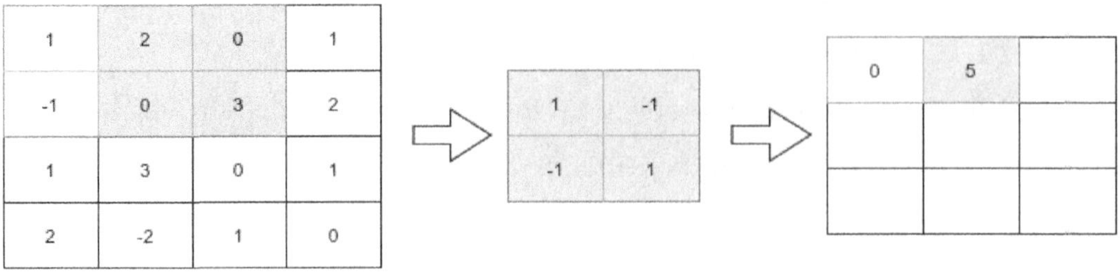

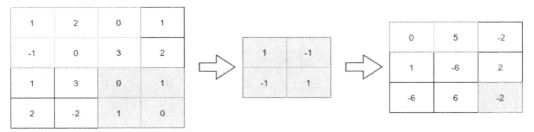

Figure 8.4: Convolution: 2ⁿᵈ step

And this operation takes place for each "*box*" in the input matrix. And at last, we have the following result:

Figure 8.5: Convolution result

Now let's study how the convolution layer is implemented using deep learning frameworks:

TensorFlow >>>>>>>>>

Let's do the same, but using TensorFlow for 2-D convolution implementation **ch8/ tf/layers/conv2d.py**:

```
import tensorflow as tf
import numpy as np
from tensorflow.keras.layers import Conv2D


A = tf.constant(
    [[
        [[1], [2], [0], [1]],
        [[-1], [0], [3], [2]],
        [[1], [3], [0], [1]],
```

```
        [[2], [-2], [1], [0]]
    ]]
    ,
    dtype = tf.float32
)

# A.shape = (1, 4, 4, 1)

conv2d = Conv2D(
    filters = 1,
    kernel_size = (2, 2),
    use_bias = False
)

# Initializing Convolution Layer
conv2d.build(input_shape = A.shape)

# Setting 2x2 Convolution Kernel
w = np.array([[[[1]], [[-1]]],
             [[[-1]], [[1]]]])
conv2d.set_weights([w])

# Executing Convolution
B = conv2d(A)

print(B.numpy())
```

Result

```
[[[[ 0.] [ 5.] [-2.]]
  [[ 1.] [-6.] [ 2.]]
  [[-6.] [ 6.] [-2.]]]]


TensorFlow >>>>>>>>>>


PyTorch >>>>>>>>>>
```

Let's do the same, but using PyTorch for 2-D convolution implementation **ch8/pt/layers/conv2d.py**:

```
import torch
from torch.nn.parameter import Parameter

A = torch.tensor([[[[1, 2, 0, 1],
                    [-1, 0, 3, 2],
                    [1, 3, 0, 1],
                    [2, -2, 1, 0]]]]).float()

# Convolution Layer
conv2d = torch.nn.Conv2d(1, 1, kernel_size = 2, bias = False)

# Setting 2x2 Kernel to Convolution Layer
conv2d.weight = Parameter(torch.tensor([[[[1, -1], [-1, 1]]]]).float())

# Executing Convolution
output = conv2d(A)


print(output.tolist())
```

Result

```
[[[[0.0, 5.0, -2.0], [1.0, -6.0, 2.0], [-6.0, 6.0, -2.0]]]]
>>>>>>>>>> PyTorch
```

Despite their simplicity, convolution layers allow to extract very complex patterns and dependencies from a dataset. In addition to 2D convolutions, there are 1D and 3D convolutions. These convolutions are calculated according to the same principle as 2D convolutions:

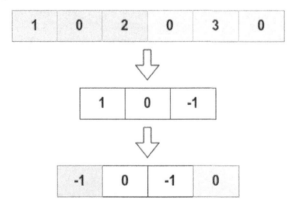

Figure 8.6: 1D convolution example

Convolution layer can have multiple output channels; it means that multiple kernel tensors are applied to the input tensor:

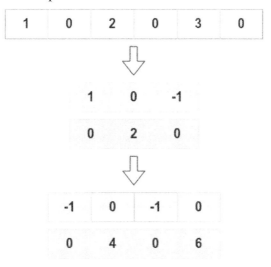

Figure 8.7: *1D convolution with two out channels*

Let's take a look at how the calculations shown in *Figure 8.7* are implemented:

TensorFlow >>>>>>>>>> ch8/tf/layers/conv1d.py

```
import tensorflow as tf
import numpy as np
from tensorflow.keras.layers import Conv1D

A = tf.constant([
    [[1], [0], [2], [0], [3], [0]]
], dtype = tf.float32)

conv2d = Conv1D(
    filters = 2,
    kernel_size = 3,
    use_bias = False
)

# Initializing Convolution Layer
conv2d.build(input_shape = A.shape)
```

```python
# Setting Convolution Kernels
w = np.array([[[1, 0]],
              [[0, 2]],
              [[-1, 0]]])
conv2d.set_weights([w])

# Executing Convolution
B = conv2d(A)

print(B.numpy())
Result
[[[-1.   0.]
  [ 0.   4.]
  [-1.   0.]
  [ 0.   6.]]]
```

>>>>>>>>> TensorFlow

PyTorch >>>>>>>>>> ch8/pt/layers/conv1d.py

```python
import torch
from torch.nn.parameter import Parameter

A = torch.tensor([[[1, 0, 2, 0, 3, 0]]]).float()

conv1d = torch.nn.Conv1d(1, out_channels = 2, kernel_size = 3, bias =
False)
conv1d.weight = Parameter(torch.tensor([[[1, 0, -1]], [[0, 2, 0]]]).
float())

output = conv1d(A)

print(output.tolist())
```

Result

```
[[[-1.,   0., -1.,   0.],
  [ 0.,   4.,   0.,   6.]]]
```

>>>>>>>>>> PyTorch

Another parameter of the convolution layer is the **kernel_size**. Usually, **kernel_size** value lies in the range of 3 to 11. For 1D convolution, **kernel_size=3** defines a vector with 3 elements as a kernel; for 2D convolution, **kernel_size=3** defines a 3×3 matrix as a kernel, and for 3D convolution, **kernel_size=3** defines 3×3×3 tensor as a kernel.

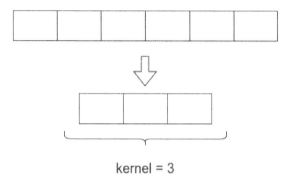

kernel = 3

***Figure 8.8**: Convolution kernel*

In the examples above, we have set weights manually, but it was done only to provide some examples of calculations. Convolution weights are being adjusted during neural network training, so normally, you don't have to set these values by yourself.

Pooling

Pooling is an aggregation technique that aims to reduce the size of the input tensor. The pooling layer tries to extract main tensor *features* and reduce the computation costs.

The most popular pooling layers are Max Pooling and Average Pooling. The pooling layer has the kernel size. Regarding this kernel size, the aggregation action is taken. The most common kernel size of the pooling layer is 2.

Let's consider 2D Max Pooling layer in action:

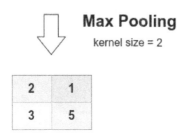

Figure 8.9: *2-D Max Pooling with kernel size=2*

Figure 8.9 demonstrates that the Max Pooling layer splits the input tensor into four 2×2 squares and selects the maximum value in each square:

TensorFlow >>>>>>>>>>

Here is the Max Pool layer implementation using TensorFlow **ch8/tf/layers/ pool_max.py**:

```python
import tensorflow as tf
from keras.layers import MaxPool2D

A = tf.constant(
    [[
        [[1], [2], [-1], [1]],
        [[0], [1], [-2], [-1]],
        [[3], [0], [5], [0]],
        [[0], [1], [4], [-3]]
    ]])

max_pool = MaxPool2D(pool_size = 2)

out = max_pool(A)

print(out.numpy())
```

Result

```
[[[[2] [1]]
  [[3] [5]]]]
```

>>>>>>>>>> TensorFlow

PyTorch >>>>>>>>>>

Here is the Max Pool layer implementation using PyTorch **ch8/pt/layers/pool_max.py**:

```
import torch

A = torch.tensor([[
    [1, 2, -1, 1],
    [0, 1, -2, -1],
    [3, 0, 5, 0],
    [0, 1, 4, -3]
]]).float()

max_pool = torch.nn.MaxPool2d(2)
out = max_pool(A)

print(out.tolist())
```

Result

```
[[
[2.0, 1.0],
[3.0, 5.0]
]]
```

>>>>>>>>>> PyTorch

Average pooling acts by the same principle but uses an average aggregation function instead of max:

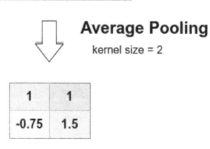

Figure 8.10: 2-D Average Pooling with kernel size=2

As you may have noticed, the Max Pooling and Average Pooling layers do not have any adjustable weights and act purely as functions.

Dropout

Dropout is an excellent regularization technique. A neural network is prone to overfitting. Overfitting leads to the problem when a model is trained, and it works so well on training data that it negatively affects the performance of the model on unobserved data. To overcome the problem of overfitting, a dropout layer can be used. The dropout layer is based on a straightforward principle: in the training mode, this layer drops out random elements of the input tensor with probability p. The left tensor elements are multiplied by $\frac{1}{1-p}$. The dropout layer does not affect the input tensor in the evaluation mode:

```
TensorFlow >>>>>>>>>>
```

Here is the example of dropout layer in action **ch8/tf/layers/dropout.py**:

```
import tensorflow as tf
from keras.layers import Dropout

tf.random.set_seed(0)

t = tf.range(1, 6, dtype = tf.float32)
```

```
print(f'Initial Tensor: {t.numpy()}')

dropout = Dropout(rate = .5)

# Training Mode
r = dropout(t, training = True)
print(f'Dropout Train: {r.numpy()}')

# Evaluation Mode
r = dropout(t)
print(f'Dropout Eval: {r.numpy()}')
```

Result

```
Initial Tensor: [1. 2. 3. 4. 5.]
Dropout Train: [0. 0. 6. 8. 0.]
Dropout Eval: [1. 2. 3. 4. 5.]


>>>>>>>>>> TensorFlow


PyTorch >>>>>>>>>>
```

Here is the example of dropout layer in action **ch8/pt/layers/dropout.py**:

```
import torch
from torch.nn import Dropout

torch.manual_seed(1)

t = torch.randint(10, (5,)).float()
print(f'Initial Tensor: {t.numpy()}')

dropout = Dropout(p = .5)

dropout.train()
r = dropout(t)
print(f'Dropout Train: {r.numpy()}')

dropout.eval()
r = dropout(t)
print(f'Dropout Eval: {r.numpy()}')
```

Result

```
Initial Tensor: [5. 9. 4. 8. 3.]
Dropout Train: [10. 18. 0. 16. 0.]
Dropout Eval: [5. 9. 4. 8. 3.]
```

```
PyTorch >>>>>>>>>>
```

Flatten

Flatten is a simple operation that converts a multi-dimensional tensor into a one-dimensional vector:

TensorFlow >>>>>>>>>>

Here is the implementation of flatten operation using TensorFlow **ch8/tf/layers/flat.py**:

```
import tensorflow as tf
from tensorflow.keras.layers import Flatten

x = tf.random.uniform((1, 16, 10))

flat = Flatten()

y = flat(x)

print(f'initial shape: {x.shape}')
print(f'flatten shape: {y.shape}')
```

Result

```
initial shape: (1, 16, 10)
flatten shape: (1, 160)
```

```
>>>>>>>>>> TensorFlow
```

```
PyTorch >>>>>>>>>>
```

Here is the implementation of flatten operation using PyTorch **ch8/pt/layers/flat.py**:

```
import torch

x = torch.rand((1, 16, 10))
```

```
y = torch.flatten(x, start_dim = 1)

print(f'initial shape: {x.shape}')
print(f'flatten shape: {y.shape}')
```

Result

```
initial shape: torch.Size([1, 16, 10])
flatten shape: torch.Size([1, 160])
```

```
>>>>>>>>>> PyTorch
```

Activations

An activation function is a function that is added to a neural network computational graph to help a model learn complex nonlinear dependencies. A typical activation function should be differentiable and continuous everywhere. Next, we provide some classic examples of activation functions.

ReLU

ReLU or Rectified Linear Function performs a simple operation:

$$\text{ReLU}(x) = max(0, x).$$

ReLU is one of the simplest and most efficient activation functions:

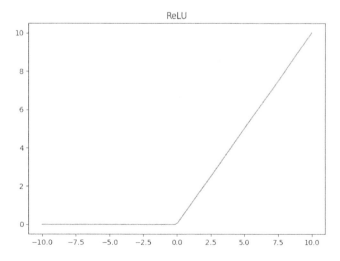

Figure 8.11: ReLU

Sigmoid

Sigmoid is one of the common nonlinear activation functions. The sigmoid function is mathematically represented as follows:

$$sigmoid(x) = \frac{1}{1 + e^{-x}}$$

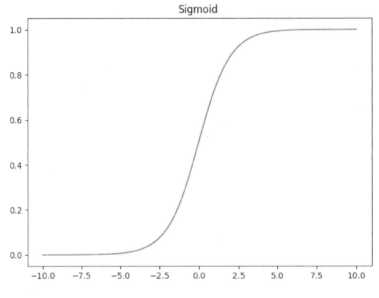

Figure 8.12: Sigmoid

The output range of the **sigmoid** function is (0, 1).

Tanh

Tanh or hyperbolic tangent function is similar to the **sigmoid** function, but it returns values in the range (−1, 1):

$$tanh(x) = \frac{e^x - e^{-x}}{e^x + e^{-x}}$$

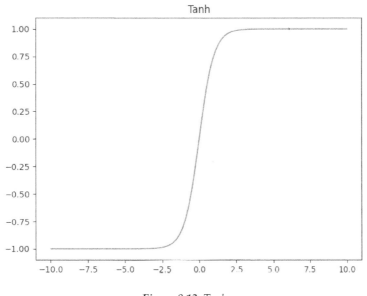

Figure 8.13: Tanh

The benefit of **tanh** over **sigmoid** is that the negative inputs will be mapped strictly to negative, and the positive inputs will be mapped strictly to positive:

TensorFlow >>>>>>>>>>

Here are the implementations of activation functions using TensorFlow **ch8/tf/ layers/activations.py**:

```
import tensorflow as tf
import matplotlib.pyplot as plt


x = tf.linspace(-10.0, 10.0, 1000)


# ReLU
plt.title('ReLU')
plt.plot(x.numpy(), tf.nn.relu(x).numpy())
plt.show()


# Sigmoid
plt.title('Sigmoid')
plt.plot(x.numpy(), tf.nn.sigmoid(x).numpy())
plt.show()
```

```
# Tanh
plt.title('Tanh')
plt.plot(x.numpy(), tf.nn.tanh(x).numpy())
plt.show()
```

>>>>>>>>>> TensorFlow

PyTorch >>>>>>>>>>

Here are the implementations of activation functions using PyTorch **ch8/pt/ layers/activations.py**:

```
import torch
import matplotlib.pyplot as plt

x = torch.linspace(-10, 10)

# ReLU
relu = torch.nn.ReLU()
plt.title('ReLU')
plt.plot(x.tolist(), relu(x).tolist())
plt.show()

# Sigmoid
sigmoid = torch.nn.Sigmoid()
plt.title('Sigmoid')
plt.plot(x.tolist(), sigmoid(x).tolist())
plt.show()

# Tanh
tanh = torch.nn.Tanh()
plt.title('Tanh')
plt.plot(x.tolist(), tanh(x).tolist())
plt.show()
```
>>>>>>>>>> PyTorch

Nonlinear activation functions, like sigmoid and tanh, suffer from a big computational problem called the vanishing gradient problem. Vanishing gradient makes it very difficult to train and adjust the initial layers' parameters in the network. This problem worsens as the number of layers in the network increases. The vanishing gradient is the main cause that makes sigmoid or tanh activations unsuitable for deep learning models. ReLU activation function does not suffer from vanishing gradient because the derivative is always 1 for positive inputs. So, always consider using ReLU as the activation function at the first drafts of your model design.

Softmax

Softmax activation function performs exponential normalization, and it is expressed as follows:

$$softmax(x_i) = \frac{e^{x_i}}{\sum_j e^{x_j}}$$

The *softmax* activation function calculates the relative probabilities. That means it uses initial estimations and converts them to probabilities. Let's study how the softmax activation function acts. Say we have an *Escape Maze* competition, in which three players participate. The player who escapes the maze first wins. Each player has the following characteristics: *speed, memory,* and *intelligence.* These characteristics can be presented in the following table:

	Player 1	**Player 2**	**Player 3**
Speed	9	10	8
Memory	7	9	10
Intelligence	9	10	8
Total	25	29	26

Table 8.1: Player characteristics

And the *softmax* function can be used to indicate the winning probability of each of the players.

```
TensorFlow >>>>>>>>>>
```

Let's calculate the probability of winning using the softmax function in TensorFlow **ch8/tf/layers/soft_max.py**:

```
import tensorflow as tf

player_characteristics = tf.constant([
    [9, 7, 9],   # Player 1
    [10, 9, 10],   # Player 2
    [8, 10, 8]   # Player 3
], dtype = tf.float32)

# Total Characteristics
```

```
player_total = tf.reduce_sum(player_characteristics, axis = 1)

softmax = tf.nn.softmax

player_prob = softmax(player_total)

# Probabilities
print(player_prob.numpy())
```

Result

	Player 1	Player 2	Player 3
Probability	1.71%	93.62%	4.66%

Table 8.2: Winning probabilities

```
>>>>>>>>>> TensorFlow


PyTorch >>>>>>>>>>
```

Let's calculate the probability of winning using the softmax function in PyTorch **ch8/pt/layers/soft_max.py**:

```
import torch

player_characteristics = torch.Tensor([
    [9, 7, 9],   # Player 1
    [10, 9, 10],  # Player 2
    [8, 10, 8]   # Player 3
])

# Total Characteristics
player_total = player_characteristics.sum(dim = 1)

softmax = torch.nn.Softmax()

player_prob = softmax(player_total)

# Probabilities
print(player_prob.numpy())
```

Result

	Player 1	**Player 2**	**Player 3**
Probability	1.71%	93.62%	4.66%

Table 8.3: Winning probabilities

>>>>>>>>>> PyTorch

Softmax function plays an important role in classification tasks. We will often use it for reinforcement learning problems estimating the probability of the best action for a state.

Neural Network Architecture

In the previous section, we explored the main layers used in deep learning models: Linear, Convolution, Pooling, Dropout, Flatten, ReLU, Sigmoid, Tanh, and Softmax. Of course, these are not all the layers used that build neural networks. But even the building blocks that are mentioned above are enough to construct quite effective deep learning models. The architecture of a neural network is a particular sequence of layers that create a computational graph. There are many different architectures of neural networks, and each of them is a solution to a specific problem.

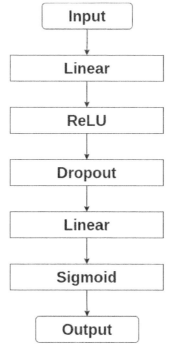

Figure 8.14: Fully connected neural network

Figure 8.14 depicts a sequence of layers that form a simple neural network. The series of linear layers and activation functions between them is often referred to as the fully connected Neural Network. The following chapters will show that even such simple models can effectively solve complex problems.

Supervised learning and loss function

Supervised learning uses a training dataset to teach models to return the desired output. This training dataset includes inputs (x) and correct outputs (y), which allow the model (m) to learn over time. In supervised learning, the model learns to adjust the weights of its layers so that the value of $m(x)$ returned by the model m is close enough to the correct value of y.

Supervised learning can be divided into two types of problems classification and regression.

Classification

The classification problem assumes mapping a category for some input x. For example, the domestic animals' classification task: *"according to the image x, it is necessary to map the animal depicted on it: cat, dog, pig, etc.".* The classification problem is close to reinforcement learning problems. For example, in *Chapter 5, Blackjack in Monte Carlo*, we mapped an action to a particular hand: Hit or Stick.

Regression

The regression problem implies that we must map some number y by input x. For example, if you need to map an age by an image of a person.

Loss function

Another key concept of deep learning is loss function. The loss function measures how close the neural network's answer $m(x)$ is to the correct answer y. The loss function helps answer the question *how close are the outputs m(x) of model m to the correct answers of y.*

Absolute Loss

Absolute loss is the simplest metric of the distance between two vectors:

$$absolute\ loss(y,\ z) = \frac{\sum |y_i - z_i|}{n}$$

Absolute loss is the average sum of all differences between two vectors:

```
TensorFlow >>>>>>>>>>
```

In TensorFlow, the absolute loss function is implemented the following way **ch8/ tf/loss/abs_loss.py**:

```
import tensorflow as tf

a = tf.constant([1, 2], dtype = tf.float32)
b = tf.constant([1, 5], dtype = tf.float32)

abs_loss = tf.keras.losses.MeanAbsoluteError()
abs_error = abs_loss(a, b)

print(f'abs: {abs_error.numpy()}')

>>>
abs: 1.5


>>>>>>>>>> TensorFlow


PyTorch >>>>>>>>>>
```

In PyTorch, the absolute loss function is implemented the following way **ch8/pt/ loss/abs_loss.py**:

```
import torch

a = torch.tensor([1, 2]).float()
b = torch.tensor([1, 5]).float()

abs_loss = torch.nn.L1Loss()
abs_error = abs_loss(a, b)

print(f'abs: {abs_error.item()}')

>>>
abs: 1.5


>>>>>>>>>> PyTorch
```

Mean squared error

Mean squared error, or simply MSE, is the most commonly used loss function for regression problems:

$$mean\ squared\ error(y, z) = \frac{\sum(y_i - z_i)^2}{n}$$

Mean squared error is the average sum of all squared differences between two vectors:

TensorFlow >>>>>>>>>>

Here is the implementation of mean squared error loss function in TensorFlow **ch8/tf/loss/mse_loss.py**:

```
import tensorflow as tf


a = tf.constant([1, 2], dtype = tf.float32)
b = tf.constant([1, 5], dtype = tf.float32)


mse_loss = tf.keras.losses.MeanSquaredError()
mse_error = mse_loss(a, b)


print(f'mse: {mse_error.numpy()}')


>>>
mse: 4.5


>>>>>>>>>> TensorFlow


PyTorch >>>>>>>>>>
```

Here is the implementation of mean squared error loss function in PyTorch **ch8/pt/loss/mse_loss.py**:

```
import torch


a = torch.tensor([1, 2]).float()
b = torch.tensor([1, 5]).float()


mse_loss = torch.nn.MSELoss()
```

```
mse_error = mse_loss(a, b)


print(f'mse: {mse_error.item()}')


>>>
mse: 1.5
```

 PyTorch

Cross-entropy loss

Cross-entropy loss is an important cost function used to optimize classification models. It measures how far a probability prediction vector is from an actual vector.

Let's say we have a model that classifies images of cats and dogs. For each input image, the model returns the probabilities for each class using the softmax function:

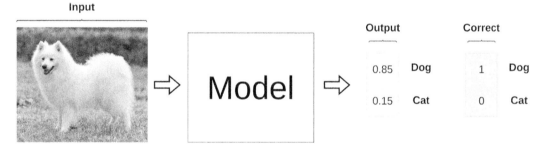

Figure 8.15: *Cats vs dogs classification model*

The higher the probability of the correct answer, the lower the value of the cross-entropy loss function:

TensorFlow >>>>>>>>>>

Now, let's calculate cross-entropy loss between two vectors from *Figure 8.15* using TensorFlow **ch8/tf/loss/ce_loss.py**:

```
import tensorflow as tf


prob_vector = tf.constant([0.85, 0.15])


# Correct class vector
correct_vector = tf.constant([1, 0])


ce_loss = tf.keras.losses.CategoricalCrossentropy()
```

```
ce_error = ce_loss(correct_vector, prob_vector)

print(f'ce: {ce_error.numpy()}')

>>>
ce: 0.1625
>>>>>>>>>> TensorFlow
```

PyTorch >>>>>>>>>>

Now, let's calculate cross-entropy loss between two vectors from *Figure 8.15* using PyTorch **ch8/pt/loss/ce_loss.py**:

```
import torch

prob_vector = torch.tensor([[0.85, 0.15]]).float()

# number of correct class
correct_class = torch.tensor([0])

ce_loss = torch.nn.CrossEntropyLoss()
ce_error = ce_loss(prob_vector, correct_class)

print(f'ce: {ce_error.item()}')

>>>
ce: 0.4031
>>>>>>>>>> PyTorch
```

In the upcoming chapters, we will often use the cross-entropy loss function for our deep reinforcement learning problems.

Training and optimizer

Roughly speaking, training is a weight adjustment by processing input dataset samples and known correct "*answers*". During the training, the model results are compared with the actual ones, and using loss function, it is possible to understand how "*far*" current model weights are from being "*good*". The weight adjustment is realized through error backward propagation process or shortly backpropagation.

This method calculates the gradient of the error function concerning the neural network's weights.

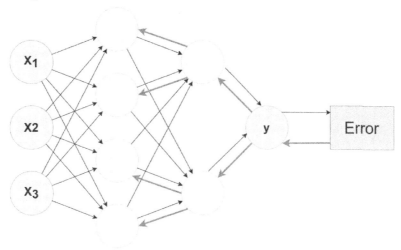

Figure 8.16: *Backpropagation*

We have to define an **optimization** function that will shift model weights in a gradient descent direction to perform training.

Optimizers

The main purpose of an optimizer is to shift the model's weight parameters to minimize the loss function. The selection of a suitable optimizer depends entirely on the architecture of the neural network and the data on which the training occurs. Below are examples of popular optimizers that we will use in this book:

- **Adagrad**: Adagrad is a gradient-based optimization algorithm that adapts the learning rate to the parameters. It performs smaller updates for parameters associated with frequently occurring features and larger updates for parameters associated with rare features.

- **Adadelta**: Adadelta is the advanced version of the Adagrad algorithm. Adadelta seeks to minimize its aggressive, monotonically decreasing learning rate. Instead of accumulating all past gradients, Adadelta limits the window of accumulated past gradients to some fixed size.

- **Adam**: Adaptive Moment Estimation or Adam is another optimization method that computes adaptive learning rates for each parameter. In addition to saving an exponentially decaying average of past squared gradients like Adadelta, Adam keeps an exponentially declining average of previous gradients.

- **Stochastic Gradient Descent (SGD)**: SGD randomly picks one data row from the whole input dataset at each training iteration to decrease computation time. It also samples a small number of data rows instead of just one row at each step. This approach is called *mini-batch* gradient descent. Mini-batch descent tries to place a balance between the goodness of gradient descent and the speed of SGD.

Epoch and batch size

Deep learning model training consists of three main steps:

- **I**: The model returns the results y for the input dataset x.

- **II**: The Loss function is applied to the model's output dataset y and the correct answers y. The result of applying the loss function is an error value.

- **III**: The optimizer shifts the model's weights based on the received error value and the gradient descent algorithm.

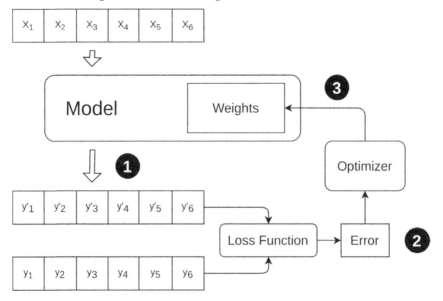

Figure 8.17: Training epoch

This whole process is called training epoch or simply epoch. Neural network training can perform various numbers of epochs; sometimes 10 epochs are enough to train a model well, and sometimes 1000 000 training epochs are needed to achieve the desired result.

In some cases, the training dataset is too large to load all the data into memory. In this case, batch training is used for practical purposes. In batch training, the dataset is split into batches of a fixed size, and in this case, the training iteration takes place on each of the batches. *Figure 8.18* demonstrates how batch training works:

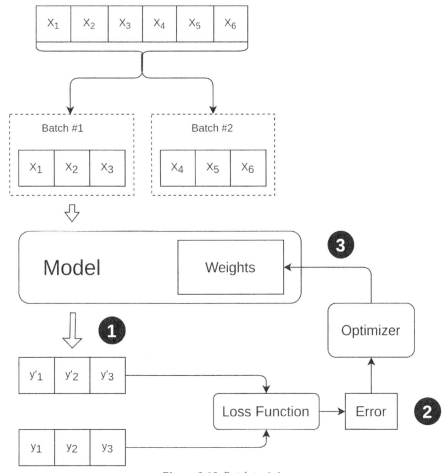

Figure 8.18*: Batch training*

The most common are batches whose size is a power of 2: 16, 32, 64, 128, 256, 512, ... Batch training approach significantly reduces the computational resources required to train the neural network.

Handwritten digit recognition Model

Well, we had enough theory, and it is time to finally build our first neural network, which will solve an important real-world problem. This section will pull all the knowledge from this chapter together and create an efficient deep learning model. We will pick the handwritten digit recognition problem or the so-called MNIST problem as an example. The MNIST problem is a classification task, according to which the model must correctly classify the digit by the image: 1, 2, 3, 4, 5, 6, 7, 8, or 9. Let's take a look at what the images from the MNIST dataset look like.

> **We will use the tensorflow-datasets library for TensorFlow and PyTorch implementations to load the dataset. The tensorflow-datasets library simply loads the MNIST dataset and does not affect deep learning model logic, so this library can be shared with the PyTorch implementation.**

We can observe samples of the MNIST dataset using this script:

```python
import tensorflow_datasets as tfds

ds, info = tfds.load('mnist', split = 'train', with_info = True)
fig = tfds.show_examples(ds, info)
fig.show()
```

Result

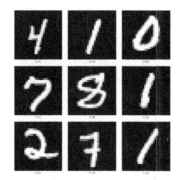

Figure 8.19: MNIST samples

Looking at *Figure 8.19*, you can think this is not a difficult task. If you really think so, take a look at the samples in *Figure 8.20*:

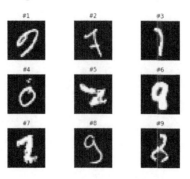

Figure 8.20: MNIST hard samples

Well? Now it's not as easy as it seems, right? For example, can you correctly classify sample #5 in picture 8.20? It is very tricky. Therefore, you should not require 100% accuracy from our future neural network in this task.

Each sample is a 28×28 black and white image. The color of each pixel is determined by a value from 0 (black) to 255 (white):

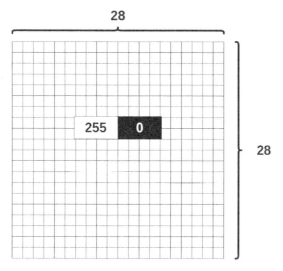

Figure 8.21: *MNIST image as tensor*

Therefore, each image can be represented by a size tensor (28, 28, 1). The first two values define the pixel coordinates, and the third value defines the pixel color.

The concepts of *training* and *test* datasets are used to understand the model performance. The training dataset is used exclusively for neural network training. After training, the quality of the model is verified on the test dataset.

Let's examine the training and test datasets for the MNIST problem **ch8/utils.py**:

```
import tensorflow_datasets as tfds


if __name__ == '__main__':

    ds = tfds.as_numpy(tfds.load(
        'mnist',
        batch_size = -1,
        as_supervised = True,
    ))
```

```
(x_train, y_train) = ds['train']
(x_test, y_test) = ds['test']


print(f'x_train shape: {x_train.shape}')
print(f'y_train shape: {y_train.shape}')
print(f'x_test shape: {x_test.shape}')
print(f'y_test shape: {y_test.shape}')
```

Result

```
x_train shape: (60000, 28, 28, 1)
y_train shape: (60000,)
x_test shape: (10000, 28, 28, 1)
y_test shape: (10000,)
```

Let's take a closer look at the **x_train**, **y_train**, **x_test**, and **y_test** variables from the script above:

- **x_train**: **ndarray** with shape: (60000, 28, 28, 1). This array contains 60 000 images (tensors of shape 28×28×1).

- **y_train**: **ndarray** with shape: (60000). This array contains 60 000 correct answers to images from **x_train** dataset.

- **x_test**: **ndarray** with shape: (10000, 28, 28, 1). This array contains 10 000 images (tensors of shape 28×28×1).

- **y_test**: **ndarray** with shape: (10000). This array contains 10 000 correct answers to images from **x_test** dataset.

We defined the task and examined the dataset we will operate with. Now, let's implement a deep learning model to solve the MNIST classification problem. One of the first architectures that successfully solved the problem of recognizing handwritten digits was the LeNet model, and its architecture is as follows:

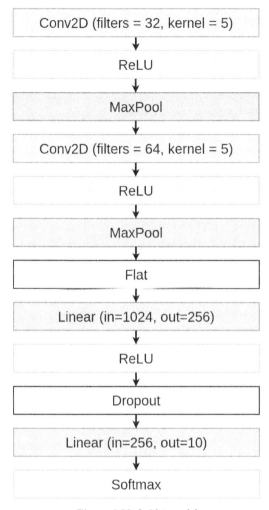

Figure 8.22: LeNet model

So, let's construct our first deep learning model!

```
TensorFlow >>>>>>>>>>
```

Let's look at the implementation of the LeNet model using TensorFlow **ch8/tf/ mnist/model.py**.

We import the necessary packages:

```
import tensorflow as tf
```

```
from tensorflow.keras import Model
```

```
from tensorflow.keras.layers import Conv2D, Dense, Dropout, Flatten,
MaxPool2D
```

Each TensorFlow deep learning model implements **tensorflow.keras.Model**:

```
class MnistClassifier(Model):

    def __init__(self):
        super().__init__()
```

Each layer of the neural network must be assigned to some model property:

```
# 1st convolution layer
self.conv1 = Conv2D(
    filters = 32,
    kernel_size = 5,
    activation = tf.nn.relu
)

# max pool layer
self.pool = MaxPool2D(pool_size = 2)

# 2nd convolution layer
self.conv2 = Conv2D(
    filters = 64,
    kernel_size = 5,
    activation = tf.nn.relu
)

# Flatten Layer
self.flatten = Flatten()

# 1st linear layer
self.lin1 = Dense(
    units = 256,
    activation = tf.nn.relu
)

# Dropout Layer
self.drop = Dropout(rate = .5)
```

```
# 2nd Linear Layer
self.lin2 = Dense(
    units = 10,
    activation = tf.nn.softmax
)
```

And then, we must determine the order in which the model layers will be called. They will be called in the **sequence** shown in *Figure 8.22*:

```
def call(self, x, **kwargs):
    x = self.conv1(x)
    x = self.pool(x)
    x = self.conv2(x)
    x = self.pool(x)
    x = self.flatten(x)
    x = self.lin1(x)
    x = self.drop(x)
    return self.lin2(x)
```

That's it! Our first deep learning model is ready! But that was only part of the job. Now we need to train the neural network and test its ability to recognize handwritten digits **ch8/tf/mnist/train.py**.

We import the necessary packages:

```
import tensorflow as tf
from sklearn.metrics import accuracy_score
from ch8.tf.mnist.model import MnistClassifier
from ch8.utils import mnist_dataset
import numpy as np
```

Making script reproducible:

```
tf.random.set_seed(0)
```

Initializing Classifier Model:

```
mnist_clf = MnistClassifier()
```

Next, we have to prepare training and test datasets:

```
(x_train, y_train), (x_test, y_test) = mnist_dataset()
dataset_size = x_train.shape[0]
```

To build model computation graph, we have to pass a shape of input tensor:

```
mnist_clf.build(input_shape = x_train.shape)
```

Model weights are extracted for the optimization process:

```
variables = mnist_clf.variables
```

Initializing the **Adam** optimizer:

```
optimizer = tf.keras.optimizers.Adam(learning_rate = 0.001)
```

Initializing cross-entropy loss function:

```
loss = tf.keras.losses.CategoricalCrossentropy()
```

Train dataset contains 60,000 samples. It is a rather large dataset, and we will implement batch training with **batch_size = 512**:

```
batch_size = 512
```

Main epoch loop with 10 epochs:

```
for epoch in range(1, 10 + 1):
```

We will construct random batch permutations for each epoch:

```
    permutation = np.random.permutation(dataset_size)
```

Secondary batch loop:

```
    for bi in range(1, dataset_size, batch_size):
```

Batch indices for new batch:

```
        indices = permutation[bi:bi + batch_size]
```

Constructing new training batches:

```
        batch_x, batch_y = x_train[indices], y_train[indices]
```

TensorFlow cross-entropy loss function works with one-hot vectors. This means we must convert the correct class number into a sequence of 0s and 1s. For example: [4] => [0, 0, 0, 0, 1, 0, 0, 0, 0, 0]:

```
        batch_y_one_hot = tf.one_hot(batch_y, depth = 10)
```

Registering derivatives:

```
        with tf.GradientTape() as tape:
```

Executing the classifier model. The shape of the output tensor is (**batch_size, 10**), which means the output tensor contains the probability of matching each of the 10 classes:

```
output = mnist_clf(batch_x)
```

Computing error between model's answers and correct answers using cross-entropy loss function:

```
error = loss(batch_y_one_hot, output)
```

Adjusting model weights using Adam optimizer:

```
gradient = tape.gradient(error, variables)
optimizer.apply_gradients(zip(gradient, variables))
```

Progress of current epoch:

```
print(f'Epoch: {epoch}: {round((hi / dataset_size ) * 100, 2)}%')
```

After the completion of each epoch, we measure the performance of the model on the whole train dataset:

```
# Model output contains probabilities for each class on whole train
dataset
# output.shape = (60000, 10)
output = mnist_clf(x_train)
```

The next step is a tricky one. The output tensor contains the probabilities of each of the classes, but we need a concrete answer. For this, the **tf.math.argmax** function is used, which returns the position (index) of the largest value in the vector, that is: **[0.01, 0.97, 0.02] => 1**:

```
predict = tf.math.argmax(output, axis = 1)
```

Computing accuracy between model's answers and correct answers:

```
accuracy = round(accuracy_score(predict, y_train), 4)
print(F'Epoch: {epoch}| Accuracy: {accuracy}')
```

After completing the training, we have to test the model on data that the model has never seen before, that is, on test dataset:

```
# Model output contains probabilities for each class for all 10 000 test
images
# output.shape = (10000, 10)
output = mnist_clf(x_test)
```

The next step is to convert the output tensor to a concrete class prediction using the **tf.math.argmax** function:

```
# predict tensor contains classes with highest probability
# predict.shape = (10000, 1)
predict = tf.math.argmax(output, axis = 1)
```

Computing accuracy between predicted and correct answers:

```
accuracy = round(accuracy_score(predict, y_test), 4)
print(F'Test Accuracy: {accuracy}')
```

Result

```
Test Accuracy: 0.9915
>>>>>>>>>> TensorFlow


PyTorch >>>>>>>>>>
```

Let's look at the implementation of the LeNet model using PyTorch **ch8/pt/mnist/ model.py**. We need only one module to define the model:

```
from torch import nn
```

Each PyTorch deep learning model implements **torch.nn.Module**:

```
class MnistClassifier(nn.Module):

    def __init__(self):
        super(MnistClassifier, self).__init__()
```

Each layer of the neural network must be assigned to some model property:

```
        # 1st Convolution Layer
        self.conv1 = nn.Conv2d(1, 32, kernel_size = 5)

        # Max Pool Layer
        self.max_pool = nn.MaxPool2d(2)

        # Dropout Layer
        self.dropout = nn.Dropout(p = .5)

        # ReLU Activation
        self.relu = nn.ReLU()
```

```
# 2nd Convolution Layer
self.conv2 = nn.Conv2d(32, 64, kernel_size = 5)


# Flatten Layer
self.flatten = nn.Flatten()


# 1st Linear Layer
self.lin1 = nn.Linear(1024, 256)


# 2nd Linear Layer
self.lin2 = nn.Linear(256, 10)


# SoftMax Activation
self.softmax = nn.Softmax(dim = 1)
```

And then, we must determine the order in which model layers will be called. They will be called in the sequence shown in *Figure 8.22*:

```
def forward(self, x):
    x = self.relu(self.conv1(x))
    x = self.max_pool(x)
    x = self.relu(self.conv2(x))
    x = self.max_pool(x)
    x = self.flatten(x)
    x = self.relu(self.lin1(x))
    x = self.dropout(x)
    x = self.lin2(x)
    return self.softmax(x)
```

That's it! Our first deep learning model is ready! But that was only part of the job. Now we need to train the neural network and test its ability to recognize handwritten digits **ch8/pt/mnist/train.py**.

We import the necessary packages:

```
import torch
import torch.optim as optim
from sklearn.metrics import accuracy_score
from ch8.pt.mnist.model import MnistClassifier
from ch8.utils import mnist_dataset
```

Making script reproducible:

```
torch.manual_seed(0)
```

Initializing Classifier Model:

```
mnist_clf = MnistClassifier()
```

Next, we have to prepare training and test datasets:

```
(x_train, y_train), (x_test, y_test) = mnist_dataset()
x_train = torch.from_numpy(x_train).float()
y_train = torch.from_numpy(y_train).long()
x_test = torch.from_numpy(x_test).float()
y_test = torch.from_numpy(y_test).long()


# Permute dimensions for PyTorch Convolutions
x_train = torch.permute(x_train, (0, 3, 1, 2))
x_test = torch.permute(x_test, (0, 3, 1, 2))


dataset_size = x_train.shape[0]
```

Initializing the **Adam** Optimizer:

```
optimizer = optim.Adam(mnist_clf.parameters(), lr = 0.001)
```

Initializing cross-entropy loss function:

```
loss = torch.nn.CrossEntropyLoss()
```

Enabling Training Mode:

```
mnist_clf.train()
```

Train dataset contains 60,000 samples. It is a rather large dataset, and we will implement batch training with **batch_size = 512**:

```
batch_size = 512
```

Main epoch loop with 10 epochs:

```
for epoch in range(1, 10 + 1):
```

We will construct random batch permutations for each epoch:

```
    permutation = torch.randperm(dataset_size)
```

Secondary batch loop:

```
    for bi in range(1, dataset_size, batch_size):
```

Batch indices for new batch:

```
indices = permutation[bi:bi + batch_size]
```

Constructing new training batches:

```
batch_x, batch_y = x_train[indices], y_train[indices]
```

Resetting optimizer gradient to zero:

```
optimizer.zero_grad()
```

Executing the classifier model. The shape of the output tensor is (**batch_size, 10**), which means the output tensor contains the probability of matching each of the 10 classes:

```
output = mnist_clf(batch_x)
```

Computing error between model's answers and correct answers using cross-entropy loss function:

```
error = loss(output, batch_y)
```

Adjusting model weights using Adam optimizer:

```
error.backward()
optimizer.step()
```

Progress of current epoch:

```
print(f'Epoch: {epoch}: {round((bi / dataset_size ) * 100,
2)}%')
```

After the completion of each epoch, we measure the performance of the model on the whole train dataset:

```
# Model output contains probabilities for each class on whole train
dataset
# output.shape = (60000, 10)
output = mnist_clf(x_train)
```

The next step is a tricky one. The output tensor contains the probabilities of each of the classes. But we need a concrete answer. For this, the **torch.Tensor.argmax** method is used, which returns the position (index) of the largest value in the vector, that is, **[0.01, 0.97, 0.02] => 1**:

```
predict = output.argmax(dim = 1, keepdim = True)
```

Computing accuracy between model's answers and the correct answers:

```
accuracy = round(accuracy_score(predict, y_train), 4)
print(f'Epoch: {epoch}| Accuracy: {accuracy}')
```

After completing the training, we have to test the model on data that the model has never seen before, that is, on test dataset.

Resetting model to evaluation mode:

```
mnist_clf.eval()
```

```
# Model output contains probabilities for each class for all 10 000 test
images
# output.shape = (10000, 10)
output = mnist_clf(x_test)
```

The next step is to convert the output tensor to a concrete class prediction using the **torch.Tensor.argmax** method:

```
# predict tensor contains classes with highest probability
# predict.shape = (10000, 1)
predict = output.argmax(dim = 1, keepdim = True)
```

Computing accuracy between predicted and correct answers:

```
accuracy = round(accuracy_score(predict, y_test), 4)
print(f'Test Accuracy: {accuracy}')
```

Result

```
Test Accuracy: 0.9905
>>>>>>>>>> PyTorch
```

Congratulations! You have just built your first neural network! The deep learning model we made recognizes handwritten digits with 99% accuracy, which is an excellent result.

Conclusion

If you are completely new to deep learning, then at this point of time, you have quite a lot of new information to comprehend. Do not be discouraged if some moments remain unusual. In the upcoming chapters, we will continue to use neural networks, and you will understand how deep learning models work. We will also study how deep learning can help reinforcement learning and construct our first Deep Q-Network.

Points to remember

- The main feature of TensorFlow and PyTorch is the ability to calculate derivatives of composite multivariable functions.

- Tensor is the main object of TensorFlow and PyTorch.

- Dropout layers are used as a regularization technique in order not to fall into an overfitting problem.

- ReLU activation function does not suffer from the vanishing gradient problem.

- Batch training approach significantly reduces the computational resources required to train the neural network.

Multiple choice questions

1. Say we have the following tensor:

   ```
   [
       [1, 0, 0],
       [0, 1, 0],
       [0, 0, 1]
   ]
   ```

   What function could produce the tensor above?

       a.   tf.ones(3) or torch.ones(3)

       b.   tf.eye(3,3) or torch.eye(3,3)

       c.   tf.eye(3) or torch.eye(3)

2. Say we have the following input tensor:

   ```
   [2, 5, 5, 7]
   ```

   And the following output tensor:

   ```
   [0, 10, 0, 14]
   ```

   What layer could produce this result?

       a.   Max Pooling

       b.   Linear

       c.   Dropout

3. Which activation function has a constant derivative?

       a.   ReLU

       b.   Sigmoid

       c.   Tanh

Answers

1. c
2. c
3. a

Key terms

- **Tensor**: Are multi-dimensional arrays

- **Linear layer**: Applies classical linear mapping of the input tensor

- **Convolution layer**: Applies convolution kernel to extract features from the dataset

- **Pooling layer**: Aggregates *"cell"* of the tensor to reduce the input tensor size

- **Dropout layer**: Randomly *"drops out"* elements from the input tensor

- **Flatten layer**: Flattens the input tensor to one-dimensional tensor

- **ReLU activation**: Linear activation

- **Sigmoid activation**: Nonlinear activation in range (0, 1)

- **Tanh activation**: Nonlinear activation in range (-1, 1)

- **Softmax activation**: Normalizes input vector into a probability distribution

- **Supervised learning**: Uses a training dataset to teach models to return the desired output

- **Classification problem**: Assumes mapping a category for some input x

- **Regression problem**: Implies that we must map some number y by input x

- **Loss function**: Measures how close the neural network's answer is to the correct answer

- **Absolute loss**: Is the average sum of all differences between two vectors

- **Mean squared error**: Is the average sum of all squared differences between two vectors.

- **Cross-Entropy loss**: Is an important cost function used to optimize classification models and measures how far a probability prediction vector is from an actual vector

- **Adagrad**: Is a gradient-based optimization algorithm that adapts the learning rate to the parameters

- **Adam**: Is another optimization method that computes adaptive learning rates for each parameter

- **SGD**: Randomly picks one data row from the whole input dataset at each training iteration to decrease computation time

CHAPTER 9

Deep Q-Network and Lunar Lander

In this chapter, you will learn about one of the most popular deep reinforcement learning algorithms called Deep Q-Network or DQN. Many advanced deep reinforcement learning algorithms are based on DQN. DQN is the starting point where reinforcement learning and deep learning meet each other. This approach significantly expands the scope of reinforcement learning problems that can be practically solved. Researchers at Google's DeepMind developed DQN algorithm to play Atari games in 2013. This chapter studies what a Deep Q-Network is and its application in the reinforcement learning area.

Structure

In this chapter, we will discuss the following topics:

- Neural networks in reinforcement learning
- Convergence of temporal difference and DQN training loss function
- Replay buffer
- DQN implementation
- Lunar landing using DQN agent

Objectives

After completing this chapter, you will have learned how to apply Deep Q-Network to reinforcement learning problems with continuous state spaces. You will have mastered the principles of construction, training, and practical application of the Deep Q-Networks.

Neural networks in reinforcement learning

In the introduction, we already mentioned Atari games, so let's start right away by describing one of them. In this section, we will examine the Breakout game environment. This is a simple game in which you need to destroy all the bricks. The player in this game can move the platform to the right or left to hit the ball. In the Breakout environment, the state is expressed as the sequence of 4 screen pixels 84×84 of 256 gray levels. We need to understand the direction of ball movement. And that is why the state is expressed by a sequence of four screens instead of a single screen. The single screen of the Breakout game is shown in *Figure 9.1*:

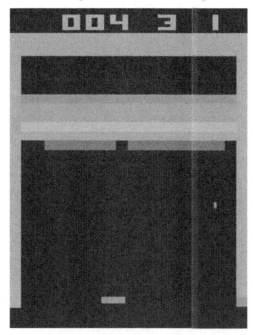

Figure 9.1: Breakout screen

Now, let's calculate the size of the state space for the Breakout game (i.e., all possible states that can occur in this game): $256^{4\times84\times84} \approx 10^{65\,000}$. To understand how large this number is, I'd like to tell you that the number of atoms in our universe is 10^{81}! Yes, the number of different states of an elementary arcade game exceeds the number of atoms in our universe. And this applies to all complex environments. Of course, the classical Q-learning approach is not suitable for solving such problems. It is physically impossible to iterate the game so many times to determine the effective action for each state. But the Q-learning approach itself has already proven its effectiveness. We just need a few modifications to apply it to tasks with a large space state.

The primary assumption for environments with a large number of states is: *The agent must act in the same way in close states in most cases* or *With minor changes in the state, the agent's actions change slightly.* Take a look at *Figure 9.2*:

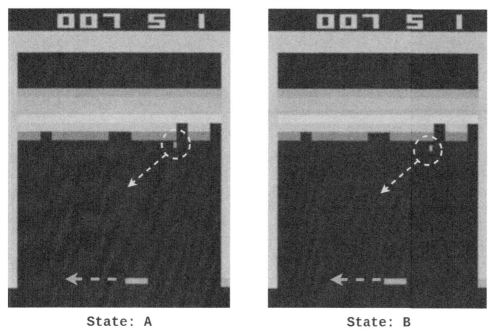

State: A   State: B

Figure 9.2: *Breakout; two close states*

Figure 9.2 contains two close states: **State A** and **State B**. The *"ball"* is slightly lower in **State B** but is moving in the same direction as **State A**. Although these are two different states, it is still the best solution for the platform to start moving to the left. This example describes the principle that the agent's behavior does not change in close states. But how can this environment property help us? And here's how, we do not have to iterate through all the states of the environment, it is enough to train the Agent to act correctly in the central states, and then he will already learn how to act in similar ones. We can call it the Experience Distribution. If the Agent knows that it is necessary to make the green decision in **state A**, then for the states closest to **A**, the Agent will surely make the same decisions. *Figure 9.3* illustrates this principle:

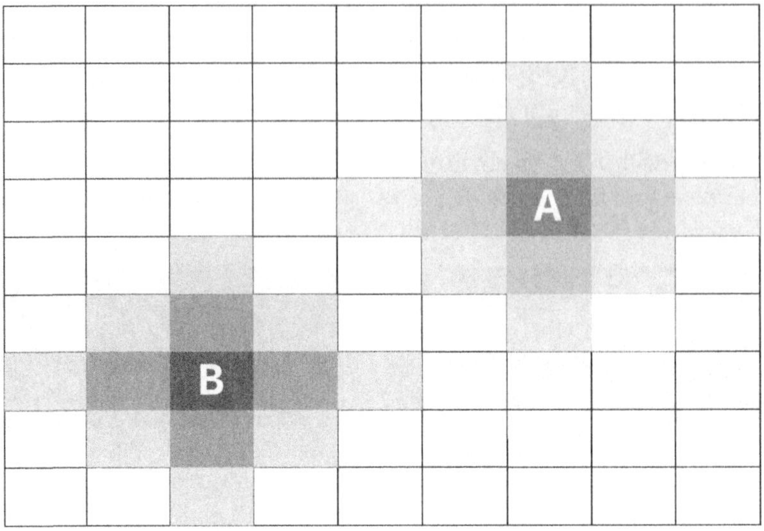

Figure 9.3: Experience distribution

And this is where neural networks come to the rescue! The neural network can correctly distribute existing experience to events the agent has never visited in exploration. The deep learning approach can be integrated into Q-learning without changing the basic principles. We cannot build the $Q(s, a)$ function the classical way, but we can make it using a neural network. The neural network models the $Q(s, a)$ function as follows: it takes input s and returns a vector a (one-dimensional tensor), where each value of this tensor represents the value of corresponding a_i action for state s, as shown in *Figure 9.4*:

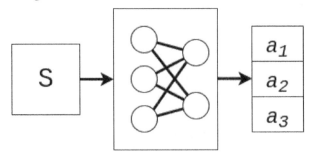

Figure 9.4: Neural Network as the Q(s, a) function

The basic implementation of this approach is Deep Q-Network or DQN is that a model implements an agent's actions using Neural Network as the $Q(s, a)$ function. Let's study how to design and train a neural network to model the $Q(s, a)$ function effectively.

Convergence of temporal difference and DQN training loss function

We will need to go back to the theory for a while to understand exactly how to train a neural network to implement a Q-learning approach. Consider the rule again for updating the value of $Q(s, a)$ function:

$$Q(s, a) \leftarrow Q(s, a) + \alpha \; temporal\_difference,$$

where: $temporal\_difference = r + \gamma \; max_{a'} Q(s', a') - Q(s, a) = r + \gamma \; V(s') - Q(s, a)$.

There is a law: *If temporal_difference converges to zero then Q(s, a)-function is being successfully trained.* It may be intuitively clear that the longer the exploration runs, the less new information the `temporal_difference` value provides. Let's reexamine the Maze Problem from *Chapter 6, Escaping Maze With Q-learning*. You can run the script that trains the agent to escape the maze: `ch9/td/q_learning_explore.py`. This script collects information about the temporal difference at each episode step. *Figure 9.5* shows that the temporal difference values gradually converge to zero. This means that $Q(s, a)$ stops updating from a particular moment, indicating that the $Q(s, a)$ function correctly determines the best action for each state.

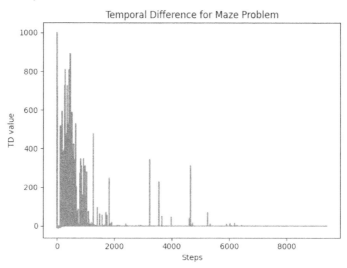

Figure 9.5: Temporal difference convergence

The fact that the temporal difference converges to zero in successful training is used to train the neural network that models the $Q(s, a)$ function. $Q(s, a)$ function must satisfy the following condition: $temporal\_difference = r + \gamma \; max_{a'} Q(s', a') - Q(s, a) \approx 0$, for historical exploration samples. And exactly this expression is used: $temporal\_difference = r + \gamma \; max_{a'} Q(s', a') - Q(s, a)$ as a loss function for neural network training of DQN model.

Replay buffer

In classical Q-learning, $Q(s, a)$ is updated based on the values s, a, r, and s', where:

- **s**: Existing state
- **a**: Action taken
- **r**: Reward after action a in state s
- **s'**: Next state after action a in state s

In DQN, many (s, a, r, s') samples are used for training. These samples are collected during exploration in a special buffer called **Replay Buffer**. It is called this because it replays events that have been already happened and allows the agent to retrain using collected historical data. Replay Buffer collects each (s, a, r, s') sample and returns some random *batch* from this collection for neural network training, as shown in *Figure 9.6*:

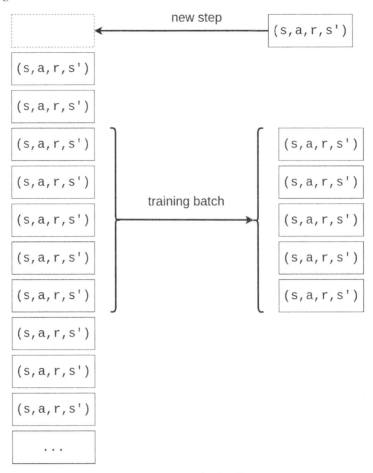

Figure 9.6: Replay Buffer

Here is the Python implementation of **ReplayBuffer** data structure **ch9/dqn/ replay_buffer.py**.

We import the necessary modules:

```
import numpy as np

import random

from collections import namedtuple, deque
```

The **ReplayBuffer** class is initialized with two variables:

- **buffer_size**: Maximum buffer size

- **batch_size**: Size of training batch

```
class ReplayBuffer:


    def __init__(self, buffer_size, batch_size):
        self.memory = deque(maxlen = buffer_size)
        self.batch_size = batch_size
        self.experience = namedtuple("Experience", field_names =
    ["state", "action", "reward", "next_state", "done"])
```

Adding new experience sample:

```
    def add(self, state, action, reward, next_state, done):
      e = self.experience(state, action, reward, next_state, done)
      self.memory.append(e)
```

The following method randomly samples a batch of experiences from memory:

```
    def sample(self, batch_size = None):
        """Randomly sample a batch of experiences from memory."""
        if batch_size is None:
            batch_size = self.batch_size

        experiences = random.sample(self.memory, k = batch_size)

        states = np.vstack([e.state for e in experiences if e is not None])
        actions = np.vstack([e.action for e in experiences if e is not None])
        rewards = np.vstack([e.reward for e in experiences if e is not None])
        next_states = np.vstack([e.next_state for e in experiences if e
is not None])
```

```
        dones = np.vstack([e.done for e in experiences if e is not
None]).astype(np.uint8)


        return states, actions, rewards, next_states, dones


    def __len__(self):
        """Return the current size of internal memory."""
        return len(self.memory)
```

As we can see, **ReplayBuffer** is a pretty simple data structure that just collects experience samples. **ReplayBuffer** is a primary component of DQN model.

DQN implementation

Similar to the previous chapter, in this chapter, we will provide two implementations of the DQN model: TensorFlow and PyTorch. Let's study one tensor method that will help us further. This method is called **gather**. The gather method collects values from the input tensor according to the passed indices. *Figure 9.7* illustrates the gather method in action:

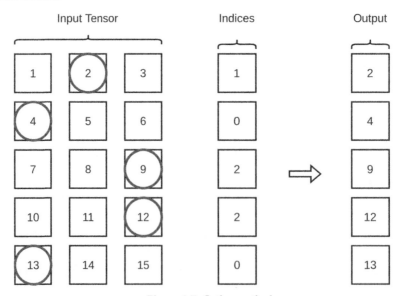

Figure 9.7: Gather method

TensorFlow and PyTorch have built-in **gather** methods, but their implementations are slightly differ. Therefore, here is a standard working style of this method:

```
TensorFlow >>>>>>>>>>
```

In TensorFlow, the **gather** method can be implemented using the helper function, as follows **ch9/utils.py**:

```
import tensorflow as tf


def tf_2d_gather(params, idx):
    idx = tf.stack([tf.range(tf.shape(idx)[0]), idx[:, 0]], axis = -1)
    out = tf.gather_nd(params, idx)
    out = tf.expand_dims(out, axis = 1)
    return out
```

Here is an application of this method **ch9/tf_gather.py**:

```
import tensorflow as tf
from ch9.utils import tf_2d_gather


params = tf.constant([[1, 2], [3, 4]])
idx = tf.constant([[0], [1]])


out = tf_2d_gather(params, idx)


print(out.numpy())
```

Result

```
[[1] [4]]
>>>>>>>>>> TensorFlow


PyTorch >>>>>>>>>>
```

PyTorch has a built-in **gather** method, and here is its application **ch9/pt_gather. py**:

```
import torch


params = torch.tensor([[1, 2], [3, 4]])
idx = torch.tensor([[0], [1]])
out = torch.gather(params, dim = 1, index = idx)


print(out.numpy())
```

Result

```
[[1] [4]]
```

`>>>>>>>>>> PyTorch`

The Neural Network is the computational core of DQN model. We will call it QNet. DQN can use various QNet architectures. QNet architecture of DQN model depends on the environment with which the agent interacts. Usually, fully connected or convolution neural networks are used for DQN model. This chapter will focus on a fully connected neural network with three linear layers as QNet implementation.

TensorFlow `>>>>>>>>>>` ch9/dqn/tf/q_model.py

```python
import tensorflow as tf
from keras.layers import Dense

class TfQNet(tf.keras.Model):
    """Q-Network. TensorFlow Implementation"""

    def __init__(self, state_size, action_size, fc1_units = 64, fc2_units = 64):
        """
            state_size: Dimension of state space
            action_size: Dimension of action space
            fc1_units: First hidden layer size
            fc2_units: Second hidden layer size
        """
        super(TfQNet, self).__init__()
        self.fc1 = Dense(units = fc1_units, activation = tf.nn.relu)
        self.fc2 = Dense(units = fc2_units, activation = tf.nn.relu)
        self.fc3 = Dense(units = action_size)

    def call(self, state, **kwargs):
        x = self.fc1(state)
        x = self.fc2(x)
        return self.fc3(x)
```

`>>>>>>>>>> TensorFlow`

PyTorch `>>>>>>>>>>` ch9/dqn/pt/q_model.py

```python
import torch.nn as nn

class PtQNet(nn.Module):
    """Q-Network. PyTorch Implementation"""

    def __init__(self, state_size, action_size, fc1_units = 64, fc2_
units = 64):
        """
            state_size: Dimension of state space
            action_size: Dimension of action space
            fc1_units: First hidden layer size
            fc2_units: Second hidden layer size
        """
        super(PtQNet, self).__init__()
        self.relu = nn.ReLU()
        self.fc1 = nn.Linear(state_size, fc1_units)
        self.fc2 = nn.Linear(fc1_units, fc2_units)
        self.fc3 = nn.Linear(fc2_units, action_size)

    def forward(self, state):
        x = self.relu(self.fc1(state))
        x = self.relu(self.fc2(x))
        return self.fc3(x)
>>>>>>>>>> PyTorch
```

Since we are dealing with two implementations (TensorFlow and PyTorch) of the DQN model, the general logic of the Agent is located in a separate base class: **BaseDqnAgent**. Let's examine its implementation **ch9/dqn/base_dqn_agent.py**.

We import the necessary modules:

```python
import random
import numpy as np
from ch9.dqn.replay_buffer import ReplayBuffer
```

DQN Agent is initialized using the following parameters:

- state_size: The size of environment state
- action_size: The size of action space
- degp_epsilon: Initial epsilon value for decayed epsilon-greedy policy
- degp_decay_rate: Ddecay rate for decayed epsilon greedy policy

- degp_min_epsilon: Minimal epsilon value
- learn_period: How often QNet is trained

```python
class BaseDqnAgent:

    def __init__(
            self,
            state_size,
            action_size,
            degp_epsilon = 1,
            degp_decay_rate = .9,
            degp_min_epsilon = .1,
            train_batch_size = 64,
            replay_buffer_size = 100_000,
            gamma = 0.99,
            learning_rate = 5e-4,
            learn_period = 1
    ):

        self.state_size = state_size
        self.action_size = action_size

        self.degp_epsilon = self.degp_initial_epsilon = degp_epsilon
        self.degp_decay_rate = degp_decay_rate
        self.degp_min_epsilon = degp_min_epsilon

        # Q-Network initialized in init_q_net method
        self.q_net = None
        self.optimizer = None
        self.loss = None
        self.learn_period = learn_period
        self.init_q_net(state_size, action_size, learning_rate)

        # Replay memory
        self.memory = ReplayBuffer(replay_buffer_size, train_batch_size)

        # Initialize time step (for updating every UPDATE_EVERY steps)
```

```
            self.training_steps_count = 0
            self.train_batch_size = train_batch_size
            self.replay_buffer_size = replay_buffer_size
            self.gamma = gamma
```

init_q_net is a framework-specific method that initializes QNet, its optimizer and loss function:

```
    def init_q_net(self, state_size, action_size, learning_rate):
        ...
```

Before each episode, *epsilon* is decreased according to decaying policy:

```
    def before_episode(self):
        self.degp_epsilon *= self.degp_decay_rate
        self.degp_epsilon = max(self.degp_epsilon, self.degp_min_
epsilon)
```

The **step** method is executed after each action taken by the agent. This method saves *(s, a, r, s')* sample to Replay Buffer and trains QNet.

```
    def step(self, state, action, reward, next_state, done):

        # Save experience in replay memory
        self.memory.add(state, action, reward, next_state, done)

        self.training_steps_count += 1
```

QNet is retrained according to the **self.learn_period** value:

```
        if self.training_steps_count % self.learn_period == 0:

            if len(self.memory) > self.train_batch_size:
                self.learn()
```

Agent takes actions according to epsilon-greedy policy. If Agent runs in train mode and random value is lower than **self.degp_epsilon**, then random action is taken. Otherwise, Agent selects action according to greedy policy:

```
    def act(self, state, mode = 'train'):
        """
        Returns the action
        mode = train|test
        """
```

```
r = random.random()
random_action = mode == 'train' and r < self.degp_epsilon

if random_action:
    # Random Policy
    action = random.choice(np.arange(self.action_size))
else:
    action = self.greedy_act(state)

return action
```

The **greedy_act** is a framework-specific method that returns action according to greedy policy for given state:

```
def greedy_act(self, state):
    return None
```

The **learn** method is a framework-specific method that trains QNet:

```
def learn(self):
    ...
```

The **save** method is a framework-specific method that saves QNet to path:

```
def save(self, path):
    ...
```

The load is a framework-specific method that loads QNet from path:

```
def load(self, path):
    ...
```

Next, we can proceed to the concrete implementations of the DQN model using TensorFlow and PyTorch.

TensorFlow >>>>>>>>>> ch9/dqn/tf/dqn_agent.py

We import the necessary modules:

```
import numpy as np
import tensorflow as tf
from ch9.dqn.base_dqn_agent import BaseDqnAgent
from ch9.dqn.tf.q_model import TfQNet
from ch9.utils import tf_2d_gather
```

TensorFlow implementation of DQN Agent inherits the **BaseDqnAgent** class:

```
class DqnTfAgent(BaseDqnAgent):

    def __init__(self, *args, **kwargs):
        super(DqnTfAgent, self).__init__(*args, **kwargs)
```

Initializing QNet, optimizer, and loss function:

```
    def init_q_net(self, state_size, action_size, learning_rate):
        self.q_net = TfQNet(state_size, action_size)
        self.q_net.build(input_shape = (1, state_size))
        self.optimizer = tf.keras.optimizers.Adam(learning_rate =
learning_rate)
        self.loss = tf.keras.losses.MeanSquaredError()
```

Greedy action evaluates QNet(*state*) $\rightarrow [a_1, .., a_n]$ and picks the index i, which has a maximum a_i value:

```
    def greedy_act(self, state):
        state = tf.constant(state, dtype = tf.float64)
        state = tf.expand_dims(state, axis = 0)
        action_values = self.q_net(state)
        return np.argmax(action_values.numpy())
```

And here, we come to the most intriguing part, which is the training process:

```
    def learn(self):
```

Agent receives history **samples** from **ReplayBuffer**:

```
        samples = self.memory.batch()
        s, a, r, s_next, dones = samples
```

Extracting QNet variables for optimization:

```
        variables = self.q_net.variables
```

Next, we have to minimize temporal difference: $r + \gamma V(s') - Q(s, a)$.

Calculating $V(s')$ value:

```
        v_s_next = tf.expand_dims(tf.reduce_max(self.q_net(s_next), axis
= 1), axis = 1)

        with tf.GradientTape() as tape:
```

Calculating $Q(s, a)$ value using the **gather** method:

```
q_sa_pure = self.q_net(s)
q_sa = tf_2d_gather(q_sa_pure, a)
```

Calculating Temporal Difference:

```
td = r + (self.gamma * v_s_next * (1 - dones)) - q_sa
```

Error value indicates how far Temporal Difference is from zero:

```
error = self.loss(td, tf.zeros(td.shape))
```

Optimizing QNet weights:

```
gradient = tape.gradient(error, variables)
self.optimizer.apply_gradients(zip(gradient, variables))
```

Additional **save** and **load** methods:

```
def save(self, path):
    self.q_net.save(path)


def load(self, path):
    self.q_net = tf.keras.models.load_model(path)
```

```
>>>>>>>>>> TensorFlow
```

```
PyTorch >>>>>>>>>> ch9/dqn/pt/dqn_agent.py
```

We import the necessary modules:

```
import numpy as np
import torch
import torch.optim as optim
from ch9.dqn.base_dqn_agent import BaseDqnAgent
from ch9.dqn.pt.q_model import PtQNet
```

PyTorch implementation of DQN Agent inherits the **BaseDqnAgent** class:

```
class DqnPtAgent(BaseDqnAgent):


    def __init__(self, *args, **kwargs):
        super(DqnPtAgent, self).__init__(*args, **kwargs)
```

Initializing QNet, optimizer, and loss function:

```
def init_q_net(self, state_size, action_size, learning_rate):
    self.q_net = PtQNet(state_size, action_size)
```

```
        self.optimizer = optim.Adam(self.q_net.parameters(), lr =
learning_rate)
        self.loss = torch.nn.MSELoss()
```

Greedy action evaluates QNet(*state*) → [a_1, .., a_n] and picks the index *i*, which has a maximum a_i value:

```
    def greedy_act(self, state):
        state = torch.from_numpy(state).float().unsqueeze(0)


        self.q_net.eval()


        with torch.no_grad():  # disabling gradient computation
            action_values = self.q_net(state)
        self.q_net.train()


        action = np.argmax(action_values.data.numpy())
        return action
```

And here, we come to the most intriguing part, which is the training process:

```
    def learn(self):
```

Agent receives history **samples** from **ReplayBuffer**:

```
        samples = self.memory.batch()
        s, a, r, s_next, dones = samples
```

Converting samples to PyTorch Tensors:

```
        s = torch.from_numpy(s).float()
        a = torch.from_numpy(a).long()
        r = torch.from_numpy(r).float()
        s_next = torch.from_numpy(s_next).float()
        dones = torch.from_numpy(dones).float()
```

Next, we have to minimize temporal difference: $r + \gamma\,V(s') - Q(s, a)$.

Calculating *V(s')* value:

```
        v_s_next = self.q_net(s_next).detach().max(1)[0].unsqueeze(1)
```

Calculating *Q(s, a)* value using the **gather** method:

```
        q_sa_pure = self.q_net(s)
```

```
q_sa = q_sa_pure.gather(dim = 1, index = a)
```

Calculating Temporal Difference:

```
td = r + (self.gamma * v_s_next * (1 - dones)) - q_sa
```

This **error** value indicates how far Temporal Difference is from zero:

```
error = self.loss(td, torch.zeros(td.shape))
```

Optimizing QNet weights:

```
self.optimizer.zero_grad()
error.backward()
self.optimizer.step()
```

Additional **save** and **load** methods:

```
def save(self, path):
    torch.save(self.q_net.state_dict(), path)


def load(self, path):
    self.q_net.load_state_dict(torch.load(path))
>>>>>>>>>> PyTorch
```

Amazing! We have created a DQN model, and now it's time to try it out on real problems.

Lunar Landing using DQN agent

Now, let's consider a rather sophisticated task of a lunar landing. Gym framework has a special environment called **LunarLander-v2**. The agent's goal in this environment is to land the spacecraft on the dedicated platform on the moon. The screen of LunarLander-v2 is shown in *Figure 9.8*:

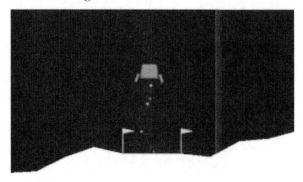

Figure 9.8: LunarLander-v2 environment screen

Environment generates a different landscape for each episode, but it has a flat pad between the yellow flags. A lunar lander must be landed on this flat pad.

States

State of the **LunarLander-v2** environment is represented by eight values:

- **s[0]**: This is the horizontal coordinate (*float*)
- **s[1]**: This is the vertical coordinate (*float*)
- **s[2]**: This is the horizontal speed (*float*)
- **s[3]**: This is the vertical speed (*float*)
- **s[4]**: This is the angle (*float*)
- **s[5]**: This is the angular speed (*float*)
- **s[6]**: 1 if first leg has contact, else 0 (*boolean*)
- **s[7]**: 1 if second leg has contact, else 0 (*boolean*)

As we can see, the number of different states of lunar lander is infinite. (Of course, it is finite, but it contains a huge number of states). The DQN model is a good application for this problem.

Actions

Four discrete actions are available for the agent:

- **do nothing**: Lander moves down
- **fire left orientation engine**: Lander moves right
- **fire main engine**: Lander moves up
- **fire right orientation engine**: Lander moves left

Environment

Fuel is infinite. A landing pad always has coordinates (0, 0). Lander coordinates are the first two numbers in the state vector (**s[0]**, **s[1]**). The reward for moving from the top of the screen to the landing pad with close to zero speed is about 100-140 points. If the lander moves away from the landing pad, it loses reward. The episode finishes if the lander crashes or comes to rest, receiving additional -100 or +100 points. Each leg ground contact gives 10 points. Firing the main engine costs -0.3 points for each frame. Yes, fuel is infinite, but it is better to save it. The episode is solved if the agent collects more than 200 points. Landing outside the landing pad is possible.

DQN application

The following source code folder contains trained DQN models for TensorFlow and PyTorch: **ch9/lunar_lander/saved_models** and before we start training a DQN agent, I would like to demonstrate how a trained agent solves the lunar landing problem.

TensorFlow:

```
$ python ch9/lunar_lander/eval_trained_tf.py
```

PyTorch:

```
$ python3 ch9/lunar_lander/eval_trained_pt.py
```

Nice, isn't it? Agent balances the lander straight to the pad. So, let's train the DQN model to do the same! The following is the training script of the DQN model **ch9/lunar_lander/train.py**.

We import the necessary modules:

```
import os
import random
import gym
import numpy as np
import matplotlib.pyplot as plt
from ch9.dqn.tf.dqn_agent import DqnTfAgent
from ch9.dqn.pt.dqn_agent import DqnPtAgent


cwd = os.path.dirname(os.path.abspath(__file__))
```

Initializing the environment:

```
env = gym.make('LunarLander-v2')
seed = 1


random.seed(seed)
env.seed(seed)
```

TensorFlow implementation (comment this if you are using PyTorch):

```
# TensorFlow Implementation
agent = DqnTfAgent(state_size = 8, action_size = 4)
save_path = cwd + '/saved_models/dqn_tf_agent'
```

PyTorch implementation (uncomment this if you are using PyTorch):

```
# PyTorch Implementation
# agent = DqnPtAgent(state_size = 8, action_size = 4)
# save_path = cwd + '/saved_models/dqn_pt_agent.pth'
```

Exploration process has 500 episodes:

```
episodes = 500


scores = []


for e in range(1, episodes + 1):


    state = env.reset()
    score = 0
```

Decaying epsilon value before each episode:

```
    agent.before_episode()


    while True:
```

Asking agent for next action:

```
        action = agent.act(state)
```

Passing action to **environment**:

```
        next_state, reward, done, _ = env.step(action)
```

Passing new data to agent and retraining it:

```
        agent.step(state, action, reward, next_state, done)
        state = next_state
        score += reward
        if done:
            break
```

Saving score for statistics:

```
    scores.append(score)

    if e % 10 == 0:
        print(f'Episode {e} Average Score: {np.mean(scores[-100:])}')
```

```
Saving trained DQN model:
agent.save(save_path)
Training results:
plt.plot(np.arange(len(scores)), scores)
plt.ylabel('Score')
plt.xlabel('Episode')
plt.show()
```

Result

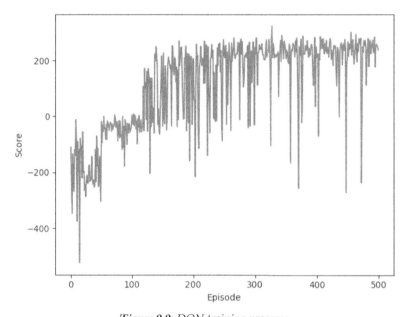

Figure 9.9: *DQN training progress*

Figure 9.9 demonstrates the training progress of the DQN model. Remember that the agent uses epsilon-greedy policy during exploration, which implies random actions. This explains a large number of deviations in the DQN Training Progress (*Figure 9.9*). In the last episodes of the exploration process, the agent achieved more than 200 points, which means that it learned to solve the problem successfully. And so, let's witness how a trained DQN agent controls the Lunar Lander **ch9/lunar_lander/ train.py**. (Full code is provided in corresponding source file.)

TensorFlow implementation (comment following lines if you are using PyTorch):

```
# TensorFlow Implementation
agent = DqnTfAgent(state_size = 8, action_size = 4)
load_path = cwd + '/saved_models/dqn_tf_agent'
```

PyTorch implementation (uncomment the following lines if you are using PyTorch):

```
# PyTorch Implementation
# agent = DqnPtAgent(state_size = 8, action_size = 4)
# load_path = cwd + '/saved_models/dqn_pt_agent.pth'
```

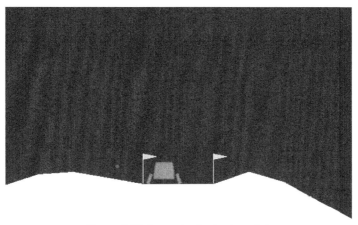

Figure 9.10: *Lunar lander in done state*

Voila! We just solved a rather tricky problem using deep reinforcement learning. The agent lands the lunar lander successfully in all cases. The solution we have just constructed confirms the promise of the deep reinforcement learning approach. You may think that this problem is too artificial, but the solution that was used in this chapter enabled you to make significant progress in the development of self-driving cars, robotics, and other areas of life. DQN method was first introduced only in 2013. Many problems are waiting for deep reinforcement learning to be solved. Therefore, you still have every chance to use it to create a solution for an entirely new problem.

Conclusion

In this chapter, we made a significant breakthrough! Markov's reward process theory and Q-learning are relatively old. deep learning techniques are younger but not new. In contrast, the Deep Q-Network approach is a brand new child of two different machine learning areas and opens up a new world, allowing us to construct sophisticated solutions to practical problems. This chapter introduced you to the basic principles of constructing a Deep Q-Network. These principles will be used in the upcoming chapters and will greatly help you develop your own custom models.

Points to remember

- To implement deep reinforcement learning for a problem with a large number of states, the agent must act in the same way in close states in most cases.

- Temporal difference converges to zero if the agent is being successfully trained.

Multiple choice questions

1. What is Replay Buffer is used for?

    a. To measure agent performance

    b. Collect history samples for QNet training

2. How does QNet indicate the best action for state s?

    a. Evaluates QNet(s) $\rightarrow$ [a_1,..., a_n] and picks the index i, which has a maximum a_i value

    b. Evaluates QNet(s) $\rightarrow$ [a_1,..., a_n] and picks a_1 value

Answers

1. **b**

2. **a**

Key terms

- **DQN (Deep Q-Network)**: Reinforcement learning based on neural networks that utilizes a deep Q-learning approach

- **QNet**: Core neural network of DQN model

    Replay Buffer: Collects agent's experience

CHAPTER 10

Defending Atlantis with Double Deep Q-Network

The previous chapter demonstrated that deep reinforcement learning significantly expands the scope of the problems to be solved. In this chapter, we will move to the most fascinating area of reinforcement learning problems: playing video games. This is an exciting challenge! I know many of us played video games before, and we remember how complicated the gameplay of certain levels was. This makes it interesting to see how artificial intelligence can learn to play video games. In this chapter, we will study more advanced techniques for building deep reinforcement learning models. We will learn to choose the right Q-Network architecture depending on the task and make the Double Deep Q-Network, a more advanced version of the Deep Q-Network. Finally, we'll apply our new knowledge to the Atari Atlantis video game.

Structure

In this chapter, we will discuss the following topics:

- Atlantis gameplay
- Atlantis environment
- Capturing motion

- Convolution Q-Network

- Double Deep Q-Network

- Defending Atlantis using DDQN

Objectives

After completing this chapter, you will learn how to apply deep reinforcement learning techniques to video games. You will also be able to construct Convolution Q-Networks and Double Deep Q-Networks Agents for complex reinforcement learning problems.

Atlantis gameplay

Atari games are the wonderful world of retro video games. Mature reinforcement learning professionals especially love Atari's game environments because it's an opportunity to revisit childhood for a while. In any case, the construction of agents for Atari games requires considerable effort and theoretical solutions, which can be applied in various real-world problems. In this chapter, we will examine the retro game called Atlantis. In this game, three cannons protect their artifacts from enemy planes. The game ends when the enemy planes have destroyed all of the player's artifacts. The game's goal is to collect as many points as possible by destroying the enemy planes. The screenshot of this game is shown in *Figure 10.1*:

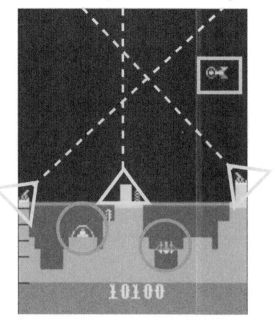

Figure 10.1: *Atlantis screen*

Figure 10.1 shows the following objects:

- **Protected artifacts**: Red circles
- **Guns**: Blue triangles
- **Planes**: Green rectangles

You can observe a Random Agent gameplay with the following script **ch10/ atlantis_env/random_play.py**:

```
import random
from time import sleep
import gym


env = gym.make('Atlantis-v0')
action_size = env.action_space.n


# Random Agent
env.reset()
while True:
    env.render()
    sleep(.05)
    img, reward, done, _ = env.step(random.randint(0, action_size - 1))
    if done:
        break
```

Even though this is an old game, it looks like a modern timekiller mobile application. In the next section, we will consider this game as a reinforcement learning environment.

Atlantis environment

Considering the video game Atlantis as a reinforcement learning environment, we need to define three key properties: *reward, action space,* and *state*.

Reward is the number of points received by the player for destroying the enemy plane. The total score is displayed at the bottom of the screen.

Action space contains four possible actions (or buttons):

- **0**: do nothing

- **1**: central cannon strike
- **2**: right cannon strike
- **3**: left cannon strike

Now, let's move on to a much more interesting question. What is a state in the Atlantis game? The player makes decisions about their actions based only on the game screen, so the environment state is the game screen, namely, the matrix of screen pixels. Actually, you can witness that the **Atlantis-v0** environment returns an array of the following size (210, 160, 3) in this script **ch10/env_state.py**:

```python
import gym

env = gym.make('Atlantis-v0')
action_size = env.action_space.n

state = env.reset()
print(state.shape)


>>> (210, 160, 3)
```

The color of each pixel in an colorful image can be represented in RGB (Red-Green-Blue) format; for example, white is (255,255,255), black is (0,0,0), yellow is (255,255,0), etc. This is why the first dimension of the tensor is screen height, the second is screen width, and the third is a color dimension in RGB format. *Figure 10.2* illustrates this concept:

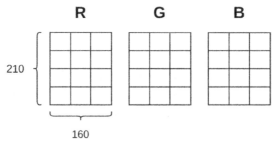

Figure 10.2: *Atlantis screen tensor*

Now, let's take a closer look at the Atlantis screen. Typically, the player only focuses on specific areas of the screen, which can be called **primary game areas**. The secondary areas of the screen have additional information, but they do not benefit the player during gameplay. It is better to help the agent's neural network by removing unnecessary parts from the screen before training. Below, we will investigate which parts of the screen are of primary importance to the player and whether something can be simplified to improve the agent's neural network training. Let's consider the following script **ch10/atlantis_env/screen_transformation.py**.

We import modules:

```
import random
import gym
import matplotlib.pyplot as plt
```

This script uses a helper method **image_rgb_to_grayscale**, to convert the image to grayscale and crop it. The details of its usage are given as follows:

```
from ch10.utils import image_rgb_to_grayscale
```

Initializing environment:

```
env = gym.make('Atlantis-v0')
action_size = env.action_space.n
```

Receiving environment state (screen) after 1000 random actions:

```
env.reset()
for _ in range(1000):
    img, reward, done, _ = env.step(random.randint(0, action_size - 1))
```

Let's visualize the state of the environment and examine it:

```
# Displaying RGB Full Game Screen
print(f'RGB image: {img.shape}')
plt.title("RGB Full Screen")
plt.xticks([])
plt.yticks([])
plt.imshow(img)
plt.show()
```

***Figure 10.3**: Atlantis RGB Full Screen*

Figure 10.3 illustrates the state of the environment after 1000 random actions. Let's try to isolate only useful information from it. Old fellows like me remember playing video games on black and white TVs. It may seem very strange to the new generation, but we used to play video games on black and white TVs. That happened because color TVs were a great luxury at that time. But often, the lack of color did not affect the player at all and sometimes, it even helped. Atlantis is one of the games that can be played in a grayscale format without damage. Therefore, we can convert the image to black and white:

```
# Displaying Grayscale Full Game Screen
gs_img = image_rgb_to_grayscale(img)
print(f'Gray Scale image: {gs_img.shape}')
plt.title("Grayscale Full Screen")
plt.xticks([])
plt.yticks([])
plt.imshow(gs_img, cmap = plt.get_cmap("gray"))
plt.show()
```

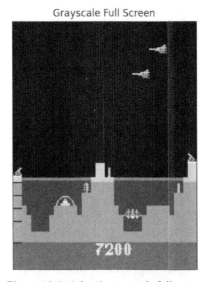

Figure 10.4: *Atlantis grayscale full screen*

Figure 10.4 shows the grayscale screen of the Atlantis game, and this screen allows the player to continue to play effectively despite the lack of RGB color. Indeed, guns, planes, and artifacts are perfectly distinguishable. We have reduced the number of elements in the state by three times: from (210, 160, 3) to (210, 160), but we still have room for optimization. The reader can notice that the bottom of the screen doesn't provides much useful information during gameplay. And since the main actions take place at the top of the screen, it seems reasonable to cut off the unnecessary part of the screen from the bottom by 80 pixels:

```
# Displaying Cropped Grayscale Game Screen
gs_img_cropped = image_rgb_to_grayscale(img, crop_down = 80)
plt.title("Grayscale Cropped Screen")
print(f'Gray Scale image Cropped: {gs_img.shape}')
plt.xticks([])
plt.yticks([])
plt.imshow(gs_img_cropped, cmap = plt.get_cmap("gray"))
plt.show()
```

Figure 10.5: *Atlantis cropped grayscale full screen*

Figure 10.5 demonstrates the most minimalist Atlantis gameplay ever. We reduced the amount of data in the state from $210 \times 160 \times 3 = 100800$ to $130 \times 160 = 20800$. Almost five times less data without losing any important data. This not only simplifies agent training but also significantly saves computational resources. In complex environments like the Atlantis game, state transformation plays an important role in building a successful reinforcement learning model.

Capturing motion

In the previous section, we explored the Atlantis game environment. We parsed the environment's state and developed an appropriate transformation to support the Q-Network to model the $Q(s)$ function better. However, another technique can significantly improve the performance of a reinforcement learning model. Let's look at *Figure 10.5* again. In which direction are the planes flying? Yes, we can suggest that planes are moving to the left since every plane has a front and a back. But for a neural network, this can be a tough challenge. It is challenging to learn the direction of an object's movement in a static image. So, we have to add motions to the state of the environment. But how can we achieve this goal? Well, the easiest way is to capture several pictures in a row. This method allows you to determine the direction of movement of objects and is especially important for self-driving cars.

We can see the data structure for the motion capturing **ch10/dqn/screen_motion.py**:

```
from collections import deque

import numpy as np


class ScreenMotion:
```

Number of frames in motion capture:

```
    frame_number = 5

    def __init__(self) -> None:
```

We will store one more image so that we can return the previous state:

```
        self.frames = deque(maxlen = ScreenMotion.frame_number + 1)
```

Adding state (image):

```
    def add(self, state):
        self.frames.append(state)
```

The following method returns **[1, 2, 3, 4, 5]** frames:

```
    def get_frames(self):
        F = ScreenMotion.frame_number
        stacks = []
        for i in range(1, F + 1):
            stacks.append(self.frames[i])
        return np.stack(stacks)
```

And the **get_prev_frames** method returns **[0, 1, 2, 3, 4]** frames, which is the previous state:

```
    def get_prev_frames(self):
        F = ScreenMotion.frame_number
        return np.stack([
```

```
            self.frames[i]
            for i in range(0, F)
        ])

    def is_full(self):
        return len(self.frames) == ScreenMotion.frame_number + 1
```

And so, we can now consider how motion capturing works **ch10/atlantis_env/ screen_frames.py**.

Importing modules:

```
import random

import gym

import matplotlib.pyplot as plt

from ch10.dqn.screen_motion import ScreenMotion

from ch10.utils import image_rgb_to_grayscale
```

Initializing environment:

```
env = gym.make('Atlantis-v0')

action_size = env.action_space.n
```

Declaring **ScreenMotion** object:

```
motion = ScreenMotion()
```

Executing 100 random actions in **Atlantis** environment and registering the motion:

```
env.reset()

for i in range(100):
    img, reward, done, _ = env.step(random.randint(0, action_size - 1))
    gs_img_cropped = image_rgb_to_grayscale(img, crop_down = 80)
    motion.add(gs_img_cropped)
```

Displaying last motion:

```
frames = motion.get_frames()

for i, f in enumerate(frames):
    plt.title(f"Frame: {i}")
    plt.xticks([])
    plt.yticks([])
    plt.imshow(f, cmap = plt.get_cmap("gray"))
    plt.show()
```

Figure 10.6 demonstrates the motion capture of **Atlantis**. It's simply five images in a row. The aircraft is moving right in these images. However, if we consider them as a whole, we can understand the object's movement direction. We will use the motion capture object as the state for the reinforcement learning model that will train an agent to play Atlantis. This means the environment state will be a tensor of size (5, 130, 160):

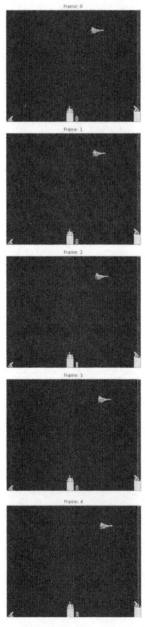

Figure 10.6: *Atlantis motion capture*

Convolution Q-Network

In this chapter, we are dealing with images and pattern recognition. Therefore, the Fully Connected Neural Network that we used as the Q-Network in *Chapter 9, Deep Q-Network and Lunar Lander,* is not suitable in this case. The neural architecture we used in the Handwritten Digit Recognition Problem in *Chapter 8, TensorFlow, PyTorch, and Your First Neural Network* is more appropriate for this task. Q-Network architecture is based on convolution layers, so we call it Convolution Q-Network:

```
TensorFlow >>>>>>>>>>
```

Convolution Q-Network has the following TensorFlow implementation **ch10/dqn/ tf/q_conv_model.py**.

Importing modules:

```
import tensorflow as tf
from keras.layers import Dense, Conv2D
from tensorflow.python.keras.layers import MaxPool2D, Flatten


class TfQConvNet(tf.keras.Model):
    """Actor (Policy) Model."""

    def __init__(self, action_size):
        super(TfQConvNet, self).__init__()
```

Declaring model layers:

```
        self.conv1 = Conv2D(
            filters = 8,
            kernel_size = 7,
            activation = tf.nn.relu
        )

        self.pool = MaxPool2D(pool_size = 3)

        # 2nd convolution layer
        self.conv2 = Conv2D(
            filters = 16,
            kernel_size = 5,
```

```
            activation = tf.nn.relu
    )


    # Flatten Layer
    self.flat = Flatten()


    self.fc1 = Dense(units = 256, activation = tf.nn.relu)
    self.fc2 = Dense(units = 32, activation = tf.nn.relu)
    self.fc3 = Dense(units = action_size)
```

Running neural network:

```
def call(self, x, **kwargs):
    """Build a network that maps state -> action values."""
    x = self.conv1(x)
    x = self.pool(x)
    x = self.conv2(x)
    x = self.pool(x)


    x = self.flat(x)


    x = self.fc1(x)
    x = self.fc2(x)
    x = self.fc3(x)
    return x


>>>>>>>>>> TensorFlow


PyTorch >>>>>>>>>>
```

Convolution Q-Network has the following PyTorch implementation **ch10/dqn/ pt/q_conv_model.py**.

Importing modules:

```
import torch
import torch.nn as nn
import torch.nn.functional as F
```

```
class PtQConvNet(nn.Module):
    """Actor (Policy) Model."""

    def __init__(self, frames, action_size):

        super(PtQConvNet, self).__init__()
```

Declaring model layers:

```
        self.conv1 = nn.Conv2d(
            in_channels = frames,
            out_channels = 8,
            kernel_size = 7
        )
        self.conv2 = nn.Conv2d(
            in_channels = 8,
            out_channels = 16,
            kernel_size = 5
        )

        self.flat = nn.Flatten()

        self.fc1 = nn.Linear(2880, 256)
        self.fc2 = nn.Linear(256, 32)
        self.fc3 = nn.Linear(32, action_size)
```

Running neural network:

```
    def forward(self, x):

        x = torch.relu(self.conv1(x))
        x = F.max_pool2d(x, 3)
        x = torch.relu(self.conv2(x))
        x = F.max_pool2d(x, 3)

        x = self.flat(x)

        x = torch.relu(self.fc1(x))
```

```
x = torch.relu(self.fc2(x))
x = self.fc3(x)
return x
```

>>>>>>>>>> PyTorch

Double Deep Q-Network

Deep Q-Network has one major issue that arises in some environments. It is called action-value overestimations. The problem of overestimations is that the Agent always chooses the non-optimal action in any given state because it has the maximum Q-value. That happens because the Agent knows nothing about the environment in the beginning. Initial Q-Networks have many noises, and we can't guarantee that the chosen action *a* in state *s* chosen by Q(s) function is the best one. These noises and deviations in Q(s) function make the training process very tough and unpredictable.

To prevent this issue, there is a technique that stabilizes the training process, and it is called **Double Deep Q-Network (DDQN)**. The essence of this technique is that the Agent uses two neural networks for training: Q_{main} (or Q_{local}) and Q_{target}. DDQN utilises Q_{main} and Q_{target} neural networks to reduce overestimation by decomposing the max operation in the target into action selection and action evaluation. Only the Q_{main} network is trained; Q_{target} is a copy of the Q_{main} network with some lag. Agent is trains Q_{main} minimizing the following expression:

$$r + \gamma \, max_{a'} Q_{target}(s', a') - Q_{main}(s, a)$$

Q_{main} optimizes its weights at each step according to Q_{target} values. And every N step, Q_{main} updates Q_{target}, bypassing its weights. *Figure 10.7* describes this concept:

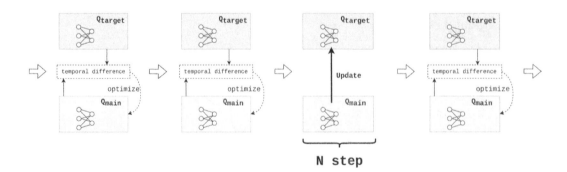

Figure 10.7: Double Deep Q-Network training

Q_{target} is several steps behind Q_{main}. Q_{target} plays the role of an anchor, which does not allow Q_{main} to deviate too much after each training iteration. This technique helps stabilize the learning process. Let's study the implementation of an agent using the Double DQN technique:

TensorFlow >>>>>>>>>>

TensorFlow implementation of DDQN is close to the DQN model we've studied in *Chapter 9, Deep Q-Network and Lunar Lander,* so we omit some code segments in the book. The following script implements the DDQN model using TensorFlow framework **ch10/dqn/tf/ddqn_conv_agent.py**.

```
class DqnConvTfAgent:
```

...

Initializing the Q_{main} and Q_{target} networks:

```
        self.net_main = TfQConvNet(action_size)

        self.net_target = TfQConvNet(action_size)


        self.net_main.build(input_shape = (train_batch_size, 130, 160,
frames))
        self.net_target.build(input_shape = (train_batch_size, 130, 160,
frames))
```

The Q_{main} network is trained using the following **learn** method:

```
    def learn(self):
```

Preparing data samples from **RepeatBuffer**:

```
        samples = self.memory.sample()

        s, a, r, s_next, dones = samples


        s_next = tf.transpose(s_next, perm = [0, 2, 3, 1])

        s = tf.transpose(s, perm = [0, 2, 3, 1])
```

Calculating $max_a\, Q_{target}(s', a)$ value:

```
        v_s_next = tf.expand_dims(tf.reduce_max(self.net_target(s_next),
axis = 1), axis = 1)


        variables = self.net_main.variables


        with tf.GradientTape() as tape:
```

Calculating $Q_{main}(s, a)$ value:

```
q_sa_pure = self.net_main(s)
q_sa = tf_2d_gather(q_sa_pure, a)


# td = r + gamma * V(s') - Q(s,a)
td = r + (self.gamma * v_s_next * (1 - dones)) - q_sa


# Compute loss
# TD -> 0
error = self.loss(td, tf.zeros(td.shape))
```

Executing Q_{main} optimization:

```
gradient = tape.gradient(error, variables)
self.optimizer.apply_gradients(zip(gradient, variables))
```

Updating Q_{target} each N steps:

```
if self.training_steps_count % self.update_period == 0:
    # update target network
    self.soft_update()
```

Q_{target} is updated using the **soft_update** method, which updates Q_{target} weights by the following expression:

$$W_{target} = \tau \times W_{main} + (1 - \tau) \times W_{target},$$

where τ is hyperparameter from 0 to 1.

```
    def soft_update(self):
        target_params = self.net_target.variables
        net_params = self.net_main.variables
        for i, (t_param, n_param) in enumerate(zip(target_params, net_
params)):
            blending_params = self.tau * n_param.numpy() + (1.0 - self.
tau) * t_param.numpy()
            target_params[i] = tf.Variable(blending_params)

        self.net_target.set_weights(target_params)


>>>>>>>>>> TensorFlow


PyTorch >>>>>>>>>>
```

PyTorch implementation of DDQN is close to the DQN model we've studied in *Chapter 9, Deep Q-Network and Lunar Lander,* so we omit some code segments in the book. The following script implements the DDQN model using PyTorch framework **ch10/dqn/pt/ddqn_conv_agent.py**:

```
class DdqnConvPtAgent:
```

...

Initializing the Q_{main} and Q_{target} networks:

```
        self.net_main = PtQConvNet(frames, action_size)
        self.net_target = PtQConvNet(frames, action_size)
```

The Q_{main} network is trained using the following learn method:

```
    def learn(self):
```

Preparing data samples from **RepeatBuffer**:

```
        samples = self.memory.sample()


        s, a, r, s_next, dones = samples


        # to PyTorch Tensors
        s = torch.from_numpy(s).float()
        a = torch.from_numpy(a).long()
        r = torch.from_numpy(r).float()
        s_next = torch.from_numpy(s_next).float()
        dones = torch.from_numpy(dones).float()
```

Calculating $max_a\,Q_{target}(s', a)$ value:

```
        v_s_next = self.net_target(s_next).detach().max(1)[0].
unsqueeze(1)
```

Calculating $Q_{main}(s, a)$ value:

```
        q_s = self.net_main(s)
        q_sa = q_s.gather(dim = 1, index = a)

        # td = r + gamma * V'(s') - Q(s,a)
        td = r + (self.gamma * v_s_next * (1 - dones)) - q_sa


        # Compute loss
```

```
# TD -> 0
loss = self.loss(td, torch.zeros(td.shape))
```

Executing Q_{main} optimization:

```
self.optimizer.zero_grad()
loss.backward()
self.optimizer.step()
```

Updating Q_{target} each N steps:

```
if self.training_steps_count % self.update_period == 0:
    # update target network
    self.soft_update()
```

Q_{target} is updated using the **soft_update** method, which updates Q_{target} weights by the following expression:

$$W_{target} = \tau \times W_{main} + (1 - \tau) \times W_{target},$$

where τ is hyperparameter from 0 to 1.

```
def soft_update(self):
    target_params = self.net_target.parameters()
    net_params = self.net_main.parameters()
    for t_param, n_param in zip(target_params, net_params):
        blending_params = self.tau * n_param.data + (1.0 - self.tau)
* t_param.data
        t_param.data.copy_(blending_params)
```

```
>>>>>>>>>> PyTorch
```

Since the DDQN model is ready, we can start training it to play the **Atlantis** game.

Defending Atlantis using DDQN

DDQN Agent training is not much different from DQN Agent training. The only difference we have for the Atlantis environment is using state transformation (grayscaling and cropping) and motion capture. Let's train the agent to play Atlantis videogame using the following script **ch10/train.py**.

Importing modules:

```
import os
```

```
import random
import gym
import numpy as np
import matplotlib.pyplot as plt
from ch10.dqn.screen_motion import ScreenMotion
from ch10.dqn.pt.ddqn_conv_agent import DdqnConvPtAgent
from ch10.dqn.tf.ddqn_conv_agent import DdqnConvTfAgent
from ch10.utils import image_rgb_to_grayscale
```

```
cwd = os.path.dirname(os.path.abspath(__file__))
```

Initializing Atlantis environment:

```
env = gym.make('Atlantis-v0')
action_size = env.action_space.n
seed = 1
```

```
random.seed(seed)
env.seed(seed)
```

DDQN Agent is initialized with the following parameters:

- **frames**: Number of frames in motion capture (is set to 5)
- **action_size**: Number of actions in action space (4 for Atlantis environment)
- **update_period**: How often Q_{target} is updated
- **train_batch_size**: Number of samples taken from **ReplayBuffer** for training
- **degp_min_epsilon**: Minimal epsilon value for decayed epsilon greedy policy
- **degp_epsilon**: Initial epsilon value for decayed epsilon greedy policy
- **degp_decay_rate**: Decay rate for decayed epsilon greedy policy
- **learning_rate**: Optimizer learning rate
- **replay_buffer_size**: **ReplayBuffer** capacity

```
# TensorFlow Implementation
agent = DqnConvTfAgent(
    frames = ScreenMotion.frame_number,
    action_size = action_size,
    update_period = 5,
    train_batch_size = 64,
    degp_min_epsilon = .1,
    degp_epsilon = .3,
    degp_decay_rate = .9,
    learning_rate = .0001,
    replay_buffer_size = 3_000
)
save_path = os.path.abspath(__file__) + '/saved_models/dqn_tf_
agent.tfh'
```

Please uncomment these lines to use PyTorch implementation of DDQN Agent:

```
# PyTorch Implementation
# agent = DdqnConvPtAgent(
#     frames = ScreenMotion.frame_number,
#     action_size = action_size,
#     update_period = 5,
#     train_batch_size = 64,
#     degp_min_epsilon = .1,
#     degp_epsilon = .3,
#     degp_decay_rate = .9,
#     learning_rate = .0001,
#     replay_buffer_size = 3_000
# )
# save_path = cwd + '/saved_models/dqn_pt_agent.pth'
```

We will use 50 episodes for training. This process can take hours:

```
# Training
training_episodes = 50
scores = []
avg_scores = []
```

```
last_best_average = 0
```

Iterating episodes:

```
for e in range(1, training_episodes + 1):

    state_rgb = env.reset()
    # converting image
    state = image_rgb_to_grayscale(state_rgb, crop_down = 80)
    score = 0

    agent.before_episode()

    motion = ScreenMotion()
```

New episode:

```
    while True:
```

We do not do anything until the motion container has minimum six frames:

```
        if not motion.is_full():
            action = 0  # none
        else:
            action = agent.act(motion.get_frames())
```

Sending action to environment:

```
        next_state_rgb, reward, done, _ = env.step(action)
```

Converting image:

```
        next_state = image_rgb_to_grayscale(next_state_rgb, crop_
down = 80)
```

Adding image to motion frames:

```
        motion.add(next_state)

        # If motion is full then perform agent.step
        if motion.is_full():
            agent.step(
                motion.get_prev_frames(),
                action,
```

```
                    reward,
                    motion.get_frames(),
                    done
                )

            state = next_state
            score += reward
```

Exit the episode loop on done:

```
            if done:
                break
```

Collecting statistics:

```
        scores.append(score)
        avg_scores.append(np.mean(scores[-min(10, len(scores)):]))

        print(f'Episode: {e}. Score: {round(score)}. '
              f'Avg Score: {round(avg_scores[-1])}')
```

Displaying training results:

```
plt.plot(scores)
plt.plot(avg_scores, label = 'Average Score')
plt.ylabel('Score')
plt.xlabel('Episode')
plt.plot()
plt.show()
```

Saving the agent:

```
agent.save(save_path)
```

Figure 10.8 demonstrates the DDQN Agent training progress. It shows that the agent usually achieves 25,000 scores each game episode. It is a pretty satisfactory result:

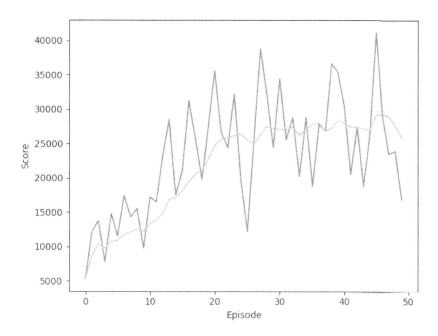

Figure 10.8: *DDQN Agent training progress*

The training process is challenging and lengthy for videogames environments. You can use the trained model to perform the battle Random Agent VS DDQN Agent. Indeed, we have to witness that DDQN Agent performs better than the Random agent, which pushes gamepad buttons randomly. Let's execute the battle using the following script **ch10/ddqn_vs_random.py**.

Importing modules:

```
import os
import random
import numpy as np
import gym
from ch10.dqn.pt.ddqn_conv_agent import DdqnConvPtAgent
from ch10.dqn.screen_motion import ScreenMotion
from ch10.utils import image_rgb_to_grayscale
```

Initializing Atlantis environment:

```
cwd = os.path.dirname(os.path.abspath(__file__))

env = gym.make('Atlantis-v0')
```

```
action_size = env.action_space.n


seed = 2

random.seed(seed)

env.seed(seed)
```

DDQN Agent setup:

```
ddqn_agent = DdqnConvPtAgent(
    frames = ScreenMotion.frame_number,
    action_size = action_size
)
load_path = cwd + '/saved_models/dqn_pt_agent_saved.pth'
ddqn_agent.load(load_path)
```

Random Agent setup:

```
def random_agent():
    return random.randint(0, action_size - 1)
```

We will execute 10 rounds (that is, **episodes**) for each agent and compare the results after:

```
ddqn_score_list = []
random_score_list = []
episodes = 10
```

Running 10 episodes for DDQN Agent:

```
for e in range(1, episodes + 1):
    state_rgb = env.reset()
    state = image_rgb_to_grayscale(state_rgb)
    score = 0
    motion = ScreenMotion()
    i = 0
    while True:
        i += 1
```

Rendering **Atlantis** screen:

```
        env.render()
        sleep(.005)
```

Smart agents usually suffer from button-jamming problems. The agent presses the same button, and the environment perceives this action as pressing the button, which leads to no action. We will release the button every odd frame:

```
if i % 2 != 0 or not motion.is_full():
    action = 0  # none
else:
    action = ddqn_agent.act(motion.get_frames(), mode = 'test')


next_state_rgb, reward, done, _ = env.step(action)


next_state = image_rgb_to_grayscale(next_state_rgb, crop_down = 80)
motion.add(next_state)
state = next_state
score += reward


if done:
    print(f'DDQN. Round {e}: {score}')
    ddqn_score_list.append(score)
    break
```

Running 10 episodes for random agent:

```
for e in range(1, episodes + 1):
    env.reset()
    score = 0
    while True:
```

Rendering **Atlantis** screen:

```
        env.render()
        sleep(.005)


        action = random_agent()
        next_state_rgb, reward, done, _ = env.step(action)
        score += reward
        if done:
            print(f'Random. Round {e}: {score}')
```

```
        random_score_list.append(score)
        break
```

Displaying results:

```
print(f'Average DDQN Score: {np.mean(ddqn_score_list)}')
print(f'Average Random Score: {np.mean(random_score_list)}')
```

The results of this battle are shown below:

	DDQN Score	Random Score
Episode 1	20 700	16 500
Episode 2	23 600	9 900
Episode 3	17 300	12 800
Episode 4	26 200	10 000
Episode 5	27 800	12 700
Episode 6	29 300	22 000
Episode 7	22 800	11 000
Episode 8	18 700	18 800
Episode 9	13 300	14 100
Episode 10	15 100	12 500
Average	21 480	14 030

Table 10.1: *DDQN Agent vs Random Agent*

Table 10.1 demonstrates that DDQN significantly outperforms Random Agent. This is a good result, which proves that the DDQN Agent learned several patterns of playing this game. If you have ever played such games, you might know how it can be challenging to win against a player who just randomly pushes gamepad buttons.

Conclusion

The principles we discussed in this chapter have far-reaching applications. Here, we considered the environment state represented not just as a set of metric data but as an image, which significantly complicates the task. Convolution Q-Networks and different variations of DQN are used for self-driving cars, autopilot, etc. In the next chapter, we will study a new approach to solving reinforcement learning problems called the Policy-Gradient method. We will see how neural networks can be used more efficiently to solve reinforcement learning problems.

Points to remember

- Image or screen can be considered as environment state.

- Convolution Q-Networks are designed to extract patterns and objects from environment's screen.

- Motion Capturing technique is used to understand the direction of object's movement.

Multiple choice questions

1. Suppose we would not use image cropping to train the DDQN agent but use the full-screen image, as shown in *Figure 10.9*.

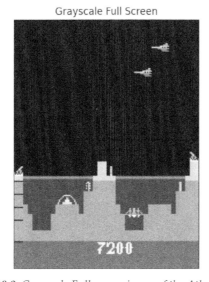

Figure 10.9: Grayscale Full-screen image of the Atlantis game

Which of the following statements is correct?

    a. It will not affect Agent's training.

    b. Agent will not be able to learn anything.

    c. It will make training more difficult, but the Agent will be able to learn.

2. Recall the soft update formula used to update the weights of the Q_{target} network:

$$W_{target} = \tau \times W_{main} + (1 - \tau) \times W_{target.}$$

What happens if we set $\tau = 1$?

   a. Agent will not be able to learn anything.

   b. It will make the training more difficult, but the agent will still be able to learn.

Answers

1. c

2. a

Key terms

- **Double Deep Q-Network (DDQN)**: A reinforcement learning model that utilizes two neural networks to reduce overestimation by decomposing the max operation in the target into action selection and action evaluation.

## CHAPTER 11

From Q-Learning to Policy-Gradient

Till now, we have been focusing on value-based approaches (that is, Q-learning) for solving reinforcement learning problems. This approach involves constructing a $Q(s, a)$ function that determines the value of each action. In the exploitation mode, the value-based approach selects the action that has the highest value. It means that the Q-learning method behaves deterministically, i.e., the agent does the same action in the same states. In this chapter, we will consider a different approach for solving reinforcement learning problems, which is called the policy-based method. This approach allows us to solve the problems in which the Q-learning method is not good enough.

Structure

In this chapter, we will discuss the following topics:

- Stochastic Policy
- Stochastic Policy vs Deterministic Policy
- Parametric Policy
- Neural network as Parametric Stochastic Policy
- Policy Gradient method

- Policy Gradient implementation

- Solving CartPole problem

Objectives

After completing this chapter, you will learn a new approach to solving reinforcement learning problems called **stochastic policies**. You will be able to construct stochastic policies and optimize them using policy gradient method.

Stochastic Policy

We will start with a description of stochastic policies. These are policies that operate only with the probabilities of actions. A stochastic policy returns the probability of each action to be taken for a given state s:

$$\pi(s) \rightarrow [p_1, p_2, p_3],$$

Where:

- p_1 is probability of action a_1

- p_2 is probability of action a_2

- p_3 is probability of action a_3.

Concrete action is chosen randomly according to the probability of each action returned by stochastic policy. *Figure 11.1* illustrates this concept:

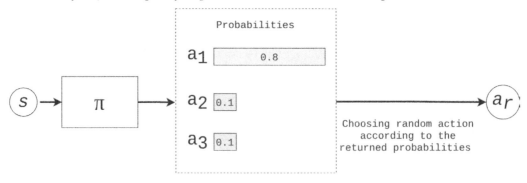

Figure 11.1: *Stochastic policy*

Stochastic policy assumes that you do not have to define unique action for each state, but you have a probability distribution for actions to take.

Stochastic Policy vs Deterministic Policy

To determine the benefits of a stochastic policy, let's compare it with a deterministic policy. A deterministic policy has no randomness and always returns the same action for the same state. Q-learning method is a deterministic policy because an action is selected according to the maximum value: $max_a Q(s, a)$.

A classic example of comparing stochastic and deterministic policies is the rock-paper-scissors game. Suppose we need to determine the optimal policy for playing *rock-paper-scissors* with a live opponent. The Q-learning method analyzed the history of 10,000 rounds and concluded that:

- **paper**: won 33.34% times

- **scissors**: won 33.33% times

- **rock**: won 33.33% times

Based on these statistics, the Q-learning method will build the following $Q(s, a)$ action-value function:

- $Q(s, paper) = 33.34$

- $Q(s, scissors) = 33.33$

- $Q(s, rock) = 33.33$

Since the Q-learning method selects only one action according to the given formula: *maxa Q(s, a)*, the agent will always show the paper. After a while, the opponent will realize that the agent is showing nothing but paper and will start showing scissors. This makes the Q-learning approach useless for this task.

Stochastic policy, after analyzing 10,000 rounds, will return the probability of each action: (paper=0.3334, scissors=0.3333, rock=0.3333). All actions are almost equally likely, so the agent will play unpredictably and will choose a random action according to the probability distribution: (paper=0.3334, scissors=0.3333, rock=0.3333).

Another good example shows the difference between determined policy and stochastic policy. Let's consider the following problem; say we have a maze, as shown in *Figure 11.2*:

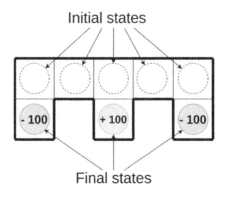

Figure 11.2: *Maze*

The agent starts the episode from a random square in the top row, with a goal to find a +100 reward cell. The agent can perform the following actions: *left*, *right*, *down*. The state of the environment is the border of the cell in which the agent is located.

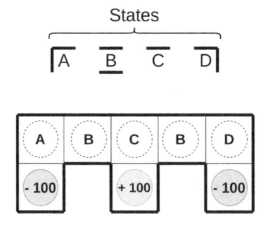

Figure 11.3: *Maze states*

Figure 11.3 shows that we have a maze environment with four different states:

    A. *Left* border and *Top* border

    B. *Top* border and *Bottom* border

    C. *Top* border

    D. *Right* border and *Top* border.

Let's try to determine the optimal deterministic policy for this problem. We need to select the optimal action for each state. Let's try to use the following policy:

- Right
- Right
- Down
- Left

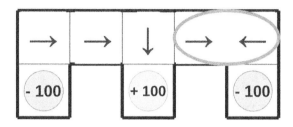

Figure 11.4: *Deterministic policy; B – right*

Figure 11.4 shows that the policy we defined above creates an infinite loop. Indeed, if an agent starts an episode from cells from the right, then it is doomed to endless movement. Obviously, this cannot be an acceptable solution. But the same thing happens if we choose *left* as the optimal action for state **B**. *Figure 11.5* demonstrates that we have an infinite loop again.

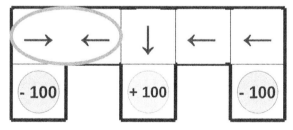

Figure 11.5: *Deterministic policy; B – left*

As we can see, no deterministic policy can properly solve this problem for any initial state.

But let's take a look at how stochastic policy solves this problem. Stochastic policy operates with probabilities, so we can define the following policy:

- *right – 100%*
- *right – 50%, left – 50%*
- *down – 100%*
- *left – 100%*

Figure 11.6 illustrates this stochastic policy:

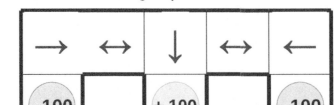

Figure 11.6: *Stochastic policy*

The stochastic policy takes random actions for B state: left or right. This saves the agent from an infinite loop. Whatever initial state the agent is in, it will be able to complete the episode with a +100 reward.

These examples show the superiority of stochastic policies over deterministic ones. Some tasks can only be solved using stochastic policies. Employing a predefined action for each state is too restrictive for the agent in deterministic policy. And every deterministic policy can be expressed in terms of a stochastic policy, but not vice versa. Indeed, *the deterministic policy taking action a in state s* is equivalent to *a stochastic policy taking action a with 100% probability in state s*. This fact will allow us to solve problems that are solved by deterministic policies (that is, Q-learning) and also effectively solve another range of reinforcement learning problems.

Parametric policy

A parametric policy is a policy whose behavior depends on parameters. This policy has some predefined rules, but these rules are based on one or several parameters. A parametric policy can be demonstrated with the following example **ch11/param_policy/policy.py**.

Say we have a simple stochastic policy π that classifies dogs and cats. It means that we have a set of cats and dogs, and stochastic policy is a tool that helps to identify an animal. π policy is receives animal's weight and returns probabilities according to the following formula:

- **dog_probability**: $\max(0, \min(1, a \times weight + b))$

- **cat_probability**: $1 - dog\_probability$

This policy depends on the following parameters: $a, b,$ and we can sign this policy as $\pi(weight; a, b)$. Policy $\pi(weight; a, b)$ is implemented the following way:

```
import random
import numpy as np
import matplotlib.pyplot as plt

class DogVsCatPolicy:
```

Policy declares **a**, **b** as its global parameters:

```
    def __init__(self) -> None:
        """

        a, b - policy parameters
        """

        super().__init__()
        self.a = .1
        self.b = -.5
```

The **act** method returns **dog_probability** and **cat_probability** by the given weight:

```
    def act(self, weight):
        dog_p = max(0, min(1, self.a * weight + self.b))
        cat_p = 1 - dog_p
        return [cat_p, dog_p]
```

The **act_sample** samples real action by given probabilities (by action, we mean the choice of dog or cat.):

```
    def act_sample(self, weight):
        probs = self.act(weight)
        action = np.random.choice([0, 1], p = [probs[0], probs[1]])
        return action
```

Let's examine the $\pi(weight; a, b)$ policy in action:

```
if __name__ == '__main__':

    agent = DogVsCatPolicy()

    # Evaluating the Policy
    seed = 1
    np.random.seed(seed)
    random.seed(seed)
```

Let's classify animal by the **weight = 7**:

```
w = 7
action = agent.act_sample(w)
if action == 0:
    print('Cat')
else:
    print('Dog')
```

Policy π(**weight; a, b)** with initial params **(a=0.1, b=-0.5)** returns **Cat** as the action for an animal with **weight = 7**, which is quite likely.

And this policy could be visualized as follows:

```
# Policy Visualization

w_list = range(0, 20)
is_dog_prob = [agent.act(w)[1] for w in w_list]
plt.title('Dog VS Cat Policy')
plt.xlabel('Weight')
plt.ylabel('Dog Probability')
plt.grid()
plt.plot(is_dog_prob)
plt.show()
```

Figure 11.7 shows the probability distribution of dog selection by animal's weight:

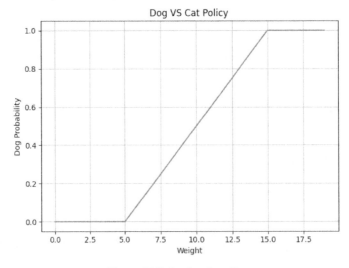

***Figure 11.7**: Stochastic policy*

Yes, this is a very primitive policy, but nevertheless, it can classify cats and dogs quite effectively. All we need is to pick policy parameters (a, b) that solve the problem with the best accuracy.

Say we have the following "*cats and dogs*" dataset **ch11/param_policy/dataset.py** representing different breeds of cats and dogs, and we can consider it representative. Therefore, if we optimize the parameters **a** and **b** for the "*cats and dogs*" dataset, we can assume that the policy π(**weight; a, b)** will operate optimally for an arbitrary individual of a cat or dog. The simplest thing we can do is iterate over all possible combinations of **a** and **b** values and choose the ones that perform best on the "*cats and dogs*" dataset. Let's perform this optimization using the following script **ch11/param_policy/optimize.py**.

We import the necessary modules:

```
import numpy as np
import random
import matplotlib.pyplot as plt
from ch11.param_policy.dataset import cats_and_dogs_dataset
from ch11.param_policy.policy import DogVsCatPolicy
```

Making script reproducible:

```
seed = 1
np.random.seed(seed)
random.seed(seed)
```

We define the set of possible **a** and **b** values as **[-5, -4.5, -4, ..., 4.5, 5]**:

```
step_num = 21
a_list = np.linspace(-5, 5, num = step_num)
b_list = np.linspace(-5, 5, num = step_num)
```

Initializing π(**weight; a, b)** policy:

```
agent = DogVsCatPolicy()
```

Iterating all (**a, b**) combinations on the *cats and dogs dataset*:

```
dataset = cats_and_dogs_dataset
accuracy_map = {}
for a in a_list:
    for b in b_list:
        accuracy = 0
        agent.a = a
```

```
agent.b = b
for el in dataset:
    action = agent.act_sample(el[0])
    if action == el[1]:
        accuracy += 1
accuracy_map[(a, b)] = accuracy
```

After the search is complete, we can visualize the results:

```
best_params = max(accuracy_map, key = accuracy_map.get)
print(f'Best params: a={best_params[0]}, b={best_params[1]}')

z = np.array([accuracy_map[(a, b)] for a in a_list for b in b_list])
Z = z.reshape(step_num, step_num)

plt.title(f'Best params: a={best_params[0]}, b={best_params[1]}')
plt.xlabel('b')
plt.ylabel('a')
plt.imshow(Z, extent = [-5, 5, -5, 5], cmap = 'gray')
plt.colorbar()
plt.show()
```

Figure 11.8 shows the optimization results. **a=0.5** and **b=-3** are optimal parameters:

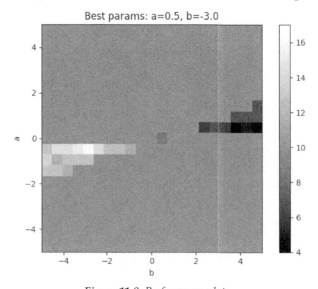

Figure 11.8: Performance plot

And finally, we can visualize the $\pi(weight; 0.5, -3)$ policy. *Figure 11.9* contains probability distribution for dog selection depending on animal's *weight*:

```
agent.a = best_params[0]
agent.b = best_params[1]
w_list = range(0, 20)
is_dog_prob = [agent.act(w)[1] for w in w_list]
plt.title('Dog VS Cat Policy')
plt.xlabel('Weight')
plt.ylabel('Dog Probability')
plt.grid()
plt.plot(is_dog_prob)
plt.show()
```

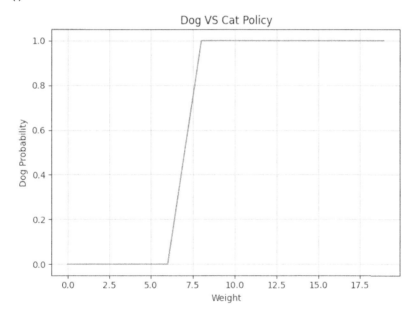

Figure 11.9: $\pi(weight; 0.5, -3)$ policy

This simple example demonstrates an illustration of stochastic policy optimization. However, we have two main problems here:

- **We are using predefined logic in the policy** π: Indeed, at the beginning, we defined the probability function as: $max(0, min(1, a \times weight + b))$. But why did we decide that this particular function would be optimal? Why not this one $max(0, min(1, a \times log(\mathbf{weight}) + b))$? Or maybe it was necessary to use a fundamentally different approach?

- **Parameter optimization**: In this case, we went through all possible combinations of parameters. But in practice, this is not feasible. Reinforcement learning problems generate too much data, and it will take a lot of time to try out each combination.

In the following two sections, we will examine how each of the above problems is solved.

Neural network as Parametric Stochastic Policy

As we have already seen, neural networks allow us to solve rather complex problems and develop complex decision-making logic. At the same time, the same architecture of the neural network can implement completely different behavior models depending on the conditions set. Therefore, it would be natural to build a parametric stochastic policy π based on the neural network architecture and use the weights of the neural network layers as policy parameters θ. *Figure 11.10* explains this concept:

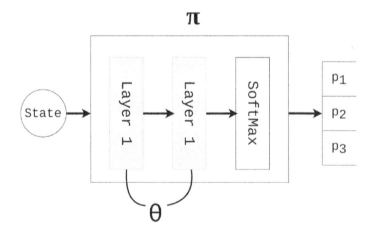

Figure 11.10: *Neural Network as Stochastic Policy Implementation*

Neural Network-based stochastic policies use the **softmax** function as final activation. Usually, these policies are noted as $\pi(\theta)$, where θ is the weights of the neural network layers.

Policy Gradient method

And now, we come to the central part of this chapter, dedicated to Policy Gradient Method. The Policy Gradient Method defines an iterative algorithm for finding optimal parameter θ for a stochastic parametric policy $\pi(\theta)$. The main goal of the Policy Gradient method is to find the θ parameter at which the agent acting according to the policy $\pi(\theta)$ collects the maximum reward. This search method performs directional shifts on the θ parameter according to the following formula:

$$\theta_{n+1} = \theta_n + \alpha \nabla_\theta(T_n; \pi(\theta_n)), \qquad\qquad (1)$$

Where:

- θ_{n+1} – new θ parameter

- θ_n – previous θ parameter

- T_n – is an experience (or trajectory) $(s_0, a_0, r_0; s_1, a_1, r_1; \dots)$ generated by policy $\pi(\theta_n)$ in Episode n.

- s, a, r denote state, action, and reward accordingly.

- $\nabla_\theta(T_n; \pi(\theta_n))$ – value that shifts parameter θ_n according to new experience T_n. It is called as policy gradient.

- α – learning rate parameter

Expression $\nabla_\theta(T_n; \pi(\theta_n))$ looks scary, but it is just a simple vector $(\theta'_{1,n}, \dots, \theta'_{m,n})$ that shifts parameter θ_n.

Policy Gradient algorithm performs the following steps:

1. Random θ parameter is initialized

2. Agent with policy $\pi(\theta)$ executes an episode collecting experience $T = (s_0, a_0, r_0; s_1, a_1, r_1; \dots)$.

3. $\nabla_\theta(T; \pi(\theta))$ – policy gradient value is calculated. This value aims to shift parameter θ for the better.

4. θ is updated according the following formula: $\theta = \theta + \alpha \nabla_\theta(T; \pi(\theta))$

5. If a terminal condition is not reached, go back to step 2.

Figure 11.11 illustrates the Policy Gradient algorithm:

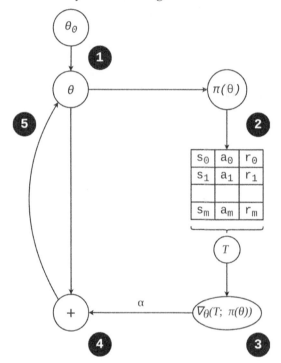

Figure 11.11: *Policy Gradient algorithm*

Everything looks nice and clear, but we need to determine how to calculate the policy gradient. We will not dive deep into mathematical calculations, but we will use a ready-made formula for calculating the policy gradient:

$$\nabla_\theta(T; \pi(\theta)) = \nabla_\theta (\sum_{i=0}^{N} \log[\pi(a_i|s_i; \theta)] G_i) \qquad (2)$$

Where:

- $\pi(a_i|s_i; \theta)$: a probability of action a_i in state s_i returned by policy $\pi(\theta)$.

- $G_i = \sum_{k=0}^{\infty} \gamma^k r_{i+k}$: discounted cumulative reward collected during episode T after a_i action. We have covered G_i expression in *Chapter 5, Blackjack in Monte Carlo*.

- ∇_θ: function's gradient by θ parameter

Well, it didn't get any easier. Let's try to look at the intention of the formula (2). Its main point is to change θ parameter so that the probability of actions with high G_t increases, and the probability of actions with low G_t decreases. *Figure 11.12* demonstrates policy gradient calculation in action:

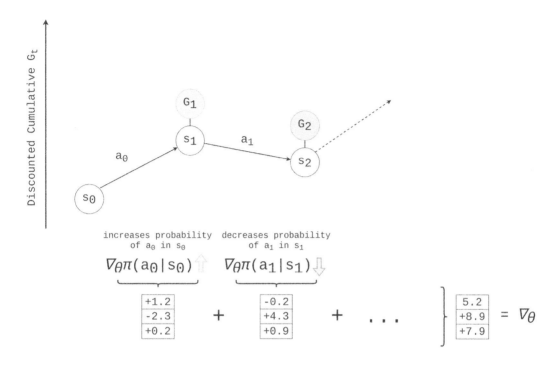

***Figure 11.12**: Policy Gradient calculation in action*

While the mathematical formulas may discourage you, the policy gradient method has a clear physical meaning. The policy $\pi(\theta)$ is adjusted after each episode to increase the expected total reward given the new experience that has appeared since the last episode. By repeating this process a sufficient number of times, the θ-parameter approaches the optimal one. Thus, policy $\pi(\theta)$ adapts to the environment, receiving the maximum possible reward.

Policy Gradient implementation

After the theoretical part, we can start implementing the policy gradient method practically. We'll start with a **Buffer** object that stores the episode's history **ch11/ utils.py**:

```
class Buffer:

    def __init__(self) -> None:
        self.rewards = []
        self.actions = []
```

```
        self.states = []

    def clear(self):
        self.rewards = []
        self.actions = []
        self.states = []

    def add(self, r, a, s):
        self.rewards.append(r)
        self.actions.append(a)
        self.states.append(s)

    def unzip(self):
        return self.rewards, self.actions, self.states
```

And now, we can start implementing using the deep learning framework:

```
TensorFlow >>>>>>>>>>
```

Let's follow this script **ch11/policy_gradient/tf_policy_net.py** with TensorFlow policy gradient method implementation.

We import the necessary modules:

```
import tensorflow as tf

import numpy as np

from tensorflow.keras.layers import Dense

from tensorflow.keras.optimizers import Adam

from tensorflow.python.ops.distributions.categorical import Categorical
```

Stochastic parametric policy $\pi(\theta)$ realized by the **TfPolicyNet** class:

```
class TfPolicyNet(tf.keras.Model):
```

Next, we define a fully connected neural network with two linear layers:

```
    def __init__(self, action_space):
        super().__init__()
        self.linear1 = Dense(32, activation = 'relu')
        self.linear2 = Dense(action_space, activation = 'softmax')
        self.opt = Adam()


    def call(self, x):
```

```
        x = tf.convert_to_tensor(x)
        x = self.linear1(x)
        x = self.linear2(x)
        return x
```

$\pi(\theta)$ acts as follows:

```
    def act_sample(self, state):
```

Neural network returns the probability of each action:

```
        prob = self(np.array([state]))
```

We build distribution **dist** using returned probabilities **prob**:

```
        dist = Categorical(probs = prob, dtype = tf.float32)
```

Sampling random action according to the distribution **dist**:

```
        action = dist.sample()
        return int(action.numpy()[0])
```

The next method updates Neural Network θ using the Policy Gradient method:

```
    def update(self, buffer, gamma):
```

Unpacking episode history:

```
        rewards, actions, states = buffer.unzip()
```

Counting discounted rewards G_t:

```
        sum_reward = 0
        discnt_rewards = []
        rewards.reverse()
        for r in rewards:
            sum_reward = r + gamma * sum_reward
            discnt_rewards.append(sum_reward)
        discnt_rewards.reverse()

        with tf.GradientTape() as tape:
```

Calculating $\nabla_\theta(T; \pi(\theta)) = \nabla_\theta (\sum_{i=0}^{N} \log[\pi(a_i|s_i; \theta)] G_i)$ value:

```
            prob = self(np.array(states), training = True)
            dist = Categorical(probs = prob, dtype = tf.float32)
            log_prob = dist.log_prob(actions)
```

```
E = log_prob * discnt_rewards
```

Since our goal is to maximize **E**, and neural network optimizers are made for minimization, we change the **E** value sign:

```
loss = -E
```

Executing gradient shift $\theta = \theta + \alpha \, \nabla_\theta (T; \pi(\theta))$:

```
grads = tape.gradient(loss, self.trainable_variables)
self.opt.apply_gradients(zip(grads, self.trainable_variables))
```

>>>>>>>>>> TensorFlow

PyTorch >>>>>>>>>>

Let's follow this script **ch11/policy_gradient/pt_policy_net.py** with PyTorch policy gradient method implementation.

We import the necessary modules:

```
import torch
import torch.nn as nn
import torch.nn.functional as F
from torch.distributions import Categorical
```

Stochastic parametric policy $\pi(\theta)$ realized by the **PtPolicyNet** class:

```
class PtPolicyNet(nn.Module):
```

Next, we define a fully connected neural network with two linear layers:

```
    def __init__(self, state_size, action_space):
        super(PtPolicyNet, self).__init__()
        self.linear1 = nn.Linear(state_size, 32)
        self.linear2 = nn.Linear(32, action_space)
        self.opt = torch.optim.Adam(self.parameters())

    def forward(self, x):
        x = F.relu(self.linear1(x))
        x = F.softmax(self.linear2(x), dim = 1)
        return x
```

$\pi(\theta)$ acts the following way:

```
def act_sample(self, state):
```

Neural network returns the probability of each action:

```
probs = self(torch.tensor(state).unsqueeze(0).float())
```

We build distribution **dist** using returned probabilities **prob**:

```
dist = Categorical(probs)
```

Sampling random action according to the distribution **dist**:

```
action = dist.sample().item()
return int(action.numpy()[0])
```

The next method updates Neural Network θ using the Policy Gradient method:

```
def update(self, buffer, gamma):
```

Unpacking episode history:

```
rewards, actions, states = buffer.unzip()
```

Counting discounted rewards G_i:

```
sum_reward = 0
discnt_rewards = []
rewards.reverse()
for r in rewards:
    sum_reward = r + gamma * sum_reward
    discnt_rewards.append(sum_reward)
discnt_rewards.reverse()
discnt_rewards = torch.tensor(discnt_rewards).float()
```

Converting **states** and **actions** to tensors:

```
states = torch.tensor(states).float()
actions = torch.tensor(actions)
```

Calculating $\nabla_\theta(T; \pi(\theta)) = \nabla_\theta(T; \pi(\theta)) = \nabla_\theta (\sum_{i=0}^{N} \log[\pi(a_i|s_i; \theta)] \, G_i)$ value:

```
probs = self(states)
sampler = Categorical(probs)
log_probs = sampler.log_prob(actions)
E = torch.sum(log_probs * discnt_rewards)
```

Since our goal is to maximize **E**, and neural network optimizers are made for minimization, we change the **E** value sign:

```
loss = -E
```

Executing gradient shift $\theta = \theta + \alpha \, \nabla_\theta(T; \pi(\theta))$:

```
self.opt.zero_grad()
loss.backward()
```

```
        self.opt.step()
>>>>>>>>>> PyTorch
```

Of course, just building an implementation of the policy gradient method is not enough for us, so let's go ahead and apply it to the real problem.

Solving CartPole problem

CartPole is a classical reinforcement learning problem that is implemented in Cart Pole-v1 Gym environment. In *Chapter 3, Training in Gym*, we have already studied this environment. The agent must balance the cart to keep the pole from falling. The agent can perform the following actions: left (0) and right (1). The state of the environment is determined by four continuous variables: (Cart Position, Cart Velocity, Pole Angle, Pole Angle Velocity). *Figure 11.13* demonstrates CartPole environment.

Figure 11.13: *CartPole Environment*

Now, we can examine how the Policy Gradient method solves CartPole problem with the following script **ch11/policy_gradient/cart_pole.py**.

Importing the necessary modules:

```
import numpy as np
import matplotlib.pyplot as plt
import gym
from ch11.policy_gradient.pt_policy_net import PtPolicyNet
from ch11.policy_gradient.tf_policy_net import TfPolicyNet
from ch11.utils import Buffer
```

Initializing environment:

```
env = gym.make("CartPole-v1")
```

Instantiating policy. TensorFlow implementation:

```
policy = TfPolicyNet(env.action_space.n)
```

Uncomment this line for PyTorch implementation:

```
# policy = PtPolicyNet(env.observation_space.shape[0], env.action_
space.n)
```

Training hyperparameters:

```
gamma = 0.99

episodes = 1_000

total_scores = []

avg_scores = []
```

We use the **Buffer** object to memorize all experience gained after episode:

```
buffer = Buffer()
```

Main training loop:

```
for e in range(1, episodes + 1):

    buffer.clear()
    # reset environment
    state = env.reset()
    epoch_rewards = 0

    while True:
        action = policy.act_sample(state)
        # use that action in the environment
        new_state, reward, done, info = env.step(action)
        epoch_rewards += reward
        # store state, action and reward
        buffer.add(reward, action, state)

        state = new_state
        if done:
            total_scores.append(epoch_rewards)
            break
```

Updating the θ parameter after each episode:

```
    policy.update(buffer, gamma)

    avg_scores.append(np.mean(total_scores[-min(100, len(total_
scores)):]))

    if e % 100 == 0:
        print(f'Episode: {e}. Average Score: {avg_scores[-1]}')
```

```
# close environment
env.close()
```

Displaying results:

```
plt.plot(total_scores)
plt.plot(avg_scores, label = 'average')
plt.title('Policy Gradient. CartPole.')
plt.ylabel('Total Reward')
plt.xlabel('Episodes')
plt.show()
```

The CartPole problem is considered solved if the agent has collected more than 200 points. *Figure 11.14* shows that the Policy Gradient method does the job well:

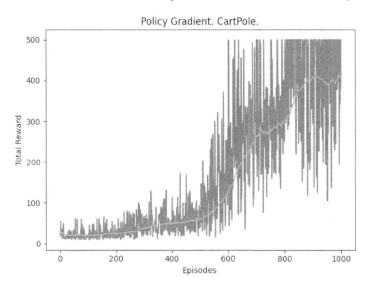

Figure 11.14: *CartPole solved with Policy Gradient method*

The policy gradient method has many interesting features. Let's list some of them:

- **Stochastic policy:** The policy gradient method generates a stochastic policy, which is more flexible in solving reinforcement learning problems.

- **Conciseness:** Despite the complexity of the formulas, you can compare the implementation of the Policy Gradient agent with other implementations: Monte-Carlo method, Q-learning, DQN, and DDQN. The Policy Gradient method really takes less code and is more elegant in implementation.

- **Hyperparameters**: Policy gradient has only one hyperparameter: reward discount factor (γ=0.99) to calculate G_t value. This saves us from the hyperparameter tuning mess.

- **Exploration and Exploitation**: The policy gradient method does not have an explicit division into exploration and exploitation stages, like Q-learning methods. The policy gradient method operates with probabilities and gradually converges to the most likely actions. However, it leaves the possibility of trying various unpopular solutions. It is similar to the Thompson sampling policy you learned about in *Chapter 3, Struggling With Multi-Armed Bandits*.

All this makes the policy gradient method favorable for further study.

Conclusion

The Policy Gradient method looks very pretty and promising, and you may wonder why we studied this method so late? There are several reasons for that. The Policy Gradient method works best when a neural network is used as the policy parameter, but the simplest way of building agents using neural networks (that is, deep reinforcement learning) is the Q-learning approach. This fact leads us to the next learning chain:

$$Q\text{-}learning \rightarrow Deep\ Q\text{-}Networks \rightarrow Policy\ Gradient\ Method.$$

In any case, we can't declare that policy-based methods are better than value-based ones. Each one works best for a specific environment, but some methods combine these two approaches, and Actor-Critic is one of them. The Actor-Critic model is the combination of value-based and policy-based approaches. *Figure 11.15* illustrates this concept:

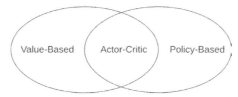

Figure 11.15: Actor-Critic method

We will explore the Actor-Critic method in the next chapter.

Points to remember

- Every deterministic policy can be expressed in terms of a stochastic policy, but not vice versa.

Multiple choice questions

1. Suppose we have the maze problem, as shown in *Figure 11.16*:

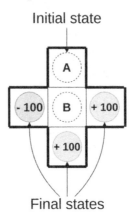

Figure 11.16: Maze problem

Which of the following policies do not guarantee a +100 reward?

    a. A: [down: 100%], B: [right: 50%, down: 50%]

    b. A: [down: 100%], B: [right: 70%, down: 30%]

    c. A: [down: 100%], B: [right: 60%, down: 30%, left: 10%]

2. Neural Network-based stochastic policies use the ... function as final activation.

    a. sigmoid

    b. softmax

    c. relu

Answers

    1. c

    2. b

Key terms

- **Stochastic policy**: Returns the probability of each action to be taken for a given state s.

- **Parametric policy**: This is a policy whose behavior depends on parameters.

- **Policy Gradient Method**: Defines an iterative algorithm for finding optimal parameter θ for a stochastic parametric policy $\pi(\theta)$.

CHAPTER 12
Stock Trading with Actor-Critic

In this chapter, we will study one of the best achievements of deep reinforcement learning. This method is called **Actor-Critic**. The Actor-Critic approach combines the best of the policy gradient method and the Q-learning technique and is one of the most significant accomplishments of reinforcement learning. This method can be applied to various real-life problems, and in this chapter, we will consider one of them. We will examine the drawbacks of the policy gradient method and how they can be fixed using the Actor-Critic model. Additionally, we will apply the Actor-Critic model to a real-life stock trading problem.

Structure

In this chapter, we will discuss the following topics:

- Policy gradient training drawbacks
- Actor-Critic theory
- A2C implementation
- A2C vs. policy gradient
- Stock trading

Objectives

After completing this chapter, you will learn about the Actor-Critic approach and Advantage **Actor-Critic** (**A2C**) as one of its implementations. You will learn how to implement the A2C model to reinforcement learning tasks, and we will consider the stock trading problem as a test for the A2C method.

Policy gradient training drawbacks

The policy gradient that we studied in the previous chapter has one very serious drawback that greatly affects its ability to learn. And that drawback lies in this formula:

$$\nabla_\theta \left(\sum_{i=0}^{N} \log[\pi(a_i|s_i; \theta)]\, G_i \right), \qquad (1)$$

Where:

- $G_i = \sum_{k=0} \gamma^k r_{i+k}$ - discounted cumulative reward collected during episode T after a_i action.

The G_i multiplier significantly affects the sum of all shifts in formula *(1)*. But it turns out that G_i is not so good at estimating the action of a_i in state s_i. To illustrate this, let's revisit how the policy gradient method solves the CartPole problem. Let's launch the script **ch12/cart_pole/pg_discounted_rewards.py** and analyze the discounted cumulative reward G_t. (For PyTorch implementation, uncomment #PyTorch Implementation lines in the script: **ch12/cart_pole/pg_discounted_rewards. py**).

In the 100th episode, the function G_t looks as shown in *Figure 12.1*:

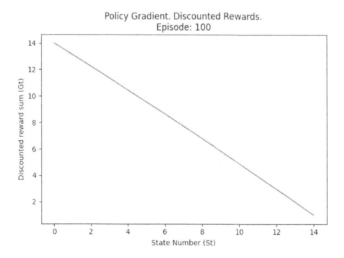

Figure 12.1: *Policy Gradient G_t function in 100th episode*

G_0 is close to the duration of the entire episode. And this makes sense since the agent gets a +1 reward after each action that did not lead to a fall. Therefore, G_t simply displays the left duration of the episode after s_t state. *Figure 12.2* illustrates the G_t function in 1000th episode.

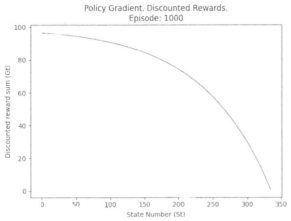

Figure 12.2: *Policy Gradient G_t function in 1000th episode*

Okay, but what's the problem here? The problem is the following. Since G_t is a multiplier in formula *(1)*, it determines the shifting weight in the sum $\nabla_\theta \left(\sum_{i=0}^{N} \log[\pi(a_i | s_i; \theta)] \, G_i \right)$. This means that the policy gradient method places too much emphasis on tuning its actions in states that the agent has already learned how to deal with. And states that critically affect the agent's performance are given little attention. *Figure 12.3* demonstrates this concept:

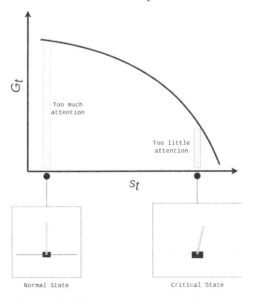

Figure 12.3: *Policy gradient unbalanced learning*

The agent already knows how to balance the pole in a vertical position. So, we can consider vertical pole position as a *normal state*. Each episode termination is accompanied by a *critical state* when the pole is going to fall. And of course, the agent has to learn to deal with a *critical state* to prolongate the episode. But the policy gradient method forces to tune states where everything is okay more than critical ones. This concept can be compared with the following real-life example. A soccer player needs to tie shoelaces correctly, but he does not need to train shoelacing every day. It is much better to take the time to train pace, striking accuracy, etc. In the next section, we'll examine how we can improve the policy gradient method to pay more attention to the really important states.

Actor-Critic theory

As we saw in the previous section, formula *(1)* has significant drawbacks, and we need to replace the G_i multiplier with something else $A(s_i, i)$:

$$\nabla_\theta (\sum_{i=0}^{N} log[\pi(a_i \mid s_i; \theta)] A(s_i, i)), \qquad (2)$$

Where:

- $A(s_i, i)$ is some function that depends on s_i and i parameters.

$A(s_i, i)$ is called *Critic*. The main task of the Critic is to correct the estimation of s_i state, which will help an agent to train better using the policy gradient method. Agent that performs actions according to $\pi(\theta)$ policy is called *Actor*. And from this combination of words, the name *Actor-Critic* model is derived.

There are various ways to express the $A(s_i, i)$ function. In this chapter, we will consider an Advantage Actor-Critic (A2C) model that expresses $A(s_i, i)$ according to the following formula:

$$A(s_i, i) = G_i - V(s_i; \varphi) \qquad (3)$$

Where:

- $V(s_i; \varphi)$ is some function that estimates s_i state depending on ϕ parameter. This function is called *baseline*.

$A(s_i, i) = G_i - V(s_i; \varphi)$ is called *advantage* as difference between G_i and *baseline*.

It turns out that the $V(s_i; \varphi)$ function can be expressed using a neural network that estimates s_i state according to neural φ weights.

Actor-Critic agent contains two neural networks:

- *Actor*(θ) returns action probabilities for a state
- *Critic*(ϕ) returns the state value

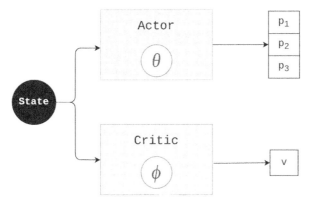

Figure 12.4: *A2C architecture*

Actor(θ) acts according to the policy gradient method, but *Critic*(φ) acts as *V(s)* state-value function from the Q-learning approach. This feature combines policy gradient and Q-learning in A2C model.

A2C algorithm is executed the following way:

0. Two neural networks *Actor*(θ) and *Critic*(φ) with random θ, φ weights are initialized.

For each training episode:

1. Actor evaluates episode according to π(θ) policy generating samples: $(s_0, a_0, r_0, s_1, a_1, r_1, \ldots, s_n, a_n, r_n)$

2. *Critic*(ϕ) calculates performed advantage: $A(s_i, i) = G_i - V(s_i; \varphi)$

3. Policy gradient is calculated: $\nabla_\theta \left(\sum_{i=0}^{N} \log[\pi(a_i|s_i; \theta)] A(s_i, i) \right)$

4. π(θ) updates its θ parameter according to: $\theta = \theta + \alpha \nabla_\theta$

5. *Critic*(ϕ) neural network minimizes its weights ϕ with the following loss function: $(G_i - V(s_i; \varphi))^2$

Figure 12.5 illustrates the A2C algorithm:

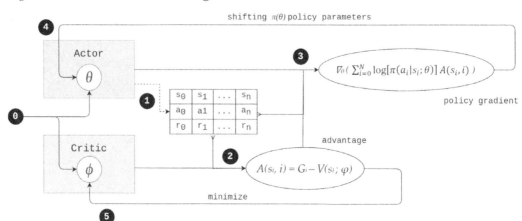

Figure 12.5: *A2C algorithm*

Don't be discouraged by the A2C model before you see its implementation. The main thing you should understand is that the model is the same policy gradient model, but with smart action estimation $A(s_i, i)$ instead of classical G_i.

A2C implementation

A2C model consists of two main components: Agent and Critic. The neural architectures of Agent and Critic correlate with each other since both of them analyze the environment state. If we are solving a video game playing problem by screen pixels analysis (*Chapter 10, Defending Atlantis with Double Deep Q-Network*), then both architectures would have to be based on convolution layers. Here, we will use a simple fully connected network as the Actor and Critic neural architecture. Let's implement the Actor component first:

TensorFlow >>>>>>>>>>

The following script provides TensorFlow implementation of Actor network using fully connected architecture **ch12/a2c/tf/actor.py**:

```
import tensorflow as tf

from tensorflow.keras.layers import Dense

class TfActor(tf.keras.Model):

    def __init__(self, action_space):
        super().__init__()
```

```
        self.linear1 = Dense(128, activation = 'relu')

        self.linear2 = Dense(256, activation = 'relu')

        self.linear3 = Dense(action_space, activation = 'softmax')


    def call(self, state):

        x = tf.convert_to_tensor(state)

        x = self.linear1(x)

        x = self.linear2(x)

        x = self.linear3(x)

        return x
>>>>>>>>>> TensorFlow
```

```
PyTorch >>>>>>>>>>
```

The following script provides PyTorch implementation of Actor network using fully connected architecture **ch12/a2c/pt/actor.py**:

```
import torch.nn as nn
import torch.nn.functional as F

class PtActor(nn.Module):

    def __init__(self, state_size, action_size):
        super(PtActor, self).__init__()
        self.state_size = state_size
        self.action_size = action_size
        self.linear1 = nn.Linear(self.state_size, 128)
        self.linear2 = nn.Linear(128, 256)
        self.linear3 = nn.Linear(256, self.action_size)

    def forward(self, state):
        x = F.relu(self.linear1(state))
        x = F.relu(self.linear2(x))
        x = self.linear3(x)
        x = F.softmax(x, dim = -1)
        return x
>>>>>>>>>> PyTorch
```

The Critic component looks similar to the Actor component, but it returns a single value that estimates the passed state instead of action probabilities.

TensorFlow >>>>>>>>>>

The following script provides TensorFlow implementation of Critic network using Fully Connected architecture **ch12/a2c/tf/critic.py**:

```python
import tensorflow as tf
from tensorflow.keras.layers import Dense


class TfCritic(tf.keras.Model):

    def __init__(self):
        super().__init__()
        self.linear1 = Dense(128, activation = 'relu')
        self.linear2 = Dense(256, activation = 'relu')
        self.linear3 = Dense(1, activation = 'relu')

    def call(self, state):
        x = tf.convert_to_tensor(state)
        x = self.linear1(x)
        x = self.linear2(x)
        x = self.linear3(x)
        return x
```

>>>>>>>>>> TensorFlow

PyTorch >>>>>>>>>>

The following script provides PyTorch implementation of Critic network using Fully Connected architecture **ch12/a2c/pt/critic.py**:

```python
import torch.nn as nn
import torch.nn.functional as F


class PtCritic(nn.Module):

    def __init__(self, state_size, action_size):
        super(PtCritic, self).__init__()
```

```
        self.state_size = state_size
        self.action_size = action_size
        self.linear1 = nn.Linear(self.state_size, 128)
        self.linear2 = nn.Linear(128, 256)
        self.linear3 = nn.Linear(256, 1)


    def forward(self, state):
        output = F.relu(self.linear1(state))
        output = F.relu(self.linear2(output))
        value = self.linear3(output)
        return value
```

>>>>>>>>>> PyTorch

The Actor-Critic agent is somewhat similar to the policy gradient agent, but it uses a slightly modified **update** method:

TensorFlow >>>>>>>>>>

A2C agent is implemented as follows using TensorFlow framework **ch12/a2c/tf/a2c_agent_tf.py**.

We import the necessary modules:

```
import numpy as np
import tensorflow as tf
from tensorflow.python.ops.distributions.categorical import Categorical
from tensorflow.keras.optimizers import Adam
from ch12.a2c.tf.actor import TfActor
from ch12.a2c.tf.critic import TfCritic


class TfA2CAgent:
    """

    TensorFlow Implementation of Advantage Actor-Critic Model
    """


    def __init__(self, state_size, action_size) -> None:
        super().__init__()
```

Agent initializes the **actor** and **critic** components:

```
self.actor = TfActor(action_size)
self.critic = TfCritic()
```

Each component has its own optimizer:

```
self.actor_optim = Adam()
self.critic_optim = Adam()
```

A2C agent has unique explicit hyperparameter: *discount rate -* for $G_i =$ calculation:

```
self.gamma = .99
```

The **action_sample** method acts the same as for policy gradient agent:

```
def action_sample(self, state):
    prob = self.actor(np.array([state]))
    dist = Categorical(probs = prob, dtype = tf.float32)
    action = dist.sample()
    return int(action.numpy()[0])
```

The **update** method is a slightly modified version of the policy gradient **update** method:

```
def update(self, final_state, buffer):
```

Unzipping episode experience from the **Buffer** object:

```
rewards, states, actions, dones = buffer.unzip()
```

Calculating discounted cumulative rewards $G_i = \sum_{k=0} \gamma^k r_{i+k}$:

```
final_value = self.critic(np.array([final_state]))
sum_reward = final_value
discnt_rewards = []
for step in reversed(range(len(rewards))):
    sum_reward = rewards[step] + self.gamma * sum_reward * (1 -
dones[step])
    discnt_rewards.append(sum_reward)
discnt_rewards.reverse()
discnt_rewards = tf.concat(discnt_rewards, 0)
```

Calculating advantage according to $A(s_i, i) = G_i - V(s_i; \varphi)$:

```
with tf.GradientTape() as critic_tape:
    values = self.critic(np.array(states), training = True)
```

```
advantage = discnt_rewards - values
critic_loss = tf.reduce_mean(tf.pow(advantage, 2))
```

Calculating policy gradient $\nabla_\theta \left(\sum_{i=0}^{N} \log[\pi(a_i|s_i;\theta)] A(s_i, i) \right)$:

```
with tf.GradientTape() as actor_tape:
    prob = self.actor(np.array(states), training = True)
    dist = Categorical(probs = prob, dtype = tf.float32)
    log_prob = dist.log_prob(actions)
    E = log_prob * advantage
```

Since our goal is to maximize **E** and neural network optimizers are made for minimization, we change the **E** value sign:

```
actor_loss = -E
```

Executing gradient shift $\theta = \theta + \alpha \nabla_\theta$:

```
actor_g = actor_tape.gradient(actor_loss, self.actor.variables)
self.actor_optim.apply_gradients(zip(actor_g, self.actor.
variables))
```

Optimizing Critic neural network:

```
critic_g = critic_tape.gradient(critic_loss, self.critic.
variables)
self.critic_optim.apply_gradients(zip(critic_g, self.critic.
variables))
```

Method returns advantage for debug purposes:

```
return advantage.numpy()
```

```
>>>>>>>>>> TensorFlow
```

```
PyTorch >>>>>>>>>>
```

A2C agent is implemented as follows using PyTorch framework **ch12/a2c/pt/a2c_agent_pt.py**.

We import the necessary modules:

```
import torch
import torch.optim as optim
from torch.distributions import Categorical
from ch12.a2c.pt.actor import PtActor
```

```
from ch12.a2c.pt.critic import PtCritic


class PtA2CAgent:
    """

    PyTorch Implementation of Advantage Actor-Critic Model
    """


    def __init__(self, state_size, action_size) -> None:
        super().__init__()
```

Agent initializes the **actor** and **critic** components:

```
        self.actor = PtActor(state_size, action_size)
        self.critic = PtCritic(state_size, action_size)
```

Each component has its own optimizer:

```
        self.actor_optim = optim.Adam(self.actor.parameters())
        self.critic_optim = optim.Adam(self.critic.parameters())
```

A2C agent has unique explicit hyperparameter: *discount rate* - γ for $G_i = \sum_{k=0} \gamma^K r_{i+k}$ calculation:

```
        self.gamma = .99
```

The **action_sample** method acts the same as for the policy gradient agent:

```
    def action_sample(self, state):
        state = torch.FloatTensor(state)
        dist = Categorical(self.actor(state))
        action = dist.sample().item()
        return action
```

The **update** method is a slightly modified version of the policy gradient **update** method:

```
    def update(self, final_state, buffer):
```

Unzipping episode experience from **Buffer** object:

```
        rewards, states, actions, dones = buffer.unzip()

        # Converting to tensors
        states = torch.tensor(states).float()
        actions = torch.tensor(actions)
```

Calculating discounted cumulative rewards $G_i = \sum_{k=0} \gamma^k r_{i+k}$:

```
final_value = self.critic(torch.FloatTensor(final_state))


sum_reward = final_value
discnt_rewards = []
for step in reversed(range(len(rewards))):
    sum_reward = rewards[step] + self.gamma * sum_reward * (1 -
dones[step])
        discnt_rewards.append(sum_reward)
discnt_rewards.reverse()


discnt_rewards = torch.cat(discnt_rewards).detach()
```

Calculating advantage according to $A(s_i, i) = G_i - V(s_i; \varphi)$:

```
values = self.critic(states).squeeze(1)
advantage = discnt_rewards - values
```

Calculating policy gradient $\nabla_\theta (\sum_{i=0}^{N} \log[\pi(a_i|s_i; \theta)] A(s_i, i))$:

```
probs = self.actor(states)
sampler = Categorical(probs)


# log(Pi(at|st))
log_probs = sampler.log_prob(actions)
E = (log_probs * advantage.detach()).mean()
```

Since our goal is to maximize **E** and neural network optimizers are made for minimization, we change the **E** value sign:

```
actor_loss = -E
```

Executing gradient shift $\theta = \theta + \alpha \nabla_\theta$:

```
self.actor_optim.zero_grad()
actor_loss.backward()
self.actor_optim.step()
```

Optimizing Critic neural network:

```
critic_loss = advantage.pow(2).mean()
self.critic_optim.zero_grad()
```

```
critic_loss.backward()
self.critic_optim.step()
```

Method returns **advantage** for debug purposes:

```
return advantage.detach().numpy()
```

>>>>>>>>>> PyTorch

Now, let's apply the A2C approach to the CartPole problem. But at the moment, we are not interested in the performance of the A2C agent but in the analysis of *advantage*: $A(s_{i}, i) = G_{i} - V(s_{i}; \varphi)$. Run the following script **ch12/cart_pole/a2c_advantage.py**. (For PyTorch implementation, uncomment **#PyTorch Implementation** lines in the script: **ch12/cart_pole/a2c_advantage.py**).

Figure 12.6 demonstrates advantage in the 800th episode:

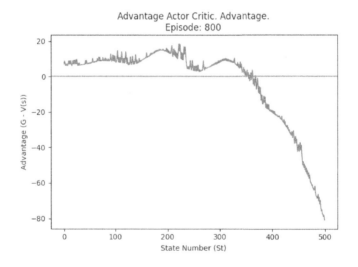

Figure 12.6: *A2C advantage plot*

Figure 12.6 can be interpreted the following way. Up to step 400, the absolute values of **advantage** are close to zero, which means that optimization of actions until 400 will not be given too much attention. However, after 400 steps, the agent loses stability and enters critical states. The **advantage** plot drops sharply, and its absolute value grows. This means that the actions in these states will receive maximum attention. *Figure 12.7* illustrates this concept.

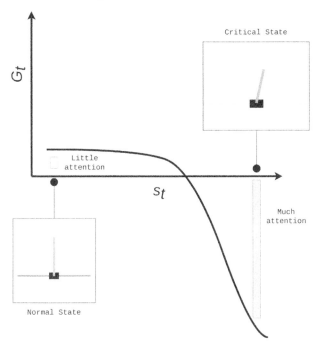

Figure 12.7: *A2C learning*

This feature allows the Advantage Actor-Critic agent to learn much more efficiently.

A2C vs. policy gradient

Well, it's all good in theory. But let's compare the performance of the A2C and policy-gradient methods in solving the CartPole problem. Let's launch the battle between A2C and policy gradient using the following script **ch12/cart_pole/a2c_vs_pg.py**.

We import the necessary modules:

```
import gym

import numpy as np

import matplotlib.pyplot as plt

from ch12.a2c.tf.a2c_agent_tf import TfA2CAgent

from ch12.pg.tf_policy_net import TfPolicyNet

from ch12.a2c.pt.a2c_agent_pt import PtA2CAgent
```

```
from ch12.pg.pt_policy_net import PtPolicyNet


# different implementations for PG and A2C buffers
import ch12.utils as a2c_utils
import ch11.utils as pg_utils
```

Initializing **CartPole-v0** environment:

```
env = gym.make("CartPole-v0").unwrapped


state_size = env.observation_space.shape[0]
action_size = env.action_space.n
```

Each agent will be trained for 200 episodes:

```
episodes = 200
total_rewards = []
```

TensorFlow implementation of policy gradient agent and A2C agent:

```
# TensorFlow Implementation
pg_agent = TfPolicyNet(action_size)
a2c_agent = TfA2CAgent(state_size, action_size)
```

PyTorch implementation of policy gradient agent and A2C agent (uncomment these lines if necessary):

```
# PyTorch Implementation
# pg_agent = PtPolicyNet(state_size, action_size)
# a2c_agent = PtA2CAgent(state_size, action_size)


a2c_buffer = a2c_utils.Buffer()
pg_buffer = pg_utils.Buffer()
```

We will collect the average reward of the last 100 episodes for each of the agents:

```
a2c_average = []
pg_average = []
```

Training A2C agent:

```
for episode in range(1, episodes + 1):
    epoch_rewards = 0
    state = env.reset()
```

```
        a2c_buffer.clear()

        while True:
            action = a2c_agent.action_sample(state)
            next_state, reward, done, _ = env.step(action)
            epoch_rewards += reward

            a2c_buffer.add(reward, state, action, done)
            state = next_state

            if done:
                total_rewards.append(epoch_rewards)
                break

        a2c_agent.update(next_state, a2c_buffer)
        a2c_average.append(np.mean(total_rewards[-min(100, episode):]))

        if episode % 10 == 0:
            print(f'A2C Average. Episode {episode}: {a2c_average[-1]}')
```

Training policy gradient agent:

```
for episode in range(1, episodes + 1):
    epoch_rewards = 0
    state = env.reset()
    pg_buffer.clear()

    while True:
        action = pg_agent.act_sample(state)
        next_state, reward, done, _ = env.step(action)
        epoch_rewards += reward

        pg_buffer.add(reward, action, state)
        state = next_state

        if done:
```

```
        total_rewards.append(epoch_rewards)
        break

    pg_agent.update(pg_buffer)
    pg_average.append(np.mean(total_rewards[-min(100, episode):]))

    if episode % 10 == 0:
        print(f'PG Average. Episode {episode}: {pg_average[-1]}')

env.close()
Displaying results:
plt.plot(a2c_average, label = 'A2C')
plt.plot(pg_average, label = 'Policy Gradient')
plt.legend()
plt.xlabel('Episodes')
plt.ylabel('Average Rewards')
plt.title('CartPole. A2C vs PG')
plt.show()
```

The battle result is shown in *Figure 12.8*:

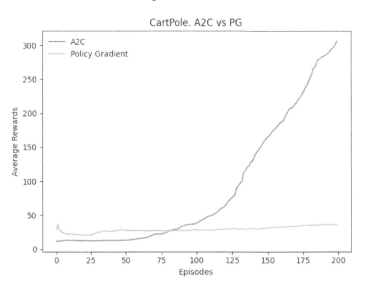

Figure 12.8: A2C vs PG

Figure 12.8 demonstrates the significant superiority of the A2C agent, which practically confirms the theoretical assumptions that we have made in this chapter. The Advantage Actor-Critic model is one of the most advanced reinforcement learning algorithms that takes best from the policy gradient and Q-learning approaches.

Stock Trading

We have come a long way by studying the various reinforcement learning methods. In all cases, we studied their application for synthetic environments. Now, let's see how you can apply reinforcement learning techniques to solve a real-life problem. Let's take the stock trading task as an example. The goal of the agent will be to trade stocks optimally. We will formulate a problem, develop a custom GYM environment and try to train an agent.

Problem

Trader's main goal is to "*buy low and sell high*" or "*sell high and buy low*"; these are the only actions that provide profit. When a trader decides to buy shares, they hope that in the following days, the price of the shares will increase, and they will be able to sell them. The difference between the *buy price* and the *selling price* is the trader's income. When a trader buys shares and then sells them, this is called a *long position*. But stock trading also allows short positions - when a trader first sells shares and then buys them back.

Stock trading rules contain many subtleties and tricks, but we will simplify the trading process. Let's say we have daily stock quotes, and at the end of each day, we take one of the following actions:

- **BUY** shares and sell them at the end of the next trading day
- **SELL** shares and buy them back at the end of the next trading day
- **NO** - do **no**thing until the next trading day

The reward is calculated as follows:

- for **BUY** action: **NEXT** trading day **PRICE** - **TODAY**'s **PRICE**
- for SELL action: **TODAY**'s **PRICE** - **NEXT** trading day **PRICE**
- for **NO** action: 0

Figure 12.9 illustrates the trading process we described above:

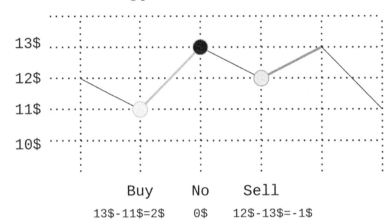

Figure 12.9: *Stock trading*

Real-life stock trading contains more complex rules, including transaction commissions, various order types. But we will not complicate the trading model too much and study this one.

Environment

Since we have identified the problem, we need to define the environment we will be dealing with. We have already defined that the action space will contain three actions: *Sell, No action, Buy*. We also determined the calculation of the reward for the action:

- $a_i = Sell : r_i = q_{n+1} - q_n$

- $a_i = No\ action : r_i = 0$

- $a_i = Buy: r_i = q_n - q_{n+1}$,

Where q_i is a stock quote on i^{th} step.

Next, we have to define an environment state. The state is presented as a sequence of n preceding quotes. For example, for i^{th} step the state is presented as: $[q_{i-n}, q_{i-n-1}, ..., q_i]$. *Figure 12.10* demonstrates stock trading state:

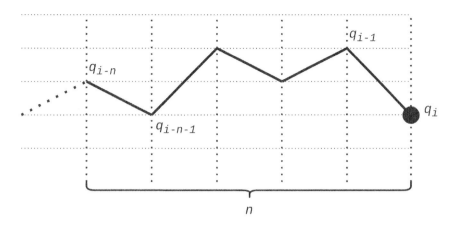

Figure 12.10: *Stock trading state*

Since we defined reward, action space, and state space, we can move on to creating a custom trading environment in Gym. One of the most important features of the environment is the possibility to visualize itself. And we'll start with it. In *Chapter 3, Training in Gym*, we already studied how to render an environment using the PyGame library. Here, we will also build a visualization using the same technique **ch12/trading_env/trading_screen.py**.

We import the necessary modules:

```
import matplotlib.pyplot as plt
```

```
import matplotlib.backends.backend_agg as agg
```

```
import pylab
```

```
import pygame
```

```
from pygame.locals import *
```

The **TradingScreen** class is responsible for displaying quotes, actions, and total reward:

```
class TradingScreen:
```

```
    def __init__(self) -> None:
```

Initializing PyGame and Display:

```
        pygame.init()
        self.scr = pygame.display.set_mode((600, 400), DOUBLEBUF)
```

The following method renders video frame:

```
def update(self, quotes, buys, sells, name, total_reward):
    self.scr.fill((255, 255, 255))  # Fill with WHITE
    fig = pylab.figure(figsize = [4, 4], dpi = 100, )
    ax = fig.gca()
    ax.title.set_text(f"{name}\nTotal: {total_reward}")
    ax.set_xticks([])
```

Displaying BUY actions:

```
    ax.scatter(
        list(buys.keys()),
        list(buys.values()),
        marker = "o",
        color = "green"
    )
```

Displaying SELL actions:

```
    ax.scatter(
        list(sells.keys()),
        list(sells.values()),
        marker = "o",
        color = "red"
    )

    ax.plot(quotes)
```

Rendering Plot as Video Frame:

```
    canvas = agg.FigureCanvasAgg(fig)
    canvas.draw()
    renderer = canvas.get_renderer()
    raw_data = renderer.tostring_rgb()

    size = canvas.get_width_height()
    surf = pygame.image.fromstring(raw_data, size, "RGB")
    self.scr.blit(surf, (0, 0))
```

```
pygame.display.update()
plt.close('all')
```

Now, let's construct Stock Trading Environment **ch12/trading_env/stock_trading_env.py**.

We import the necessary modules:

```
import random
import gym
from ch12.trading_env.trading_screen import TradingScreen
```

The **StockTradingEnv** is initialized with the following parameters:

- **quotes**: List of daily quotes
- **start_from**: The day to start trading from
- **state_size**: Number of previous days that will form the state
- **max_steps**: Max steps per episode
- **name**: Trading screen title
- **trading_screen_width**: Trading screen width

```
class StockTradingEnv(gym.Env):

    def __init__(
            self,
            quotes,
            start_from = 30,
            state_size = 10,
            max_steps = 250,
            name = '',
            trading_screen_width = 100,
    ):
        self.start_from = start_from
        self.state_size = state_size
        self.trading_screen_width = trading_screen_width
        self.name = name
        self.quotes = quotes
        self.max_steps = max_steps
        self.trading_scr = TradingScreen()
```

```
            self.current_bar = start_from
            self.total_bars = len(quotes)
            self.action_history = []
            self.total_reward = 0
            self.total_steps = 0
```

The following method returns actual environment state:

```
    def get_state(self):
        return self.quotes[self.current_bar - self.state_size: self.
current_bar]
```

Next, we implement the `step` method:

```
    def step(self, action):
```

It is convenient to transform action from (0, 1, 2) to (-1, 0, 1) to simplify the reward calculation:

```
        # Transforming (0,1,2) action to (-1,0,1) order action
        # action: 2 -> buy: 1
        # action: 1 -> no action
        # action: 0 -> sell: -1
        order_action = action - 1
        self.action_history.append(order_action)
        self.current_bar += 1
        self.total_steps += 1
        info = None
        state = self.get_state()
```

Calculating reward:

```
        diff = self.quotes[self.current_bar] - self.quotes[self.current_
bar - 1]
        reward = order_action * diff
        self.total_reward += reward
```

The **done** if no more quotes left or maximum steps per episode reached:

```
        done = (len(self.quotes) - 1 == self.current_bar) or\
            self.total_steps == self.max_steps

        return state, reward, done, info
```

The **reset** method sets the **current_bar** to a random day:

```python
def reset(self):
    # Setting random trading day
    self.current_bar = random.randint(self.start_from, self.total_
bars - self.max_steps - 1)
    self.action_history = [0] * self.current_bar
    self.total_reward = 0
    self.total_steps = 0
    return self.get_state()
```

And finally, we define the **render** method:

```python
def render(self, mode = 'human'):
    from_pos = max(0, self.current_bar - self.trading_screen_width)
    to_pos = self.current_bar + 1
    sq = self.quotes[from_pos:to_pos]
    actions = self.action_history[from_pos:to_pos]
    sells = {i: sq[i] for i in range(len(actions)) if actions[i] ==
-1}
    buys = {i: sq[i] for i in range(len(actions)) if actions[i] ==
1}
    self.trading_scr.update(sq, buys, sells, self.name, self.total_
reward)
```

We have always used a random agent to test the environment, and we will do the same this time in the following script **ch12/trading_env/random_agent.py**.

(Install the **yfinance** package before running the below script.)

We import the necessary modules:

```python
from time import sleep
from ch12.trading_env.stock_trading_env import StockTradingEnv
import yfinance as yf
import random
```

Downloading Microsoft daily quotes from Yahoo Finance:

```python
quotes = yf.download('MSFT', start = '2015-1-1', end = '2022-1-1')
close_quotes = quotes['Close'].values
```

Making script reproducible:

```
random.seed(1)
```

Initializing environment:

```
state_size = 10
# 0 - sell, 1 - none, 2 - buy
action_size = 3

env = StockTradingEnv(
    close_quotes,
    name = 'MSFT. Random Agent',
    state_size = state_size
)
init_state = env.reset()
```

Executing agent:

```
total = 0
while True:
    env.render()
    action = random.randint(0, action_size)
    state, reward, done, debug = env.step(action)
    sleep(.3)
    total += reward
    if done:
        break

env.close()

print(f'Total Reward: {total}')
```

As a result, you can see **total reward = -1.22**.

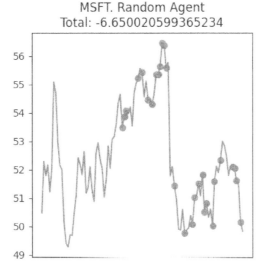

Figure 12.11: *Trading screen*

Figure 12.11 demonstrates the trading screen. Green point means BUY action, and red point means SELL action. Of course, you do not expect anything special from the random agent. Let's try to construct something more intelligent.

Solution

Now, let's use an A2C agent to solve this problem. It will be interesting to see how the Advantage Actor-Critic approach plays out in a real-world situation. Follow this script **ch12/trading_env/a2c_train.py**.

We import the necessary modules:

```python
import matplotlib.pyplot as plt

import numpy as np

import yfinance as yf

from ch12.a2c.tf.a2c_agent_tf import TfA2CAgent

from ch12.a2c.pt.a2c_agent_pt import PtA2CAgent

from ch12.trading_env.stock_trading_env import StockTradingEnv

from ch12.utils import Buffer
```

Downloading Microsoft daily quotes from Yahoo Finance:

```python
quotes = yf.download('MSFT', start = '2015-01-01', end = '2022-01-01')
close_quotes = quotes['Close'].values
```

Initializing environment:

```python
state_size = 10
# 0 - sell, 1 - none, 2 - buy
action_size = 3

env = StockTradingEnv(
    close_quotes,
    name = 'MSFT. A2C',
    state_size = state_size
)
```

Stocks have a different price range, so it is better to normalize the state by the last price, for example **[9\$, 11\$, 10\$] -> [0.9, 1.1, 1]**:

```python
def normalize_state(state):
    return np.array(state) / state[-1]


episodes = 500
avg_period = 50
avg = []
total_rewards = []
```

TensorFlow A2C implementation:

```python
a2c_agent = TfA2CAgent(state_size, action_size, lr = 0.0005)
```

PyTorch A2C implementation (uncomment this line if necessary):

```python
# a2c_agent = PtA2CAgent(state_size, action_size)
```

Executing the agent:

```python
buffer = Buffer()
for episode in range(1, episodes + 1):
    epoch_rewards = 0
    state = normalize_state(env.reset())
    buffer.clear()
```

```
    while True:
        action = a2c_agent.action_sample(state)
        next_state_dirty, reward, done, _ = env.step(action)
        epoch_rewards += reward

        buffer.add(reward, state, action, done)
        state = normalize_state(next_state_dirty)

        if done:
            total_rewards.append(epoch_rewards)
            break

    a2c_agent.update(state, buffer)

    avg.append(np.mean(total_rewards[-min(avg_period, episode):]))

    if episode % avg_period == 0:
        print(f'Episode: {episode}. Average Score: {avg[-1]}')

env.close()
```

Displaying results:

```
plt.plot(avg)
plt.axhline(y = 0, color = 'r', linestyle = '-')
plt.xlabel('Episodes')
plt.ylabel('Average Rewards')
plt.title('Stock Trading. A2C')
plt.show()
```

Figure 12.12 shows A2C stock trading performance. As we can see, the A2C agent learned some stock patterns that allowed him to trade successfully:

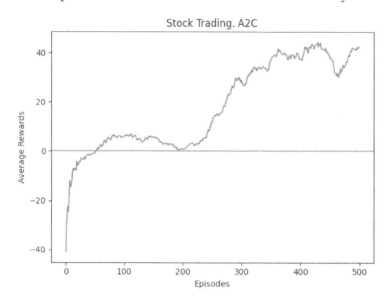

***Figure 12.12**: A2C stock trading results*

Of course, real-life trading is a much more complex and risky activity, but our goal was only to show an example of the application of deep reinforcement learning techniques to solving real problems. Developing agents and implementing them in real life is an engaging task!

Conclusion

In this chapter, we complete our study of reinforcement learning methods. An Actor-Critic model is a promising approach capable of tackling the most challenging problems. This chapter examined the A2C (Advantage Actor-Critic) model, which is just one implementation of the Actor-Critic concept. Now, you are at the beginning of your exciting journey in reinforcement learning, and you still have to learn a lot of new and exciting things, and perhaps, even invent your own problem-solving methods!

Points to remember

- Policy gradient method focuses too much on tuning its actions in states that the agent has already learned how to deal with.

- The main task of the Critic component is the correct state estimation.

- *Actor*(θ) returns action probabilities and acts according to the policy gradient method.

- *Critic*(φ) acts as $V(s)$ state-value function from the Q-learning approach.

Multiple choice questions

1. What is the benefit of the Actor-Critic approach over the policy gradient method?

    a. Actor-Critic employs two neural networks instead of one

    b. Actor-Critic pays more attention to critical states

    c. Actor-Critic uses more training episodes than the policy gradient method does

    d. None of these

Answer

1. **b**

Key terms

- **Actor-Critic**: Policy gradient method that uses following formula for gradient shift $\nabla\theta$ ($\sum_{i=0}^{N} \log[\pi(a_i|s_i; \theta)] A(s_i, i)$).

- **A2C (Advantage Actor-Critic)**: Actor-Critic method that utilizes $A(s_i, i) = G_i - V(s_i; \varphi)$ as Critic.

## CHAPTER 13

What Is Next?

We made a great journey in reinforcement learning and learned how to use its most popular methods. Of course, reinforcement learning applications continue to evolve dynamically, and in this chapter, we will see directions on what's next, that is, after completing this book.

Structure

In this chapter, we will discuss the following topics:

- Reinforcement learning overview
- Re-read
- Deep learning
- Practice

Objectives

This chapter provides suggestions for further study in reinforcement learning. The recommendations mentioned in this chapter will keep you updated about the latest advances.

Reinforcement learning overview

Reinforcement learning has several methods and approaches. In this book, we have covered only some of them. *Figure 13.1* demonstrates the Reinforcement Learning (RL) method tree:

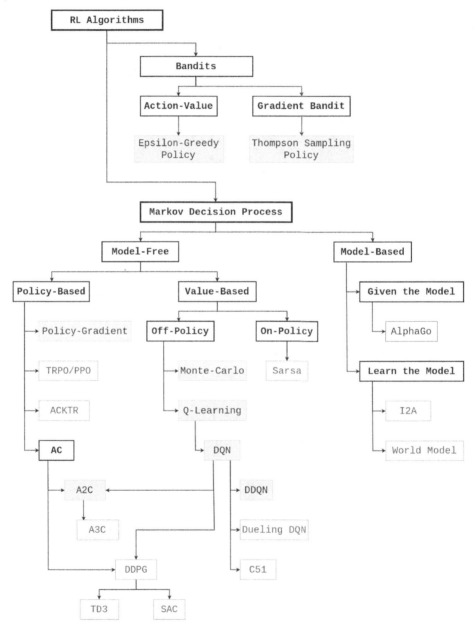

Figure 13.1: *Reinforcement learning method tree*

Let's get an overview of reinforcement learning from a global point of view and recall the methods we covered in this book.

All reinforcement learning problems can be divided into two big parts: **Bandits** and **Markov Decision Process** (**MDP**). The main difference between **Bandit** and **MDP** is that the Bandit problem actually does not have any state, and it only operates with action and reward.

Bandit problems are solved using **Epsilon-Greedy Policy** or **Thompson Sampling Policy**. We studied these methods in *Chapter 4, Struggling With Multi-Armed Bandits*.

MDP problems can be classified into the following categories: **Model-Free** and **Model-Based**. **Model-Based** Reinforcement learning refers to learning optimal behavior indirectly by learning a model of the environment by taking actions and observing the outcomes that include the next state and the immediate reward. **Model-Based** approaches try to determine internal environment rules and only then conclude optimal policy. As the name suggests, Model-Based methods are trying to model environment. **Model-Free** methods do not care about environment internals and aim to construct the optimal policy without understanding the principles an environment is based on. In this book, we have studied only Model-Free methods.

Model-Based methods are quite complex, but they are very exciting techniques; let's list some of them. **AlphaGo** is the first algorithm based on the reinforcement learning approach that defeats any professional human. **Worlds Model** suggests the fascinating idea of *learning in dreams*. This technique tries to mimic a real environment (dream) and train an agent inside the dream. And after the training, it passes imaginary experience to the actual environment.

Model-Free methods are the most popular approaches in Reinforcement Learning. They are divided into two big branches: **Value-Based** and **Policy-Based**. Value-Based algorithms construct deterministic policy, where each action depends on its value for a given state. Policy-Based algorithms result in stochastic policy, where each action has its probability.

Value-based methods have one very interesting subgroup called the **On-Policy** approach. And **SARSA** is one of its representatives. **SARSA** is an excellent method for real-world learning when the cost of error during exploration is very high. For example, when we only have 10 robots to complete a mission, each mistake results in the loss of a robot. In such conditions, we are not always worried about maximizing the reward, and all we want is to complete the mission, perhaps not even with the most optimal reward.

Off-Policy methods do not have an explicit limit on the number of episodes in exploration. The brightest representatives of **Value-Based Off-Policy** methods are **Monte-Carlo** (*Chapter 5, Blackjack in Monte Carlo*) and **Q-Learning** (*Chapter 6, Escaping Maze With Q-learning*). **Q-learning** is a fundamental algorithm that underlies many reinforcement learning methods, and its natural extension is **DQN** (*Chapter 9, Deep Q-Network and Lunar Lander*).

DQN is a combination of reinforcement learning and deep learning. The association of these two global research areas has made it possible to make a breakthrough in solving many practical problems. The ideas behind **DQN** have given rise to various concepts based on this approach: **DDQN** (*Chapter 10, Defending Atlantis With Double Deep Q-Network*), **Dueling DQN**, **C51**. **Dueling DQN** presents the architecture that explicitly separates the representation of state values and state-dependent action advantages via two separate models. **C51** implements a distributional reinforcement learning technique. It models distribution over returns explicitly instead of only estimating the mean.

Policy-Based group contains the following methods: **Policy-Gradient** (*Chapter 11, From Q-learning to Policy-Gradient*), **TRPO/PPO** (Trust Region Policy Optimization Algorithm and Proximal Policy Optimization Algorithm), **ACKTR** (Actor-Critic using Kronecker-factored Trust Region) and **AC** (Actor-Critic). **TRPO** and **PPO** algorithms solve a common problem of sample efficiency that takes a huge number of steps to optimize. Both of them optimize the size of a policy update. **ACKTR** combines three techniques: actor-critic methods, trust-region optimization for more consistent improvement, and distributed Kronecker factorization to improve sample efficiency and scalability.

AC is an approach that has several implementations, and **Advantage Actor-Critic** (**A2C**) is one of them (*Chapter 12, Stock Trading with Actor-Critic*). The idea to combine policy gradient optimization and value estimation shows excellent efficiency. **A3C** (**Asynchronous Advantage Actor-Critic**) is an extension of A2C. **A3C** consists of multiple independent agents with their own weights, who interact with a different copy of the environment in parallel. Thus, they can explore a bigger part of the state-action space in much less time.

As we see, reinforcement learning is a whole world of methods, concepts, and ideas. And in this book, we studied far from everyone. In *Figure 13.1*, the methods we learned in the book are highlighted in green. In any case, you now have a good understanding of the various approaches and can continue the journey in any direction you like.

Reread

Reinforcement learning is a fascinating yet challenging area to study. To better understand some concepts, you can reread the theory behind the various methods. You can use multiple sources and various authors to better understand the logic of the method you are using. YouTube has several helpful videos that visualize mathematical formulas that underlie reinforcement learning. They will definitely help you understand this further.

Deep learning

Deep learning is a natural tool for applying reinforcement learning in practice. And if you are new to deep learning, it is recommended to improve your skills in this area. Complex RL models contain complex logic, and you need to be good with deep learning to apply, debug, or implement your own idea in practice.

Practice

The best idea to dive into reinforcement learning is practice. You can try solving a lot of different environments. There are a lot of challenges on the internet where people compete to develop the best algorithm to solve a given environment. The most exciting thing is the development of agents playing video games. I find these environments to be some of the most compelling and out of the ordinary to tackle. It's a great idea to pick an Atari game from the Gym framework and try to teach the agent to play it. Solving this problem may not be trivial and take more than 1 day, but the experience gained will be valuable and give confidence in solving future problems.

Conclusion

This final chapter provided an overview of reinforcement learning and pointed directions for further learning. Reinforcement learning techniques are evolving rapidly, and many machine learning models use RL ideas inside. This book lays a good foundation in reinforcement learning, and we hope it can be a good start for the reader.

Index

Printed in Great Britain
by Amazon